CANNES
A FESTIVAL VIRGIN'S GUIDE

Attending the Cannes Film Festival for filmmakers
and film industry professionals

5th Edition

Benjamin Craig

Illustrations by Lee Tatham

Cinemagine Media Publishing
London

Cannes - A Festival Virgin's Guide
Attending the Cannes Film Festival for filmmakers and film industry professionals.

Disclaimer

Trademarks

Published By
Cinemagine Media Publishing
3 Castelnau Row, London SW13 9EE, United Kingdom.
www.cinemagine.com
A division of Cinemagine Media Limited

1997- 1998 (Online Editions), 1999 (1st Edition), 2000 (2nd Edition),
2001 (3rd Edition) 2002 (4th Edition), 2006 (5th Edition)

ISBN 0-9541737-3-2

Cover art by Lee Tatham
Edited by Beth White
Book design by Benjamin Craig

Enquires for sales and distribution, textbook adoption, advertising, foreign language translation, editorial, and rights permissions concerning this book should be addressed to the publisher.

Visit Cannes - A Festival Virgin's Guide Online
www.cannesguide.com

preface and acknowledgments

Welcome to the fifth edition of "Cannes - A Festival Virgin's Guide". This book was born of a first-time visit to Cannes many years ago. As a young Australian filmmaker, it seemed like a good idea at the time to drop in on the world's most festival during my travels in Europe. But as it turned out, not only was I completely confused by the festival's structure and operation, Cannes itself was not the most hospitable place for someone new to the industry and travelling on a shoestring budget. Fortunately, that particular trip was designated "reconnaissance only" and out of my discoveries, experiences, and mistakes, the seeds of the Festival Virgin's Guide were sown.

Since then I have been to Cannes many times and had lengthy conversations with others who are true Cannes veterans. The fruits of this work originally existed in the "Cannes - A Festival Virgin's Guide" web site, but are now presented for you in this book. As with all good travel guides, the tips, tricks, and recommendations change over time so I urge you to visit the site (www.cannesguide.com) now and then to see what's new. Likewise, great travel resources are born of collaborative effort so feel free to share your experiences with others through the community and feedback areas of the site.

As always, an undertaking such as "Cannes – A Festival Virgin's Guide" can never be completed in isolation. Special thanks must go to the following people who have been instrumental in helping create the book you now hold in your hands: Lee Tatham for the magnificent cover and map illustrations; Ashley Evans for the wonderful hospitality and use of Can Guitarro as a writing retreat; Emmanuelle Marvy for correcting my French; Richard Miller for advice and support; and finally, my superbly talented editor, Beth White.

Also deserved of my sincerest thanks are the group of Cannes veterans who very kindly made available a slice of their valuable time to provide their own insights into all that is the Cannes Film Festival: Lise Corriveau, Kim Dalton, Dennis Davidson, Simon Franks, Patrick Frater, Harry Hicks, Stephen Kelliher, Sarah McKenzie, Jonathan Olsberg, Bill Stephens, and Jane Wright.

I hope you find the information in this book useful and more importantly, I wish you all the best with your professional and personal exploits at the world's most famous film festival.

Benjamin Craig
Can Guitarro, Sóller, Majorca
September 2005

table of contents

Part 4 — The Lowdown

Appendices

CANNES - A FESTIVAL VIRGIN'S GUIDE

5TH EDITION

introduction

It's May. Armed with a wad of business cards, tapes of your cinematic masterpiece, a French phrase book, and huge optimism, you've decided to take the plunge and hit the Riviera for a taste of the world's most famous film festival.

Attending Cannes will be one of the most rewarding things you do for your film industry career. But at the same time it can also be a rather daunting experience. Not only do you have to stay on top of 12 days of hardcore film business, you must also cope with the fact that the event takes place in a country which doesn't speak English, in a city that isn't the largest nor the cheapest place to stay on the Riviera. So where do you start? How do you get to the festival? And where do you find that essential information that will make your visit fun, successful, and most importantly, stress free?

"Cannes - A Festival Virgin's Guide" is for filmmakers and film industry professionals who are interested in learning more about the Festival, how it operates, and how to make the most of their time in on the Riviera. We intend to demystify the city and the festival, and help make your visit both successful and enjoyable. There are four main sections in the book:

The City - covering amongst other things, getting to Cannes, getting around, places to stay, places to eat, and general information;

The Festival - its structure, how to attend, parties and hanging out, and all about the screenings;

The Biz - an overview of how the business side of the festival operates and some advice for filmmakers who are planning to head to Cannes with a project in tow;

The Lowdown - a series of interviews with a selection of Cannes veterans from across the film industry.

In addition to these sections, there is a group of appendices containing a wealth of additional information.

But before we move forward, please take a moment glance over the following notes and bear them in mind as you read through this book.

How to Pronounce "Cannes"
Hopefully you know this already, but if not, remember: *cans* are what you find in a six pack, *Khan* is the bad guy in the second Star Trek movie (Australians, take note!), and *can* is a city in the south of France, famous for its film festival. Cannes is pronounced *can* as in "can of beer."

Prices
Currency exchange rates are in constant flux, but local prices change very slowly over time. Consequently, all prices in this guide are shown in local currency - in this case Euro. More information on the Euro and obtaining/converting money in

Cannes can be found in the section on Money in part one of this book. Any price shown in dollars ($) are US dollars.

Phone Numbers

Most phone numbers in this guide are shown in the format you would use if you were to call them from within France. In order to call these numbers from abroad, you need to add your phone company's international access code, the country code for France (33), and then you must drop the leading zero on any number shown. For example, the Cannes phone number 04 23 82 92 82 would be dialled:

From USA	001 33 4 23 82 92 82
From UK	00 33 4 23 82 92 82
From Australia	0011 33 4 23 82 92 82

You should check with your own phone company for the correct international access code for your service.

And Finally...

It's worth remembering that whilst this book contains a large amount of information about Cannes and the festival, it is by no means 100% comprehensive. As time passes, recommendations change, old places close while new places open, and some suggestions may not suit all tastes. Even the festival itself changes over time - part of the fun of attending an event like Cannes for the first time is building your own library of experiences or anecdotes, and scouting out new places that you can recommend to future Cannes virgins.

cannes
a festival virgin's guide

CFVG Online

Visit Cannes — A Festival Virgin's Guide on the Web for the latest on the festival, access to up-to-the-minute information, and a suite of tools to help make your trip a success.

Hotel Booking — online bookings with real-time availability and reservations.

Accommodation Exchange — find and share lodging with other festivalgoers

Restaurant Guide — the lowdown on the best places to eat in Cannes

Travel Desk — cost-effective travel services from CFVG's partners

Message Boards — share advice and meet new Cannes contacts

www.cannesguide.com

the city

the city

For nearly 200 years Cannes has been a favourite playground for the rich and famous. The city is renowned for its expensive lifestyle, its agreeable Mediterranean climate, and of course its film festival. Tight old streets bustle with a plethora of boutiques displaying the latest from the world's leading designers, with classy restaurants and trendy cafes filling the void between. And in Cannes even a Big Mac meal can set you back in excess of $10 (and yes, you can down a beer while enjoying your Royale with Cheese).

But there is more to Cannes than your preconceptions of wealth and opulent Riviera lifestyles. Despite the presence of the well-heeled jet set, the city has managed to maintain a large degree of old world Southern European charm. It's easy to get lost in the fascinating street markets that are hidden away in quiet alleys – a little local knowledge can help uncover wonderful food that is often great value for money. And if you want to dodge the festival crowds for a day or two, the surrounding region harbours a wide array of medieval villages, abbeys, and museums, as well as wealth of other cultural and historical attractions.

history

Like most cities on the Mediterranean rim, Cannes has a long and colourful history - a history which dates back far beyond its reputation as a film industry hotspot or playground for the rich and famous.

Archaeological evidence suggests that the area now dominated by the city of Cannes gained its first significant settlement around 200 B.C. At the time the local populace of Nikaia (Nice) and Antipolis (Antibes) was immersed in a bitter territorial dispute with the nearby Oxybians.

cannes facts

Population 70,000

Average May Temperature High 20°C (68°F) Low 13.3°C (56°F)

Measurement System Metric

Time Zone Western Europe (GMT +1, +2 from late-March to late-October)

Electricity 220 volts AC, 50Hz (standard Western Europe round two-pin plugs)

Phone Country Code 33, City Code 04

The call was put out to Rome for support and the soldiers arrived soon after to make short work of the rebels. To discourage the remaining Oxybians from returning, the Romans set up a garrisoned trading post which allowed Cannes – at this point little more than a small fishing village – to grow and be transformed into a *castrum* (fortified town).

Despite the presence of the Romans, the local area still suffered attacks from the handful of left over Oxybians and their Ligurian allies and this appears to have indirectly been the origin of the town's name. To counter the threat from the remaining rebels, the people of nearby Marseilles constructed a fort on the hill of Le Suquet in the heart of what is now Cannes. The fort was named *Castrum Marsellinum* ("The Fort of Marseilles"), but this didn't really go down well with the locals, who simply referred to it as *Castrum Canoïs* due to the presence of many *canna* (reeds) at the foot of the hill. Translated into the Provençal language, this became *Canes*, which first appears on record in 1619. Although this is the generally-accepted origin of the town's name, a handful of other scholars also point to the fact that the Indo-European languages have a root *kan*, which means "to dig in" or "fortify".

Documented history in the area began around 410 A.D. with the arrival of a congregation of monks from Italy. Under the leadership of Saint Honoratus, the monks founded a monastery on a small island in what is now the Baie de Cannes (Bay of Cannes) with the intention of going about their worship in solitude. The island later became known as Ile

Saint Honorat, named for the leader of the monks.

For several hundred years the monks lived in relative isolation, conducting a small amount of trade with the Romans and local fisherman, but otherwise keeping largely to themselves. However, towards the end of the first millennium, Ile Sainte Honorat began to suffer an increasing number of attacks from marauding Saracen pirates. Around 1000 A.D., the monks took steps to counter this threat, commencing a programme of fortification works which would continue for several centuries. Although over time the Saracen threat began to dissipate and the monks remained fairly secure on their fortified island, the local area continued to remain unstable for the following centuries, experiencing reasonably frequent turmoil caused by armies in transit between the various wars in France, Italy, and Spain.

By the 14th Century, the region around Cannes had found its way into the hands of the Counts of Provence – the local aristocracy which ruled a large chunk of what is now the south of France. In 1480, the reigning monarch "Good King René" died without leaving a clear succession plan. The king's nephew, Charles du Maine, laid claim to the throne even though many believed the title was rightfully that of the Duke of Lorraine, René's grandson. Not wanting to see a civil war break out in his southern neighbour's backyard, the French king, Louis XI, stepped in and brokered a somewhat self-beneficial deal: the Duke of Lorraine was paid to renounce his inheritance and

Du Maine was forced to bequeath Provence to the French Crown "for its own protection". Charles and his supporters would have probably been fairly quick to realise that they had been given the rough end of the deal, but for the fact that the very next day, Du Maine "mysteriously" dropped dead after dining during a visit to Marseilles.

Under French rule life for the Cannois remained harsh, but relatively peaceful for the next couple of centuries until things were shaken up in 1615 when France declared war on Spain. Worried about the possibility of a large-scale naval attack on his eastern seaboard, Cardinal Richelieu, the country's ruler in all but name, ordered the construction of a fort on Ile Sainte Marguerite (the larger of the two islands in the Lérins group off Cannes) as part of a wide-ranging upgrade of France's eastern defences. But the new fort failed to keep the armada at bay, falling to Spanish forces in 1635. Fortunately for Richelieu, the fort was only held briefly by the Spaniards before being liberated by French troops in 1637.

Following the Spanish scare, Marshal Vauban – Louis XIV's leading military engineer – realised the strategic importance of the area and in 1712, order the fort to be completed reconstructed. A prison wing was also added at the same time to house a whole host of "guests of the state" in a place which was far away from the action so as to prevent them from causing trouble for the king, but not so far away that he couldn't keep an eye on them. The Fort Royale, as it became known, operated as a prison right up to the early 20th Century housing a large number of political prisoners, the most famous of which was The Man in the Iron Mask.

The plight of the infamous masked prisoner, incarcerated between 1687 and 1689, was immortalised in the Alexandre Dumas novel, "Le Vicomte de Bragelonne" ("The Viscount of Bragelonne"), but his true identity remains a mystery to this day. Some historians say he was the elder brother of Louis XIV; others that he was actually Louis' twin brother. Tales of illegitimacy also abound: some suggest that he was the fruit of some hanky-panky between Anne of Austria (the wife of Louis XIII) and the Duke of Buckingham; or the same Anne and one Cardinal Mazarin (the effective ruler of France while Louis XIV was a child). A few even believe that masked man was the illegitimate son of Charles II of England or of Louis XIV himself. Other evidence suggests that he may have been Count Matteoli (an Italian courtesan), imprisoned for espionage during the Franco-Spanish war. But the common thread that runs through all of the various rumours is that virtually everyone believed he was of royal blood, since he received preferential treatment during his time in prison.

Perhaps the most enchanting rumour of them all is the one which would have The Man in the Iron Mask as the grandfather of Napoleon Bonaparte. As the story goes, a local Cannes woman visited the masked man in his cell one night and the horizontal folk-dancing that ensued resulted in the woman bearing a son. For reasons unknown, the child was subsequently fostered out to a family in Corsica. Although the new parents knew nothing of the child's origins, they were assured that he was de buoné-parte (of good breeding) and thus named him Bonaparte.

The most recent conclusions suggest that the Man in the Iron Mask may simply have been a royal servant who was incarcerated for knowing a little too much about a series of scandalous financial dealings at the palace. At any rate, the secret died with him in the Bastille in Paris in 1703. Interestingly, one piece of trivia that does survive to this day is the fact that his famed mask was actually made of velvet rather than iron.

During the Century after the Man in the Iron Mask's death, Cannes and its surrounds once again returned to a peaceful state. In the early 19th Century, Cannes grew off the back of a strong local fishing industry, and the construction of a better port to facilitate trade with the nearby inland town of Grasse. Not long after this, Napoleon I, returning from exile on the Italian island of Elba, used the area as a bivouac for his new army before carving a route through the Alps en route to Paris. However, Cannes as we know it today was actually born in 1834 with the arrival of an Englishman by the name of Henry Brougham.

At the time, Brougham was Lord Chancellor of Great Britain, but more importantly for the future of Cannes, he was also a fan of fleeing the miserable British winter in favour of warmer climes. In 1834 Brougham set off with his daughter, Eleonore Louise, to visit Italy. Back in those days, if you were an English aristocrat travelling

to Italy, you did so by sea. Brougham and his daughter arrived in the port of Nice only to find that the Italian border had been closed by the King of Piemonte in order to contain an outbreak of cholera. Brougham decided to head for the alpine town of Grasse instead, but as it was late in the day he felt it was best to spend the night at an inn in the port of Cannes before heading inland at daybreak.

Although he originally intended a brief stop in Cannes, Brougham and Eleonore Louise were charmed by the beauty of the area and the hospitality of their hosts. They ended up staying for many days and by the time they left, Brougham had decided to build a home in the idyllic village. Two years later the toast of the British aristocracy flocked to Cannes for the inauguration of Villa Eléonore-Louise, named for his daughter. Such was Brougham's influence within London's high society, before you could say, "By George, I need a winter retreat," a colony of English villas and chateaux had sprung up in and around the town.

For the next 10 years Cannes grew steady as a British winter colony, but as time progressed it also attracted the attention of other well-to-do types in Europe. Following a brief visit in 1848, Alexandra Feodorovna Skrypitzine, the wife of the French consul to Moscow, fell in love with the town, returning a short time later with a host of Russian aristocracy in tow. The increasing number of visitors prompted construction of Cannes' first luxury hotel in 1858, the Gonnet et de la Reine, which also helped further cement the town's reputation as a resort for the wealthy.

Until 1863 the French aristocracy had taken little notice of the antics on the Riviera, so Cannes largely remained a destination for rich foreigners. But that year marked the completion of the Paris-Lyon-Méditerranée railway, and with it the town suddenly became extremely accessible to the wealthy French middle classes and Parisian socialites. French interest in Cannes received a major boost in 1865 with the arrival of Prosper Mérimée, France's Inspector of Historical Monuments. Mérimée was a friend of Brougham and well-placed in French high society. After a brief visit to the area on a mission to catalogue the historical value of the Lérins Islands, he became instrumental in promoting Cannes to his Parisian chums. Shortly after his first visit, Mérimée himself took up full-time residency in the town in order to use the area's "therapeutic climate" to help control his asthma.

Indeed, Cannes' reputation as a "health resort" had been steadily growing for several years, with many prominent British and French doctors singing the praises of the restorative powers of the region's winter climate. By 1883 the town had no less than five hydrotherapy centres, where patients came to benefit from range of water treatments targeting a whole host of ailments. Local doctors published a range of brochures and guides aimed at attracting the widest possible clientele, following the example of the best-selling book, "Winter in Cannes and Le Cannet", by Dr Antonin Buttura, which divided the town into three zones of interest for patients: the seafront ("extremely tonic, stimulating"), the foothills ("tonic, restorative") and the hill and valley zone ("tonic, calmer").

The appearance of villas, luxury hotels, and health spas was not the only change experienced by the city during the second half of the 19th Century. At time of Lord Brougham's arrival, the diversity of the local flora was fairly limited due mainly to the arid climate. For the wealthy new residents of the area, this was a problem. It was unimaginable for an Englishman to live without flowers, let alone without a lawn! But the area suffered from the lack of a reliable water supply – most of the watercourses were seasonal mountain streams that were dry for a good part of the year.

Not to let this kind of problem stand in his way, Brougham and a few colleagues formed the "General Irrigation and Water Supply Company of France Limited" to address the challenge of supplying water to their homes and gardens, and by extension, to the residents of Cannes. The company's crowing achievement was the construction of the Canal de la Siagne, which was completed in 1868 and continues to provide water for Cannes to this day.

The introduction of irrigation to the land between the Mediterranean and the mountains had a dramatic effect, transforming the area into a botanical paradise capable of sustaining a huge array of plant life. And Cannes' wealthy residents spared no expense scouring the globe for the most exotic specimens available. Soon the area was teaming with flora, including citrus trees from the Middle East, eucalyptuses from Australia, and the *Phoenix Canariensis* from Africa. Better known as the classic palm tree, these plants can now be found throughout the region and have become an icon of the city and its famous film festival.

The arrival of the 20th Century saw Cannes in persistent growth. More luxury hotels and villas were built, and the area continued to flourish as a winter health resort for Europe's elite. One piece of interesting Cannes trivia is the suggestion that the cupolas of the famous Carlton Hotel (designed by Marcellin Mayère's and built in 1910) were inspired by the architect's fascination with the reputedly ample bosom of a well-known local courtesan named La Belle Otéro.

The carefree lifestyle of Cannes was briefly interrupted during World War I, when the winter health fanatics were replaced by northern refugees and wounded soldiers. Many of the luxury hotels in town were also used as makeshift hospitals between 1914 and 1918, but by the late 1920s the festive spirit had returned to Cannes and the town also began to attract summer visitors. In answer to this new demand, the local hotel managers took the then unprecedented step of opening for the summer season in 1931 (previously all the hotels had closed during the summer), and Cannes adopted its current guise of a year-round resort.

Today Cannes is a thriving metropolis of around 70,000 people, sitting in the middle of one of France's most prosperous regions. Cannes is France's second-most important city for business tourism (after Paris), and hosts international events throughout the year for a wide variety of industries ranging from advertising and music, to tax-free goods and pharmaceuticals. The city is also a major hub for a busy regional tourism industry, hosts the world's most famous film festival, and of course is still one of the top places to be seen on the Riviera.

getting there

The city of Cannes is located in the south of France on the Mediterranean coast known as the *Côte d'Azur*, or more famously, as the "French Riviera". Being close to many major European cities, Cannes is well-serviced by a variety of modes of transport, so getting there poses few problems.

By Air
Nice-Côte d'Azur International Airport (Airport Code – NCE, www. nice.aeroport.fr) is the main entry point for those flying to the festival. Nice is France's second busiest air destination after Paris so a huge number of local and international airlines fly there directly or via one of the major European hubs. There is another airport closer to Cannes, Cannes-Mandelieu (Airport Code – CEQ, www.cannes-mandelieu. aeroport.fr), however this is used mainly by private jets and the odd European charter flight.

For the long haul crowd, major international carriers such as Delta, Air France, and QANTAS operate a daily service to Nice from many key airports. Within Europe the preference tends to be towards the various low-cost carriers which now crisscross the continent. Popular carriers include Easyjet (www.easyjet.com), Air Berlin (www.airberlin.com), and Flyglobspan (www.flyglobespan.com), but it's also worth checking out the regular airlines as well. Companies like British Airways (www.ba.com), BMI (www.flybmi.com), Aerlingus (www.aerlingus.com), and Lufthansa (www.lufthansa.com) have found themselves squeezed by their low-cost rivals and now regularly offer comparable deals.

Whilst the options on flights to Nice should be reasonably plentiful, it's important to remember that the arrival of May sees much of Europe poised for a leap into peak season. Consequently you will not only be in competition with other festivalgoers for seats, but also against people who've booked early summer holidays. To ensure that you not only get a seat, but also the best possible fare, it goes without saying that you should book your tickets as early as humanly possible. Today's airlines are masters of 'dynamic pricing', which means the closer to the flying date you book your ticket, the more you pay. Seats on flights to Nice are also put under pressure by the Monaco Grand Prix, which often clashes with the first weekend of the festival and also uses Nice as its main entry point.

Once you've arrived in Nice getting a transfer to Cannes is a piece of cake. Most people opt to make use of the shuttle service provided by Bus Rapides Côte d'Azur (Tel. 04 93 39 11 39, www.rca.tm.fr) to take them the last 25km to Cannes. The service operates between 7am and 7pm every day, with buses leaving both terminals at Nice airport at approximately 30 minute intervals. Fares are around 12.90€ and the trip to Cannes takes about 45 minutes. On arrival, you are conveniently deposited at the central bus station on Place Cornut-Gentille (outside Hôtel de Ville).

Alternatively, if you're watching the pennies you can take a local bus from the airport to Cannes for a few euros less. These have more stops and therefore take considerably longer, however can be useful if you are staying east of Cannes in places such as Antibes, Juan-les-Pins, or Golfe Juan. Note that unless you're planning on visiting the centre of Nice, catching the train from Nice to Cannes is a waste of time – the train station is in the centre of town, which is in the opposite direction to Cannes!

If you're arriving outside of the shuttle bus times, travelling in a small group, or simply want to avoid the crowds, a taxi from the airport to Cannes will set you back between 60€ - 80€ (depending on the time of day). But sadly, as with many airports around the world, there is a healthy racket in inflated fares for visitors run by some less reputable drivers. To alleviate this problem regional authorities have introduced a fixed-price voucher system which covers fares to major local destinations (including Cannes). Ask about taxi vouchers at the airport information desk after arrival.

Finally, if you're living the movie mogul lifestyle or believe that money is simply here to provide access to the better things in life, you might want to consider a helicopter transfer to Cannes. For around 400€ you and up to four "assistants" can enjoy spectacular mountain and costal views as you are whisked off to Cannes, high above the rabble for a highly civilised 20 minutes. The helicopter service is operated by Helistation de Cannes (Tel. 04 93 43 42 42; www.nicehelicopteres.com).

By Car

Driving to Cannes is a very straight-forward affair and has long been a popular method of travel for groups of indie filmmakers from Britain, Germany, and other parts of Europe. If you have a bit of time and are bringing several people, travelling to Cannes by car can also be extremely cost-effective. French roads are normally in excellent condition and largely uncongested, however be prepared for frequent wallet-crunching tolls (and the inflated cost of petrol if you're used to North American prices).

In France, motorways (aka freeways) are called *autoroutes*. They have the prefix "A" and most have *péages* (tolls). Other major roads have the prefix "N" for *Route National* and minor roads are classed as "D" roads. Just to keep everyone guessing, most road signs on major routes also show the Europe-wide numbering system starting with "E". These are best ignored if you are only driving in France, because one European route may actually use several different French roads.

The bulk of the drivers come from the UK and therefore the route usually starts at Calais. The journey from Calais to Cannes is around 1120km (696 miles) and takes approximately 11 – 15 hours on the road. You can expect to pay around 40€ in tolls each way (or up to 80€ if you opt for autoroutes all the way). For the shortest (and cheapest) route, start in Calais on the A26, simply follow the signs to Lyon (via Reims and Dijon), then the A43/A48 to Grenoble. From there, take the N75 to Sisteron (via Digne-les-Bains) and change for the N85 to Cannes. The drive along the N75/N85 *Route Napoléon* (carved out by the emperor's army on his return from exile) offers some spectacular mountain scenery. If you're travelling from Paris, take the A6 to Lyon, then take the route as from Calais. Head back the same way, following the signs for Paris until you see one for Dijon, then follow that route on via Reims to Calais (although take care as some of the turnoffs are easier to miss in the opposite direction).

If you are bringing a car from the UK or elsewhere in Europe, you should ensure that your insurance meets the minimum requirements in France. The speed limit on A-roads is 130kph (110kph in wet weather), 110kph on dual carriageway N-roads, 90kph outside built-up areas, and 50kph in towns. Emergency breakdown assistance can be obtained from Inter-Mutuelles (Tel. 0800 75 75 75) on most major routes, although not on autoroutes as these have their own breakdown services (use the orange emergency telephone boxes). Alternatively, you can contact the *Gendarmerie* (local police) for assistance.

By Train

Cannes is serviced by local,

international, and TGV (fast) trains from Paris and many other European cities. If you are travelling from within France, Switzerland, or Northern Italy, it's likely you will be able to get a fairly direct train to Cannes. Otherwise, you will need to pick up a connection in Paris (typically at Gare de Lyon). Journey times from Paris to Cannes are approximately seven hours on the sleeper train or five hours by TGV. If you're coming from London via Eurostar you'll need to add roughly 3-4 hours to the journey time.

The train station in Cannes (Gare du Cannes, Tel. 08 92 35 35 35) can be found right in the centre of town at Place de la Gare. For more information, fares, and timetables, contact France's national railway operator SNCF (www.sncf.fr), visit Rail Europe (www.raileurope.co.uk) or contact Eurostar (Tel. +44 (0)8705 186 186; www.eurostar.com). If you are under 26 you should always enquire about the possibility of discounts as many European rail services have special "youth fares" available.

By Bus

Many coach lines service Nice and Cannes from major cities within France, Europe, and the UK. Contact your local travel agent for more information on operators from a specific location, or try visiting Go By Coach (www.gobycoach. com) for timetables, fares, and online bookings. There are two bus stations in Cannes: one by the train station, generally used by inland routes; the other outside Hôtel de Ville, mainly serving local and coastal destinations. Typical journey times will be approximately 10 hours on the road from Paris and 15 hours from Calais.

In Groups

Some local filmmaking co-ops or similar organisations arrange group transport (and often accommodation) for their members. It's definitely worth contacting your local filmmaking organisation or government film office to see if there are any groups with which you can tag along. Alternatively, form your own group and transform your journey into a kick-arse European road trip!

finding your way

Given the amount of running around done by most festivalgoers in Cannes, your feet will be eternally grateful for the fact that 99% of the festival action is jammed into a few blocks of this small city.

The city itself is loosely divided into eight main districts:

Centre Ville

This district covers the area between the train station and the waterfront. 95% of the festival action is found

travel made simple

Make sure you take a few moments to visit the Travel Desk at the Cannes - A Festival Virgin's Guide web site (www.cannesguide.com) for great deals on flights from many locations around the world.

here, as are a large number of the hotels in Cannes. As you'd expect, staying in Centre Ville affords a great deal of convenience in terms of being close to the action, but convenience does of course come at a price...

Le Suquet

This area is sometimes called the "Old Town" and basically covers the veritable maze of tiny pedestrian streets that crisscross the hill at the west end of town. Le Suquet is mainly comprised of small flats for the locals, but you'll also find a good selection of restaurants here (particularly along the port and up Rue Sainte Antoine).

Pointe Croisette

A large peninsular, known as the Cap d'Antibes, forms the eastern-most boundary of the Baie de Cannes. The inland end of this district contains a high density of flats and hotels, and can be a good option if accommodation in closer areas is either hard to come by or out of your price range. Further out onto the peninsular you'll find the famed Hotel du Cap – Eden Roc where all of the A-list celebrities stay during the festival.

Californie Pezou

This district is largely comprised of expensive villas owned by the Riviera's richest residents. If you are renting an out of town villa, there is a good chance it will be in this district (as will be many of the infamous villa parties). The south end of Californie Pezou is not too far from the festival action, but the north end can be a bit of a trek.

Prado Republique

This district backs up against the train station and stretches in a thin corridor northwards until it hits the A8 autoroute (unofficially the boundary between Cannes and the town of Mougins). The south end of Prado offers a good range of less expensive hotels, and is still within walking distance of the Centre Ville.

Carnot

Like Prado Republique, the Carnot district also backs up to the train station and stretches northwards. Boulevard Carnot cuts a dead straight line up the middle of this area, and again is home to a range of reasonably priced hotels and restaurants where locals eat. The south end is within easy walking distance of the festival action.

Petit Juas

This district sits behind Le Suquet and stretches northwest back to the A8. It's occupied mainly by flats and houses for the locals, but there are also a few posh villas in the area, including Lord Borougham's Villa Eléonore-Louise (now a private residence), so you might find also yourself at a party in this area.

Croix des Gardes

A large, mainly residential district which stretches northwest from behind Le Suquet. The area is dominated by a large municipal park housing a range of expensive villas. As you move north through this district you can almost watch the wealth evaporate – the north end of the district is occupied by locals who may be living close to the Riviera, but are very far from the dream.

In addition to the districts of Cannes itself you may also come across references to some of the surrounding areas (particularly in relation to accommodation):

Cannes la Bocca
Le Cannet
Antibes-Juan les Pins
Golfe Juan
Mandelieu-la-Napoule
Mougins
Vallauris

All of these areas are suitable alternatives for accommodation if you can't get something closer to town. If you do opt for a hotel in one of these areas, you will need to take into account the transport options as none of them are within walking distance of Centre Ville. The time required to get from these towns to Cannes is probably between 15 – 45 minutes, depending on where exactly you are staying and the traffic conditions at the time you travel.

In terms of finding your way around the Centre Ville, a basic map can be found in the back of this book. This lists the key streets and locations in the city. However your first mission upon arrival should be to seek out a proper map. These are available free of charge at either branch of the official tourist office:

Palais des Festivals
Esplanade Georges Pompidou
Tel. 04 92 99 84 22
Open seven days, 9am to 8pm

Gare du Cannes (train station)
Place de la Gare
Tel. 04 92 99 19 77
Open Monday to Friday, 9am to 7pm.

The entrance to the tourist office at the Palais can be found to the right of the blue Théâtre Debussy steps; the tourist office at the train station is on the ground floor at the east end of the building (on the right if you are facing the station from Rue Jean Jaurès), and is generally a better option as the staff tend to be friendlier (due to not being constantly harassed).

With map in hand and a basic understanding of the main districts of the city, you should take a bit of time shortly after your arrival to familiarise yourself with the location (and pronunciation) of the following places. Some of these are used for various functions of the festival itself, others you will simply find it useful to know their locations.

City Buildings and Streets

Boulevard de la Croisette – "The Croisette" is the main beach-front drag and is dotted with classy hotels, expensive restaurants, and crowds several miles deep. Most of the festival action takes place along this road and people-watching can be a great pass-time. *Croisette* is pronounced: KWA-SET.

Rue d'Antibes - located a couple of blocks inland from the Croisette, Rue d'Antibes is the retail backbone of Cannes. All manner of expensive shops line this tight street and it's here you will find it effortlessly simple to part with your hard-earned cash. However, Rue d'Antibes is important for another reason: most of the banks (and consequently ATMs) can be found here. *Antibes* is pronounced: ON-TEEB.

Hôtel de Ville - knowing the location of this building is important, not because you might consider staying there (it's actually the town hall, not a hotel), but rather because the main bus station (Gare Routière) is right outside in Place Bernard Cornut Gentille. *Hôtel de Ville* is pronounced: OH-TEL DE VILL.

Gare du Cannes – AKA *Gare SNCF*. Aside from the obvious reason, you should also be familiar with the location of the train station because, firstly, it is used as a reference point for many places described elsewhere in this book; secondly, because it generally separates the business area of Cannes (for festival purposes anyway) from the rest of the city; and finally, because the other main bus station is located out the front. The train station can be found on Rue Jean Jaurès. *Gare* is pronounced: GAR.

Gare Maritime – knowing the location of the ferry port is useful if you want to take a few hours off and head out to the islands, but it also houses the accreditation centre for Cinéphiles and day passes. The ferry port is located on the west end of the Croisette, near the corner with Rue du Maréchal Joffre. *Maritime* is pronounced: MARI-TEEM.

Major Hotels – even if you're not staying in one, it's important to know where the various major hotels are located. You may need to attend a meeting, or even decide to do some networking in one of the bars (assuming your credit card is prepared for the assault). Almost all of the majors can be found along The Croisette: the Majestic Barrière

at the corner with Rue des Serbes; the Grand Hôtel near the corner with Rue Commandant André; the Noga Hilton at the corner with Rue Frédéric Amouretti; the Carlton Intercontinental at the corner with Rue François Einesy; and the Martinez at the corner with Rue Latour-Maubourg. The odd one out is the Grey d'Albion, which can be found straddling Rue des États-Unis and Rue des Serbes.

Festival Buildings and Locations

Palais des Festivals – Officially known as the Palais des Festivals et Congrès, but more commonly referred to as "The Bunker", "The Fortress", or simply, "The Palais", this massive conference centre is located on the waterfront, smack in the middle of town. The Palais is home to the main festival action including the official screenings, festival administration, the press centre, and a good deal of the Market action. Access to the Palais is strictly controlled by the festival's blue-blazered, no-nonsense security men. An accreditation badge or official invitation is required to enter the Palais and in today's heightened security climate expect some delay in entering while bags are searched and you and your fellow festivalgoers are scanned (and occasionally frisked) for metal objects. The Palais is open from 9am to 6pm daily during the festival. *Palais des Festivals* is pronounced: PAL-AY DE FEST-EE-VAL

Riviera – Recently built to take up the overflow from the Palais this brand-spanking new building has 7,000 square meters of exhibition space and eight state of the art screening theatres. The Riviera now houses the bulk of the Market activities, including market screenings and the tradeshow floor. You will find the Riviera directly behind the Palais, accessible either through the bowels of its older brother or via its own entrance on the east side of the building. You will need your accreditation badge to enter.

Cinemas

In addition to the various theatres and screening rooms in the Palais and Riviera there are seven other venues where films are screened in Cannes during the festival. These are dealt within the "Screenings" section, later in this guide.

Le Club – The festival's official lounge for accredited attendees. Quieter than other parts of the Palais or Riviera, Le Club provides snacks and beverages as well as wi-fi Internet access and several screens on which you can watch the Festival TV channel in French or English. Entry to Le Club is generally prioritised for holders of press accreditation, but it normally isn't a problem for other festivalgoers to gain entry upon presentation of your badge. Le Club can be found on Level 4 of the Palais.

Village International – aka "the pavilions". At festival time, a veritable Bedouin village springs up on the waterfront in Cannes as many national film commissions and other organisations pitch their tents outside the Palais. Whilst entry to some pavilions is by invitation only, the bulk of them offer a range of facilities for informal meetings, Internet access, seminars, and quick snacks. Services tend to be targeted towards nationals of the respective countries they represent, but are normally open to all accredited festivalgoers. More details on specific pavilions can be found in the section on "Parties and Hanging Out".

Village International Pantiero – as the number of pavilions now far exceeds the space available outside the Palais, the festival has set up a second Village International at La Pantiero in front of the old port. The Village International Pantiero houses the pavilions of the various sponsors and the myriad of French organisations that are involved in the festival, but is also home to the new *Cinéma de la Monde*. An accreditation badge is usually required to enter the area. *Pantiero* is pronounced: PAN-TEE-AIR-OH.

Festival Boutique – official Cannes-branded merchandise, including clothing, posters and gifts, is available from the Festival Boutique, located at the far eastern end of the Village International. The boutique is open to both festivalgoers and the general public.

Festival and other relevant venues and locales are marked on the Cannes map at the back of this book. You can also find a map of key festival venues in the accreditation pack provided when you pick up your badge.

For additional information on festival locations, check out one of the various information booths (called *Points d'Informations*, marked with a yellow "i") which are dotted around the Palais and Riviera buildings. Multi-lingual hostesses are also available to answer your questions.

getting around

Cannes is a relatively small city, and since most of the festival action is concentrated in a few compact blocks between the train station and the waterfront, getting around town poses little or no problem. If you are staying in town then the easiest way to get around is the old two-leg method. Out of town, public transport will probably be your best bet for getting between your accommodation and festival central.

Buses

The main operator in Cannes is Bus Azur. With routes all over the city and to neighbouring towns, buses run approximately every 15-20 minutes between 6am and 9pm. The service is less frequent on Sundays and public holidays, and the last buses leave at around 7pm. Overall, the bus system is fairly reliable, although the lack of after-hours services does put you in taxi territory when coming back from an evening screening or late party.

Fares on Bus Azur are a standard 1.35€ for a single journey. If you're planning to use the buses extensively, you can save a bit by buying either a 10-trip ticket (*La Carte 10 Voyages*, 9€) or a weekly pass (*La Carte Palm'Hebdo*, 10€). The weekly pass is valid for seven days from the date you first use it. Buy your passes at Gare Routière or at a range of bars and tabacs around the city including:

Bar Tabac Saint-Antoine
6 Place Cornut-Gentille

Forville Presse
12 Rue Louis Blanc

Régence Tabac
10 Rue Maréchal Foch

Tabac de Luxe le 116
69 Rue Félix Faure

Tabac du Lycée
129 Boulevard de la République

Trains

If you are staying reasonably close to a station, the train service operated by SNCF provides a great alternative to the buses. Unlike their four-wheeled compadres the trains are incredibly reliable and operate until midnight (except on Sundays and public holidays). Although they won't really be useful for getting around town (as there's only one line), they significantly reduce the hassle of staying out of town in certain areas. Local train fares are 1.60€ - 3.00€ for an *aller simple*, *deuxieme class* (single, second class ticket).

Taxis

Unless you are lucky enough to be staying in town, after 9pm taxis become the main mode of transport between festival central and a cosy bed. Rates are pretty much on par with what you'd expect to pay in most modern cities. It's around 2.40€ at flag-fall, then about 1.50€ per kilometre. Cannes taxis will also charge extra if you have luggage (normally around 0.65€ per item) and surcharges apply late at night or in the wee hours of the morning.

Most French taxi drivers are hard-working, honest folk, but there will always be someone who'll try to extract a few extra euros given the opportunity. The most common trick amongst European taxi drivers is insisting that there is a fixed fare for your destination. Of course, this fare is usually higher than the meter would be, so unless you know you are buying a fixed-price trip (i.e. from the airport), always ensure the meter is running when you start your journey. Tipping is not necessary with French taxis and the taxi passenger charter prevents drivers from demanding a tip. However like everyone else, drivers will be appreciative of a little extra if you feel that the service they provided was good.

One key difference between taxis in France and those in other countries is you cannot hail a French taxi from the roadside. By law they are not allowed to pick you up (although inevitably some will). To get a taxi you should find one of the official taxi ranks which are located all over the city. The rank outside Hôtel de Ville is a good option, particularly when every taxi within a mile of the Palais is fair game for the post-screening hoards. Alternatively, you can order your own (24/7) from:

Allô Taxi Cannes
103 Avenue Georges Clémenceau
Tel. 04 92 99 27 27
www.taxicannes.com

Driving (and Parking)
Forget about driving in Cannes. Tight streets, thick crowds, and road closures near Festival Ground Zero (the Palais) make driving a nightmare best avoided. And this is before you face the problem of finding somewhere to park. So the advice is: if you're staying in Cannes itself you don't need a car because virtually everywhere you need to go will be within reasonable walking distance. If you're staying away from the centre of town, or in one of the neighbouring areas, your best bet is to use your car to come into town in the morning then join the foot-crowd for the rest of the day.

There around 5,500 spaces in the various car parks around town. This might sound like a lot, but given that around 1,400 go to official vehicles in the Palais and Pantiero car parks, and that there are around 200,000 people in Cannes during the festival, it doesn't leave a lot to go around. The moral of the story is of course get there early. Parking rates vary a little between car parks but are generally in region of 2€ - 3€ per hour. A full day's parking, multiplied by the number of days you are in Cannes can add up to a small fortune – another reason why it's best to avoid using a car if at all possible. The following car parks are all within walking distance of festival-central:

Parking Croisette (280 places)
Enter off Port Canto, La Croisette

Parking Ferrage (400 places)
Enter off Boulevard Victor Tuby

Parking Forville (700 places)
Enter off Rue Pastour, Avenue Sainte Louis, or Rue de la Miséricorde

Parking Lamy (400 places)
Enter off Rue d'Antibes or Boulevard de Lorraine

Parking Laubeuf (350 places)
Enter off Boulevard Jean Hilbert

Parking République (126 places)
Enter off Rue Docteur Calmette

Parking Vauban (280 places)
Enter off Rue Raphaël, Avenue de Grasse

Gray d'Albion (475 places)
Enter off Rue des Serbes

Gare SNCF (660 places)
Enter off Rue Jean Jaurès

Parking du Noga Hilton (458 places)
Enter off La Croisette or Rond-Point Duboys d'Angers

If you have any issues with your car in one of the car parks, you can either contact the local police or the city's car park operator:

Unipark
Tel. 04 93 38 52 12
www.interparking-france.com

In addition to the car parks, metered street parking is available in the areas surrounding Centre Ville. In most cases the maximum stay is limited to a few hours and traffic wardens are active across the city during the festival. There are a few unmetered spaces around the place, but as you can imagine, they fill up very quickly. As with most cities, the parking restrictions tend to be relaxed in the evenings and on Sundays or public holidays. However for obvious reasons, you should never park in tow-away zone (marked by a small sign showing a tow-truck and car).

If you do return to find your car has been visited by one of the city's meter-maids (yes, for some reason they are all women with uniforms comprised of skirts which have an interesting length and level of tightness for such

an official position), then you can pay the fine at most tabacs around town. To settle your ticket you purchase stamps from the tabac, attach these to the ticket and simply pop it in a post box. If you return and you car has disappeared completely your first port of call should be the local impound depot: Fourière Municipal (Tel. Tel. 04 93 43 54 55).

Car Rental
Whilst you shouldn't need to rent a car to get around town, if you have some spare time it may be cool to grab some wheels for the day and check out the area surrounding Cannes. A few suggestions for day-trip destinations can be found in the "Getting Away" section of this book. If you do decide to go exploring make sure you get yourself a decent map of the area. The tourist office should be able to help you with this, if not, the rental companies themselves. As always, it is generally cheaper to book your rental car before you leave your home country, and you will need to be at least 25 years old (although some companies will rent to people between 21-25 for an additional premium). Try Expedia (www.expedia.com) for good deals or one of the majors (Avis, Budget, Hertz, Europcar).

In Cannes itself:

Ada Location
91 Boulevard Carnot.
Tel. 04 93 38 38 93

Avis
Place de la Gare
Tel. 04 93 39 26 38

Hertz France
147 Rue d'Antibes
Tel. 04 93 99 04 20

Europcar
3 Rue du Commandant Vidal
Tel. 04 93 06 26 30

If you're looking to head to an evening screening in style, limousines (with driver) can be hired from the following locations:

Chabé Riviera
11 Rue Latour Maubourg
Tel. 04 93 43 90 91

Limousines Agence Côte d'Azur
1 Rue Philibert Delorme
Tel. 04 93 38 11 91

Scooters

Most of the locals seem to be single-handedly keeping the scooter industry alive, as this is the main form of independent motorised transport. Easy to park, cheap to run, and simple to manoeuvre through the gridlock, scooters are probably the best way to get around if you find the old two-leg method objectionable. Rates are 28€ - 30€ per day or 175€per week and scooters can be hired from the following places:

Mistral Location
4 Rue Georges Clémenceau
Tel. 04 93 99 25 25
www.mistral-location.com

Finazzo Alain
Palais Miramar, 65 La Croisette
Tel. 04 93 94 61 94

Multi Location Service
5 Rue de Latour Maubourg
Tel. 04 93 43 60 00

Bicycles

A trusty tredley is another good way to make short work of getting around town and there are plenty of places that rent them out. Expect to pay 10€ - 14€ per day or 63€ per week.

Alliance Location Service
19 Rue des Frères Pradignac
Tel. 04 93 38 62 62
alliance.location@wanadoo.fr

Cycles Daniel
2 Rue du Pont Romain
Tel. 04 93 99 90 30

Mistral Location
4 Rue Georges Clémenceau
Tel. 04 93 99 25 25
www.mistral-location.com

HB Cannes-Holiday Bikes
32, Avenue Maréchal Juin
Tel. 04 93 94 30 34

accommodation

If you thought that making the movie was tough, have a go at trying to find somewhere to lay your beret in Cannes during the festival. This is a mission unto itself and has been known to reduce even the most battle-hardened Cannes veterans to a pile of blubbery tears. It doesn't matter whether you're an indie producer or a famous actor (as Uma Thurman found out some years ago when she apparently was grateful to accept a $30 a night room in a hostel run by local hippies) - when there's no room in the inn, there is no room in the inn. Even Robert Redford is reportedly fond of recounting how he slept on the beach at Cannes many moons ago.

Finding affordable accommodation in Cannes during the festival is difficult for several reasons. Firstly, a good deal of the rooms (particularly in the big hotels) never become available to the open market: they are protected by a myriad of opaque deals (involving everything from "sub-letting" to backhanders) that ensure that wealthy and/or influential people are able to keep their regular room for each festival. And other rooms in these hotels are block-booked by companies for use as offices during the event.

Secondly, extremely high demand for rooms has created a seller's market, so prices tend to by high and virtually all hotels in Cannes itself will only take bookings for the entire festival period. In other words, even if you only want to stay for a week, they will make you fork out for the entire 12 days. And rooms in the cheaper places tend to disappear quicker than a starlet's bikini on the public beach.

The upshot of all this is that it's pretty much essential for you to book your accommodation as far in advance as humanly possible, and to make use of every contact, option, scheme, opportunity, and excuse at your disposal.

Cannes Reservation

Fortunately for Cannes virgins, salvation comes in the form of Cannes Reservation, the accommodation booking service from the tourist office. They can find you a place to stay, often within your price range, and will make the necessary arrangements for you. Although they won't be finding you a room in the Carlton for 25€ a night, the service is free, very thorough, and as an added bonus, they speak English.

Cannes Reservation
Tel. 04 93 99 99 00
Fax. 04 93 99 06 60
centrale@cannes-reservation.com
www.cannes-reservation.com

You should contact them as soon as possible (like now), and although their English is reasonable, to avoid any confusion it's probably best to use written means when communicating with them. Remember to include details of your visit dates, the number of people, your required sleeping arrangements (i.e. how many beds), and your realistic price range.

Budget Options

For those travelling on a tight budget, your best options for cheap accommodation are hostels, caravan parks, or campsites.

There are three hostel options in Cannes, all close to the centre of town and without curfews. Rooms tend to be shared dorms which are good option for those travelling on a shoestring, but can sometimes be difficult to book. Once again, to avoid confusion it's best to use written means to contact them.

Le Chalit – Auberge de Jeunesse

Offers 16 rooms, with four, five, or eight bed configurations. Prices start at around 13€ per night and includes access to shared bathrooms and showers. There are good facilities nearby (groceries, laundry, Internet access etc), however there is a 11am – 5pm lock-out in force (for security reasons and to allow cleaning). To get there, take bus number 4 towards Le Cannet from Gare Routière and ask the driver to let you off in Gallieni.

Le Chalit - Auberge de Jeunesse
27 Avenue Maréchal Gallieni
06400 Cannes
Tel. 04 93 99 22 11
Fax. 04 93 39 00 28
le-chalit@wanadoo.fr

Les Iris

Marketing itself as "Cannes' first fusion restaurant hostel", Les Iris has nine rooms available starting from a very reasonable 13€ per night. Conveniently-located on Boulevard Carnot, there are certainly some big pluses for having your own restaurant and bar on site for those kind of prices. Les Iris is walking distance from the Centre Ville.

Les Iris
77 Boulevard Carnot
06400 Cannes
Tel. 04 93 68 30 20
Fax. 04 93 68 30 20
lesiris@hotmail.com

Logis des Jeunes de Provence

A conveniently-located and reasonably - priced complex with 137 rooms and 43 apartments. Prices start at around 25€ per night and a range of first-class facilities are on offer including Internet access, a meeting room, a restaurant, disabled access, satellite television and parking. Logis des Jeunes is located in the area behind the train station, so is easily walkable from the Centre Ville.

Logis des Jeunes de Provence
5 Rue de Mimont
06400 Cannes
Tel. 04 92 99 77 77
Fax. 04 92 99 76 15
contact@logisdesjeunes.asso.fr
www.logisdesjeunes.asso.fr

Aside from sleeping on the beach, caravan parks and campsites are probably the cheapest accommodation options in the city. And you definitely won't be alone if you decide to rough it a little – around 6pm at most places you are guaranteed to see a tuxedo or two emerge from a small tent as other festival-goers make their way into town for an evening screening. There are two main caravan parks/campsites near Cannes:

Le Ranch

The cheaper of the two with 130 sites for tents/caravans over two hectares of land and a number of fixed-caravan "chalets". The facilities are excellent with free showers, a laundry, swimming pool, and a small grocery store. Prices start at €11 per night for a campsite. To get there take Bus 10 towards Pins Parasols from Gare Routière, stay onboard for about 10-15 minutes and keep your eyes open - the bus goes right past the front gate.

Le Ranch
Chemin Saint-Joseph, L'Aubarède
06110 Le Cannet
Tel. 04 93 46 00 11
Fax. 04 93 46 44 30

Parc Bellevue

This site has around 200 places and excellent facilities including a swimming pool, disabled access, a bar and restaurant. Prices start at 15€ for a camping space. Take bus 35 from Hôtel de Ville in the direction of Lamartine Ranguin, and ask the driver to let you off in La Frayère. Get your map first.

Parc Bellevue
67 Avenue Maurice Chevalier
06150 Cannes la Bocca
Tel. 04 93 47 28 97
Fax. 04 93 48 66 25
contact@parcbellevue.com
www.parcbellevue.com

Hotels and Apartments

With tourism being the main business in Cannes the hotel density is considerably higher than that which would be found in a city of similar size elsewhere. Whilst this still doesn't make things much easier during the film festival, if money isn't really an object then arranging accommodation for the festival also shouldn't be a major problem, provided you book early enough.

Cannes has a range of hotels to cater for medium budgets and up, from two-stars through to luxurious five-star daddies. A night in a two-star hotel starts at around 45€ and goes higher than most of us would prefer to contemplate for the more swanky establishments. Most rooms however are generally in the 75€ - 200€ per night range, although bear in mind what was said previously about hotels only taking bookings for the entire festival period.

Apartment buildings, or *residences*, are another good option, particularly if you have a small group or are looking for space to work as well

as sleep. Most have at least two bedrooms, self-catering facilities and optional maid service. Once again, apartments in the Centre Ville will generally only be bookable for the entire festival period, with prices starting at around 1,000€ per week for a studio and maxing out at around 14,000€ for a luxury 3-bed apartment.

A comprehensive list of hotels and apartment buildings can be found in Appendix VI, and you should take a moment to check out the Hotel booking service at the official Cannes – A Festival Virgin's Guide web site (www.cannesguide.com).

Villas

One of the most popular options with festivalgoers is renting a villa, particular those coming in small groups or looking for a more cost-effective solution than paying for entire twelve days. Whilst there aren't any villas in the Centre Ville area, there are a wide range of options in the surrounding districts, from modest two to three bedroom places through to palatial mansions fit for royalty. Standard prices range from about 180€ - 500€ per night (unless you're looking to spend really silly money).

Staying Outside of Cannes

If you don't have the advantage of travelling on an expense account or are struggling with availability, the price of a room, or simply the fact you have to book for 12 days, another option is to stay outside of Cannes. You can often save a bit on the nightly rate and once you get out of the Centre Ville area, most hotels won't expect you to pay for the whole festival either. Staying outside of Cannes will certainly make it easier to find a room for a reasonable price. However, the flip-side is of course the added hassle of travelling between the centre of town and your accommodation. For this reason, you should choose the area carefully.

Your best bets are Antibes-Juan les Pins (the Juan les Pins end), Cannes la Bocca, Golfe Juan, Vallauris, or Le Cannet. If you get really desperate, Mougins, Mandelieu la Napoule, and Antibes itself are doable options. Whilst it is also possible to stay further away in Nice or Saint Raphaël, this really isn't advisable as you're going to be a very long way from the action and there will be places closer to Cannes with comparable, if not cheaper prices.

Contact details for the various tourist offices in these areas can be found in Appendix II, but in all likelihood, if you use Cannes Reservation, they will often place you in these areas anyway.

The Foolhardy (Or Brave)...
If, by some twist of fate, you've arrived in Cannes without pre-arranged accommodation, you should proceed immediately to the tourist office next to the train station. They can perform the same service as Cannes Reservation and are usually able to find a place in the worst of accommodation droughts. Once again, the service is free, they speak English, and they will make the necessary arrangements for you.

eating

Eating is a national pass-time in France, and French food should be a major highlight for any visitor. Cannes is no exception – the city is teaming with eateries of all types, from small family-run cafes through to multi Michelin-starred world beaters. You certainly won't be pushed for choice, regardless of the type of cuisine you desire or to a large extent, on price.

Although restaurants and cafes are dotted around all over the city, there are heavy concentrations along Rue Félix Faure (also good for late-night options), in the area around the old port (Place Bernard Cornut Gentille and Quai Saint Pierre), on the hill in Le Suquet (especially Rue Saint Antoine and the west end of Rue Meynadier), and behind the Grand Hotel on Rue Fères Pradignac and Rue de Bateguier. You'll also find quite a few places along Rue Jean Jaurès by the train station, but with the exception of the Petit Carlton and the various takeaways, these mainly cater for locals and almost all are universally poor.

accommodation exchange

If you are looking for somewhere to stay in Cannes, make sure you visit the Accommodation Exchange at the CFVG website (www.cannesguide.com). This free service lists offered/wanted accommodation, villas, and last minute deals, and is a great place to form groups and meet new Cannes contacts.

For the bulk of restaurants in Cannes, dining is a fairly informal affair, so it isn't normally necessary to make reservations unless you're planning on visiting a fairly upmarket establishment. Having said that, it can be advisable to call ahead of you're planning to bring a large group or have a desire to eat at a specific restaurant during the peak dinner period of 8pm – 10pm. In small groups you should still get a table around these times but there may be a short wait involved.

For a true French culinary experience it's best to avoid places which have menus in several languages. More often than not they are tourist joints and as a result may have variable quality or higher prices than places where locals eat. You should also be wary of restaurants or cafes which provide you with a separate menu in English. In some cases these have different prices to the French version – prices which are of course higher. The best option is to ask for *la carte en française* (the menu in French) and have your pocket phrasebook ready for some quick translations.

In fact, having a pocket phrasebook at the table with you is always a very good idea, particularly as the names of some dishes look similar to those you might get at home, when in fact they are quite different. For example, a common French dish is *steak américain*, often served *tartare avec* frites. An "American-style" steak with fries, right? Wrong. Steak tartare is raw beef mince with onions and herbs, served with a raw egg on top. If you're not one for culinary surprises the embarrassment of consulting a phrasebook will certainly outweigh the embarrassment of sending something back, or forcing down something you hate.

Another area of common confusion for foreigners in France is coffee. This black liquid is fuel to many filmmakers and it's likely that you too will be running on the stuff if you're doing Cannes with a project in tow. Make sure you know what you are ordering: *un café* is an espresso or "short black"; *café au lait* is coffee with a generous portion of milk; *café crème* is something more akin to the standard white coffee you get in English-speaking countries, but some people will interpret this as an espresso with milk, so if in doubt ask for *un grande café crème*; and decaf (what's the point?) is *un déca*. Thankfully for those with a sweet-tooth, *cappuccino* is the same in every language.

Fast-food

As with almost any modern city a range of fast-food options are available to ensure that you're fed in a cheap and speedy manner. Corporate fast-food is noticeably absent from the business areas of Cannes, with McDonalds and Subway being the only offerings. Give them a miss in favour of the smaller local fast-food joints: Chick and Chips on Rue Jean Jaurès (under the car park opposite Rue Hélène Vagliano) does staples such as burgers, roast chicken, pizza, panini (toasted sandwiches), and *sandwiches chaud/sandwiches froid* (hot/cold baguettes); Jonathan's Snack Bar, opposite the bus station (Place Bernard Cornut Gentille), has a similar menu; and Kiosque Gambetta on Rue Chaubaud also does takeaway at reasonable prices.

You can also pick up cheap eats from the various kiosks along the beach, although the prices tend to be inversely proportionate to the distance you are from the Palais (i.e. the further away you are, the cheaper the prices).

If you can't resist, you'll find Subway on Rue Hélène Vagliano and McDonalds at Square Lord Brougham (off Allées de la Liberté) where a slightly unamused statue of the city's founding father looks on as the local kids breakdance and eat their Big Macs.

Cheap and Cheerful
If you're watching the pennies, the best way to save money when eating in Cannes is to stay off the Croisette. You may not be seen in the right places, but at least you'll come out with your wallet intact. Cheaper eats can be found in nearly every area of town – it's simply about checking the menus and avoiding places that appear to be more about posing than eating.

Most restaurants in Cannes will offer one or more fixed-price menus, normally comprising of at least a starter, main, and dessert. These are simply called le menu or sometimes prix fixe (note that in French, the menu is la carte). A palatable price for le menu is 9€ - 15€, but you can pay anything up to 30€ or more. Make sure you check out the plat de jour (daily special), as these are often also available for a decent price.

For a quick snack, check out Aroma Bagel Café at 22 Rue du Commandant André (Tel. 04 93 99 72 03) or the fantastically tasty and cheap Lebanese taverna, Traiteur al Charq (on Rue Rouaze, Tel. 04 93 94 01 76). Also worth a visit is the aptly-named Asian Fast Food (Tel. 04 93 38 21 00) on Rue Felix Faure, which offers fusion oriental cuisine (Chinese/Thai/Vietnamese), is open late, and has a superb prix fixe menu for around €10. And if you're looking for a quiet and casual business meal then the resurrected Petit Carlton (Tel. 04 93 39 13 97), in its new location next to Monoprix on Place de la Gare, is a great choice.

Slightly more upmarket but still excellent value, is the Italian restaurant La Toscana, which is open 24 hours and can be found on Rue Félix Faure (Tel. 04 93 68 56 36). Other cheap Italian options include La Pizza (Tel. 04 93 39 22 56), a Cannes institution on Quai Saint Pierre; the large, but busy, La Piazza (Tel. 04 92 98 60 80) on the corner of Rue Gazagnaire and Place Cornut Gentille; and Bistrot Le Casanova (Tel. 04 93 38 30 06), on the pedestrianised Rue Casanova, which does excellent pizza, pasta, salad, and great alfresco atmosphere.

If you're after a more regional flavour to your cuisine you can't go past the value of Aux Rich-Lieu (Tel. 04 93 39 98 75) and La Fringale (Tel. 04 93 39 90 79) both of which serve cheap local seafood and grills and are located almost next to each other on Rue Meynadier. Coffee, salads and crêpes are available from La Galette de Marie (Tel. 04 93 68 15 13) at 9 Rue Bivouac Napoléon, and Restaurant Esméralda (Tel. 04 92 98 18 77), on Rue Tony Allard, is an excellent starting point if you're planning on settling in at the Petit Majestic later on. The restaurants along Rue Rouguière, particularly L'Olivier (Tel. 04 93 99 44 05) and Bar du Marin (Tel. 04 93 39 90 00), also offer regional specialities at palatable prices.

Middle of the Road
The vast majority of the eating options in Cannes fit into this category, so it tends to be more about personal preference than anything else. For starters, try the wonderful home-cooked Provençale cuisine on offer at the cosy Petit Lardon (3 Rue Batéguier, Tel. 04 93 39 06 28) or Cannes' oldest restaurant, Auberge Provençal at 10 Rue Saint Antoine (Tel. 04 93 38 52 14). For seafood with a champagne chaser, try La Marée (Tel. 04 92 98 03 33) on Boulevard Jean Hibert – it's a short walk around the port, but it has great views over the Baie de Cannes. On the way, you will also pass Gaston Gastounette (7 Quai Saint Pierre, Tel. 04 93 39 49 44) which Cannes regulars almost unanimously vote as offering the best seafood in town.

If it's great steaks you're after, then a visit to Willy's Bar (144 Rue d'Antibes, Tel. 04 93 94 12 12) should find its way on to your agenda; or if you're up for a more lively evening of food and music, a night at pub Au Bureau (Rue Félix Faure, Tel 04 93 68 56 36) for pizza, pasta, and grills should be your cup of tea. The Greek taverna Restaurant Tovel Beth-Din on Rue Dr Monod (Tel. 04 93 39 36 25), is also popular with the locals, and contemporary Chinese is available at the popular and stylish Le Jardin de Bamboo (16 Rue Macé, Tel. 04 92 98 63 06). For a truly unique dining experience try La Brochette de Grand-Mère ("Grandmother's Wheelbarrow", Tel. 04 93 39 12 10) on Rue d'Oran where you sit down at Granny's table and she keeps bringing you food until you say stop (closed Sundays).

Other tried and tested middle of the road options include:

Aux Bon Enfants
80 Rue Meynadier

Bar des Negociants
Corner, Rue Marechal Foch
and Rue Jean Jaurès
Tel. 04 93 39 06 35

Le Fregate
26 Boulevard Jean Hilbert
Tel. 04 93 39 45 39
Open 24 hours

New Croisette
17 Rue du Commandant André
Tel. 04 92 98 62 82

Restaurant Festival
52 Boulevard de la Croisette
Tel. 04 93 28 04 81

The area of Le Suquet also harbours some charming restaurants, both along Rue Saint Antoine and further up on top of the hill.

Expense Account Time
If you're travelling on expenses or someone else is keen to impress you, then it's possible to sample the finest cuisine the French Riviera has to offer. Lovers of ultra-fresh shellfish and other *fruits de la mer* should not leave Cannes without spending at least one evening at Astoux et Brun (Tel. 04 93 39 06 33) on the corner of Rue Félix Faure and Rue Louis Blanc. For a more refined dining experience, you can't go past the glamorous and elegant Le Merchant Loup (17 Rue Saint Antoine, Tel. 04 93 99 06 22),

or Neat (11 Square Mérimée, Tel. 04 93 99 29 19) which does wonderful modern French cuisine and has a wine list to match. You'll also have a great night on the terraces of any of the big hotels, particularly the Majestic and the Carlton.

Top Riviera dining is also available at many famous regional restaurants outside of Cannes. The three Michelin-starred Le Moulin de Mougins (1432 Ave Notre-Dame de Vie, Mougins, Tel. 04 93 75 78 24) is worthy of its reputation and hosts the star-studded annual AmFAR charity dinner during the festival's second week. Studio bosses and the A-List glitterati can also be found dining on the terrace at the Eden Roc (Boulevard Kennedy, Antibes, Tel. 04 93 61 39 01), which is located in the Hotel du Cap complex at the tip of the Cap d'Antibes peninsula.

Self-Catering

If you're staying in an villa or an apartment with self-catering facilities, you can buy provisions at one of the local *supermarchés* (supermarkets). A branch of the large chain Monoprix is located almost directly opposite the train station on the corner of Rue Jean Jaurès and Rue Buttura; the ground floor caters for most of your non-food needs and you'll find the food section upstairs. Down the other end of town, on Rue Volta, there's

also a branch of another grocery giant, Casino.

Alternatively, take a wander down the pedestrianised Rue Maynadier and you will find not only a Champion supermarket but also a wide selection of small purveyors of mouth-watering delights. True foodies should also take the time to visit the Forville Marché for a mouth-watering array of fresh produce (meat, seafood, fruit, and vegetables). Forville can be found in a block of its own off Rue Louis Blanc and is open every day except Mondays, from 7am – 1pm.

It's worth noting that most shops in Cannes, including the big supermarkets, are closed on Sundays and public holidays.

money

The close of the 2001 festival brought with it the end of an era for Cannes-goers: it was the last time you could blow a serious wad of francs on a round of drinks at a fancy hotel.

On 1 January 2002, French traditionalists shed a tear at the passing of the franc as it gave way to the arrival of the new Euro coins and notes. Of course, anyone who had spent time travelling in Europe let out a resounding "woo-hoo!" at this

restaurant guide

The Cannes – A Festival Virgin's Guide web site (www.cannesguide.com) includes a large database of eateries across the full spectrum of styles and prices. The database also includes reviews, contact details, and a "restaurant basket" to help you plan your Cannes eating experience.

news; no doubt casting their minds back to the hassles of carrying four different countries in one's wallet, or the ruinous exchange rates obtained at establishments offering the "convenience" of paying in multiple currencies, but who doled out the change in local chips.

Francs, like most of the other former currencies of the "Euro Bloc", ceased to be legal tender on 28 February 2002. This change-over period may seem a little aggressive when you consider that the money used by over 300 million people needed to be replaced in just two months, but Europeans had been preparing for three years. In January 1999 all of the participating countries had their currencies irrevocably pegged to the Euro as it started trading on the international currency markets. Effectively these currencies became simply smaller denominations of the Euro, albeit at slightly odd values (for example, one franc is forevermore 0.15245 Euro). The introduction of coins and notes was simply the last step in the process.

Today the change-over is complete and although many establishments still show prices both currencies for the benefit of the locals, Cannes, like the rest of France, is now completely Euro-powered. In saying that, it's always worth taking an extra moment to check your change before leaving a shop or restaurant, as some old franc coins (particularly 10F) look similar to euros and a few less-reputable establishments have been known to use this as a way of offloading their unwanted currency.

The Euro is a simple and easy currency to use. Gone are the excessively high denominations of the franc days - the Euro trades fairly closely with the US dollar in face value. The symbol for the Euro looks a bit like a capital "E" with two cross bars: €. No-one seems to have decided whether the symbol should precede or proceed the numeric figure, so expect to see prices shown as '€20', '20€', although the latter is increasingly more common.

Like most currencies, the Euro comes in a variety of coins and notes. Coins are available in one and two Euro values, and like the dollar, one Euro is made up of 100 cents, with 50c, 20c, 10c, 5c, 2c, and 1c coins. Every Euro coin carries the 12 star symbol of the European Union on one side, and member countries have been able to include a national image of their choice on the reverse side for coins they mint. However, all the coins have the same value across Europe so you are able to use any coin in any Euro country.

Notes are available in seven denominations: 500, 200, 100, 50, 20, 10, and 5 Euro. Unlike the coins, notes are uniform across Euroland and member states are not able to use their own designs (undoubtedly a measure to help in the fight against counterfeiting). Notes are distributed through normal outlets such as banks, ATMs (aka cashpoints), and Bureaux de Change (money changers). You should also be able to obtain euros at home from any establishment that normally buys and sells currency. Although exchange rates vary all the time, most major currencies maintain a reasonably stable value against each other. You should always check the current rates at the time of your trip, and remember that many banks and money changers may take a commission on the sale/purchase of foreign currency, or may make the exchange at less favourable rates than those you find published online or in newspapers. As a rough guide, you can expect your dosh to get you the following in Cannes:

Australia
$1 = 0.60€
1€ = $1.65

Canada
$1 = 0.70€
1€ = $1.40

New Zealand
$1 = 0.55€
1€ = $1.75

UK
£1 = 1.50€
1€ = £0.65

USA
$1 = 0.85€
1€ = $1.20

Euros may be better than francs, but at the end of the day, they still amount to foreign currency, which means conversions, variable exchange rates, and commissions along the way (both stated and hidden). The best way to minimise the number of fingers in your currency transaction pie is to use plastic wherever possible.

Major credit cards (Visa, MasterCard, American Express, and Diners Club) are widely accepted across town in restaurants, shops, cafes, and hotels. International debit cards such as Cirrus and Maestro are also accepted at many places (although watch out for the often horrendous transaction charges levied by your home bank). It's probably best to leave other domestic credit/debit cards at home unless you are 100% sure they will work in France.

Most of the major French and European banks have branches in Cannes, so there are plenty of ATMs. Oddly, most of the banks are congregated in a couple of blocks on the western end of Rue d'Antibes. Your best bet for securing cash is in this area as ATMs can be few and far between in other parts of the city. In France, ATMs are called *distributeurs automatique de billet* (DABs) or *ponts de l'argent* (literally, money points).

Most ATMs accept major credit cards and international debit cards, and will usually display these somewhere obvious. Many machines also offer you the chance to choose the language you would like the service in. However, bear in mind that various banks are hooked up to the international ATM network in different ways, and consequently there may be times when you card won't work, even though it is supposedly accepted by the machine in question. Don't despair – simply try your card in another machine with a different bank and in most cases, voila!

ATMs are definitely the best place to secure cash. You will get the most favourable exchange rate available because the exchange is made by your home bank, and normally you do not have to pay a commission. However, before you leave home it's definitely worth confirming with your bank that you're able to draw cash in foreign countries with your card. And while you're at it, find out what charges are involved as well.

If you have a duff ATM card or your credit rating is shot to pieces after it executive-produced your last film, you may wish to buy some travellers cheques, which are generally the next best thing to carry. Most places should accept them, they are normally replaceable if you are unfortunate enough to lose them, and you can always cash them at a bank or Bureau de Change.

Sales Tax
Like all EU countries sales tax in France is levied in the form of VAT (known as *TVA* in French). The standard rate is 19.7%. By law all taxes must be included in the price, so as in all civilised countries, the price you see is the price you pay.

If you are heading to the festival from outside of the European Union you are also eligible to claim a refund on the VAT you pay when making purchases in France. Refunds are available on purchases of over 175€ from the same shop on the same day, although certain types of goods and services are excluded from the scheme. If you're planning on claiming a VAT refund let the shopkeeper or service provider know at the time of purchase and they will provide you with the necessary forms (although not all shops participate in the scheme). Refunds are issued at the airport when you leave France. For more information on VAT refunds visit the French Customs web site: www.douane.gouv.fr.

Tipping
Restaurants and cafes in France are normally required by law to include service in the final bill (*service compris*), so there is generally no need to tip; although most people do leave a few coins on the table unless the service has been bad. Service is usually included at 10-15%, and there is no need to tip for drinks and bars or cafes.

Likewise, tipping generally isn't required for taxi drivers, porters, or maids, but everyone will be appreciative of something extra if the service they have provided is good.

language

Cannes is of course in France and that means everyone speaks French. Whilst this can certainly add to the confusion felt by first-time visitors to the festival, it's definitely not something to really worry about. Those who are lucky enough to be

online currency conversion

The Internet contains a wealth of up to the second currency information. A great place to visit is Olsen & Associates (www.oanda.com), where you can not only get the latest exchange rates, but you can print out a mini 'cheat sheet' to take with you to Cannes for help with quick on-the-spot conversions.

versed in the language of love will obviously encounter no problems. However for the rest of us, it isn't really that daunting as several factors work in favour of Anglophones visiting the festival.

Firstly, you will remember that the city was effectively founded by a Brit, so speaking English is nothing new here. Secondly, the growing strength of English as the "international language of business", and indeed the world dominance of the American media, both work to the advantage of native English-speakers in France. Finally, there's the fact that English has become the world's de facto common language, meaning that wherever visitors are found it's likely that English translations will also be available.

These days a large number of the French speak English to some degree, particular younger people and those working in jobs related to tourism. However, this doesn't mean that you should go around speaking English to all and sundry. Those who charge in as if they were at home will surely get treated like the rude and arrogant arses that they are.

The best strategy to use to ensure you encounter the pleasant and helpful side of any Francophone you meet is to try and speak French, but fail miserably. Even if you stumble on the vowels, massacre the pronunciation, or change the gender of an object, your efforts will be appreciated. And in many cases, if a French person detects that you're an Anglophone, they will often speak to you in English even if you speak to them in French (which on the flip-side,

can be annoying if you're trying to practice!).

Alternatively, if you're overly conscious of your poor French skills you can start by mastering the phrase: *parlez vous anglais?* (PAR-LAY VOO ONG-GLAY) – "Do you speak English?" After your exchange of pleasantries you should politely pop this question. The usual response is, "a little" and you're in business. But remember, when someone says "a little", they mean *a little*. Make sure you speak slowly and clearly (but not loudly) so that you are easily understood.

In general, the written word is a little easier to grasp than the spoken one. Because English is closely related to French the two languages share a large number of words, and many other French words are similar enough to their English counterparts to allow you to guess their meaning. French grammar and punctuation, on the other hand, is a little different, not to mention a slew of irregular verbs and the inexplicable practice of assigning gender to inanimate objects. However, you can often get the general idea of what signs, labels, menus, and other written words mean pretty easily.

You should at least try your hand at French while you are in Cannes. You never know, you might find that the little bit you perhaps did at school comes flooding back. The main problems with spoken French, and indeed any language are: the speed at which the natives speak and the colloquial terms found in common speech. If you get a stream of incompressible babble, you can always ask the person to repeat themselves, *répétez s'il vous plait* (REP-ET-AY SI-VOO-PLAY), or to speak a little more slowly, *Est-ce que vous pourriez parler plus lentement?* (ES-KE-VOO POO-REE-AY PARLAY PLOO LONT-MON). Finally, you could always resort to, Pardon. *Je ne comprends pas* (PAR-DON. ZJUH-NEY COM-PRON PAR) – "Sorry. I don't understand." An introduction to French, including a collection of useful words and phrases can be found in Appendix V.

You will generally find that most people in Cannes, particularly during the festival, speak at least some English. Cannes has more of an international flavour than many other French cities and with the huge influx of Americans, Canadians, Brits, Aussies, Kiwis and others, you're bound to hear plenty of understandable chatter. If you find yourself craving some English-speaking company take a visit to either the American or Irish Pavilions, or the UK Film Centre. English-language books and magazines can also be found at the Cannes English Bookshop (11 Rue Bivouac Napoléon, Tel. 04 93 99 40 08), which is run by a friendly expat Aussie.

general info

New towns (and countries) can often throw a few curveballs to visitors. Here is a collection of handy hints and tips about Cannes, and France in general, to help make your stay as smooth as possible.

Driving
The French (as with all continental Europeans) drive on the right-hand side of the road. Not a problem if you hail from North America, but filmmakers from places such as the UK, Ireland, Australia, and New Zealand should take extra care when driving and crossing the road or you may find yourself directing your next film from a wheelchair. If at all!

Weather
Cannes has a typical Mediterranean climate: warm dry summers and cool wet winters. The average maximum temperature in May is a pleasant 20°C (68°F), but it isn't uncommon for temperatures to nudge 30°C (86°F) during the festival. The sun can be quite strong so decent sunscreen is a must (looking like a less than appetising lobster is not the best way to get noticed in Cannes). However, because we're technically still in spring it's virtually guaranteed that during the festival there will be at least one or two days of fairly heavy rain and cooler temperatures (15°C - 18°C, 59°F - 64°F). As with the lobster-look, soaked-chic hasn't hit the catwalks in Cannes yet so remember to bring a brollie. Weather updates can be obtained by calling Météo (Tel. 08 92 68 12 67) or visiting Yahoo! Weather (weather.yahoo.com).

What to Wear
In general your Cannes wardrobe should comprise of comfortable, neat summer wear. The dress code during the day is fairly laid back, although if you're in town on business it's best to keep it professional. It's also worth packing a couple of warmish items, particularly if you feel the cold, as it can get a little nippy in the evening.

If you're planning to take in a gala screening or swanky party, you'll also need your formal gear. For the blokes, this means a tux with bow-tie (although you can often get away with a black suit and white shirt); for the ladies, classy and elegant evening wear.

Finally, the most important item... shoes. At least two pairs of shoes are essential for a successful visit to Cannes. The first should be the most comfortable pair you own – to provide some consolation to your feet for the amount of running around you'll be doing. The other pair should be your knock 'em dead shoes to match your Sunday best; although ladies, it's advisable to keep your glam shoes as sensible as possible, since it is conceivable that some fancy footwork may be required to pull off entry to an exclusive party.

Tabacs

Part newsagent, part grocery store, Tabacs are effectively France's corner shops. Across the country they can be easily identified by the universal Tabac symbol of an elongated orange double-triangular shape, called *la carotte* (the carrot) by the French. Get your newspapers, gum, tobacco, phone cards, and other staples from these stores.

Payphones

These are located all over the city and inside the Palais and Riviera complexes. The latter locations are a good option because the areas tend to be much quieter than outside. Virtually no French payphones accept coins, so to make calls you must use a credit card, calling card from home, or purchase a *télécarte* (local phone card). Télécartes can be picked up from post offices, Tabacs, and anywhere you see the

sign "Télécarte en vente ici". The country code for France is 33, and the access code for the international direct dial network is 00. Remember to drop any leading zero when calling numbers outside of France.

Photocopy/Fax

A business centre is located on Level 01 of the Palais and offers photocopying and fax facilities, as well as Internet access terminals. Outside of the Palais, Buro-Copy (6 Rue Notre Dame) or Telecourses Bureautique (16 Rue Louis Blanc) can service your photocopy and faxing needs. You should also check out the offices in Cannes of your country's national film commission or similar organisation. Many offer free fax, photocopy, and messaging services for their nationals.

Post Office

A mini post office is available in the Palais (Level 01) which is open daily from 9am – 6pm (including Sundays and public holidays). A full-sized post office can be found at 22 Rue Bivouac Napoléon (open Monday to Friday).

Prices/Numbers

You should be aware that most European countries use commas and decimal points in the completely the opposite way to English-speaking countries. Commas are used as decimal points, and decimal points are used as thousand separators. In the past this was not usually a source of confusion for foreigners, since the denominations of the local currency were often very high. However, the Euro has changed this. Remember, when you see 5,99€ it means 5.99€, and 5.999,99€ means 5999.99€ and so on. Occasionally you will also see 5€99.

Times

All times in France are listed in 24 hour notation (sometimes referred to as "military time"). The hours in the morning commence with 00:00 (midnight; can also be shown as 24:00), and continue 01:00 (1am) through to 11:00 (11am). Midday (12:00) is followed by 13:00 (1pm), 14:00 (2pm), 15:00 (3pm) and so on up until 23:00 (11pm). Times are usually displayed with an "h" for *heure* (hour) separator rather than the traditional colon or decimal point common in English-speaking countries. For example, *18h30* is of course 6.30pm.

Business Hours

These are a little different to many other countries in that most French businesses close for lunch from around midday until 2pm. Larger shops and chain stores will often remain open, but most offices, retailers, banks, and other establishments will close. Typical trading hours are as follows:

Banks: 9am – 12pm, then 2pm – 5pm, Monday to Friday

Shops: 9am – 12.30pm, then 2pm – 6pm Monday to Saturday.

Offices: 9am – 12pm, then 2pm – 6pm Monday to Friday.

It's also worth noting that most shops (including large supermarkets) will be closed on Sundays and public holidays, so it's important to make sure you have everything you need by the close of business Saturday.

Public Holidays

There are a couple of public holidays that can fall during the festival, depending on which dates it runs. *Victoire 1945* (celebrating the Allied victory in World War II) is the 8 May, and *Lundi de Pentecôte* (Pentecost/ Whit Monday) sometimes falls within the festival if Easter is late in the year. The front doors of banks are good places to see if there are any upcoming public holidays.

First-Aid

A first-aid post with a doctor on duty is operated by the *sapeurs-pompiers* (fire brigade) in the Palais during the festival. It can be found on Level 0, near the Artists Entrance at the rear of the building. For out of hours or serious medical assistance, contact details for local hospitals and emergency services can be found in Appendix II.

Beaches

In Cannes beaches are a bit of an oddity, particularly to non-Europeans who may be used to ample beach being available at no cost. Most of the beaches in Cannes are owned by the hotels, and consequently are reserved for the sole use of their guests. For the rest of us there is a small stretch of public beach available near the Palais and if you continue west around past the Vieux Port you will find Plage du Midi and Plage de Cannes - La Bocca, both of which are also free, cleaner, and far less crowded.

Internet Access

Checking email is now an essential daily task for most of us and thankfully getting online while you're in Cannes is entirely straight forward. During the festival free Internet terminals are available in many of the pavilions and also at several areas within the Palais. Most locations also offer wi-fi access, although you will need to obtain the relevant settings and security details from the local staff.

If you have exhausted all of the free Internet options and are just desperate to get online, there are a couple of Internet Cafes in Cannes where you can pay for your access. These are listed in Appendix II.

Electricity

The electricity supply in Europe is different to that found in North America (but compatible with that found in Australia/New Zealand and much of Asia). You will need to ensure that any electrical devices you bring to the festival are multi-region. If not, you'll need to use a transformer. European power operates with 220 volts at 50 hertz, whereas North America is on 115 volts, at 60 hertz, so there is a real danger of blowing up your device if you don't use a transformer. For compatible devices you will also need an appropriate adaptor plug to convert your locate cable to the double round pin plug used in Europe.

Time Difference

Cannes operates on standard western European time, which is one hour ahead of Greenwich Mean Time (GMT). This translates to being one hour ahead of UK time; 9 hours ahead of US Pacific Time, 8 hours ahead of US Mountain Time, 7 hours ahead of US Central Time, 6 hours ahead of US Eastern Time, and between 7-12 hours behind Australian/New Zealand time. Alternatively, if you prefer to let someone else worry about all this "four hours forward, six hours back stuff," try the World Time Server at www.worldtimeserver.com.

Vigipirate

Vigipirate is the French national anti-terrorist programme and it is in force in Cannes during the festival. It is manifested mainly in visible anti-terrorist policing (look for the guys with the sunnies, big guns, and mean-looking dogs) and also in the entry controls for the Palais and Riviera. Expect to be subjected to bag searches and metal-detectors when you enter these buildings. If you notice a suspect package you should immediately contact a member of staff in the Palais, and it goes without saying that you shouldn't leave your own items unattended as they may be destroyed.

email on the road

Many people use web-based email services, like Hotmail, which can be checked anywhere in the world as long as you have access to a web browser. For those with non-web-based email, it's still possible to check your email on the road without worrying about expensive phone calls, forwarding, or temporary Hotmail accounts. Visit a free site called Mail2Web (www.mail2web.com) and you can check your email from any web-browser, just like Hotmail. You will need your email username and password, as well as your incoming mail server address. Your ISP, technical support desk, or office geek should be able to provide you with these details, so remember to get them before you leave.

Lost Property

Items found within the Festival buildings (that haven't been blown-up by the anti-terrorist police) are taken to the police station next to Gare Maritime (Tel. 04 92 99 85 96). If you have lost an item elsewhere in town you should contact the City of Cannes lost property service at 1 Ave Saint Louis (Tel. 04 97 06 40 00).

Personal Security

Wherever there are crowds there always will be unsavoury types who are interested at making something for themselves at the expense of others. Usual common sense should see you safely through the festival, but you should pay particular attention to your personal belongings in crowds (especially after you've had a few party drinks). And in the party atmosphere always keep an eye on your drink, whether you are male or female. Incidents of violent crime in Cannes are extremely rare, but you should also take the usual precautions when travelling alone at night.

getting away

Attending any film festival can be an amazing experience, but it can also be very draining. Late nights (usually involving too much alcohol), early starts, and far too many screenings have the power to take it out of even the most seasoned campaigner. And this effect can be magnified exponentially if you're attending a festival with a business agenda.

Fortunately, many festivals take place in locations where there are a range of interesting ways to take time out and recharge and Cannes is no exception. So if after a few days you're finding the madness of festival-gripped Cannes a little too intense, then there are plenty of places nearby where you can escape the hoards and take time out to enjoy some of what the South of France has to offer.

Shopping

If the shopping experience is part of your nature, then Cannes won't disappoint. The city is brimming over with all manner of retail establishments waiting to help you part with your money. The obvious starting point is a walk along Rue d'Antibes where you'll find a range of boutiques, shoe, and gift shops. If you're credit card is feeling brave, along the Croisette, in between the hotels and restaurants, you'll find most of the big name designer stores. For more eclectic items a little exploration along the pedestrianised Rue Maynadier can be rewarding, and there are bargains to be had at the clothes market in Place Gambetta (open daily from 7am – 1pm).

Musée de la Castre

At the top of Le Suquet (also known as Mont Chevalier) is La Castre, the last incarnation of the town fortifications started in Roman times. Built in the 11th Century, the fort complex is now a museum housing a range of collections including paintings from local artists, archaeological treasures from the Mediterranean and Middle East, and over 200 antique musical instruments. The pretty 12th Century Chappelle Sainte-Anne also sits below the fort's clock tower. The Musée de la Castre is open daily (except Mondays) from 10am – 6pm, but closed for lunch from 12pm – 2pm. Tours are available in English on request. Excellent museum aside, La Castre also commands magnificent views of the city and surrounding area.

Where? On the hill above Hôtel de Ville and Gare Routière. Get there by wandering up Rue Saint Antoine from Place Cornut Gentille. A little way up the hill take the stairs on the left.
How Much? Views, free. Museum, 3€ for adults, free for students and children.
Time Requirement? A couple of hours.

Iles de Lérins
Three kilometres off the coast of Cannes two sister islands – Sainte Marguerite and Saint Honorat – form the group known as the Iles de Lérins.

Ile Sainte Marguerite, the largest of the pair (3.2km by 0.9km), is home to Aleppo pines, eucalyptus trees, tranquil walks, and Le Fort Royale. The 15th Century fort and former prison of "The Man in the Iron Mask" now houses the Musée de la Mer which provides information on the famous prisoner, and contains relics from several ancient Mediterranean ship wrecks. The museum is open daily (except Mondays) from 10.30am – 4.45pm, but closed for lunch from 1.15pm – 2.15pm.

Ile Saint Honorat (1.5km by 0.4km) sits directly behind its big sister and is named in honour of the monk St Honoratus who, along with seven disciples, settled on the island in 410 A.D. Today the island is still in monk hands, being the property

of the Cistercian Congregation of Senanque. The inhabitants of the island grow grapes and herbs, and like all good monks, produce a few varieties of speciality booze. The island is open to visitors and regular services are conducted in the 11th Century fortified monastery, Abbaye de Lérins (www.abbayedelerins.com).

Where? 3km off the coast of Cannes. Get there by ferry from Quai M. Laubeuf.
How much? Allez retour (return ticket) from Cannes – Sainte Marguerite, 10€ and Cannes – Saint Honorat, 10€. Musée de la Mer (Ile Sainte-Marguerite), 3€ for adults, free for children and students.
Time requirement? Half or full-day trip.

Château de la Napoule
Framed by its Saracen and Romanesque towers, this 14th Century seafront castle is now a museum. In 1918 the building was acquired by American sculptor, Henry Cluse, and now houses an extensive collection of art and sculpture, including works from Cluse himself. There are also extensive gardens, tea rooms, and the area around the castle is a popular bathing beach. Visit the official web site (www.chateau-lanapoule.com) for more information.

Where? 7km west of Cannes. Get there by train or Bus 16 from Place de la Gare.
How much? Museum entry circa 4€, plus bus/train fare.
Time requirement? Half day.

Mougins
300 metres above Cannes in the

Alpes-Maritimes is the old fortified village of Mougins (pronounced MOO-GAN). The village is full of great restaurants (including the famous two Michelin-starred Le Moulin de Mougins) and has great walks in the La Valmasque Forest Park. There are also a range of historical and cultural sites to visit including the Museum of Photography, Musée de l'Automobile (Motor Museum), and the beautiful churches of Saint Jacques le Majeur and Chapelle Notre-Dame de Vie.

Where? 7km north of Cannes. Get there by taking bus 3VB towards Valbonne from outside the train station.
How much? Your bus fare only, although some museums have entry fees.
Time requirement? Half to full day.

Valbonne

This well preserved 16th Century Provençale village is a great place to offload some time and enjoy the flavour of the South of France. There's a 12th Century abbey and the Roman Aqueduct of Claussonnes to visit, and the walk along the River Brague path from Valbonne village to Biot is magic.

Where? 14km northeast of Cannes. Get there by taking the train or bus (3VB from Place de la Gare).
How much? Your bus fare only.
Time requirement? Full day.

Grasse

High above Cannes (950 metres) is the world capital of the perfume industry, Grasse (pronounced GRAS). Many of the famous perfume factories conduct tours and of course are happy to sell you their product at source. If the perfume trail gets a bit overpowering, you can get some fresh air visiting the town's 12th Century Notre Dame Cathedral (home to three original Rubens), excellent maritime museum, and Princess Pauline Gardens.

Where? 17km north of Cannes. Get there on bus 610 from outside the train station or take the N85 in a car.
How much? Your bus fare only, although some museums have entry fees.
Time requirement? Full day.

Saint Paul de Vence

This scenic village is set against the mountains within fortified walls, and has been a source of inspiration for some of the world's greatest painters, including Picasso and Monet. Today the artistic influence is still alive in the town through a local centre for artists, painters, and writers, and two fascinating museums.

Where? 26km northeast of Cannes. Get there by taking the train from Cannes to Cagnes-sur-Mer and then take the bus from the station to Saint Paul.
How much? Bus/Train fare.
Time requirement? Full day

Nice

The capital of the Côte d'Azur (pronounced NEESS) is a great place to visit if you have some spare time. Museums are the name of the game in Nice: Musée Matisse (164 Ave des Arènes de Cimiez) displays a collection of paintings and sculptures in the artist's former home; Musée National Message Biblique (Ave du Dr Ménard) houses the enormous dreamscapes of Marc Chagall; portraits of Napoléon and Josephine are amongst the works at Musée d'Art et d'Histoire (65 Rue de France); and contemporary French and America art can be seen at Musée d'Art Moderne et d'Art Contemporain (on Promenade des Arts). If the museum trail gets a bit dull there are many great cafés in Nice, and a walk along the famous seaside Promenade des Anglais (remember the Steve Martin/ Michael Caine film "Dirty Rotten Scoundrels"?) is a must.

Where? 32km east of Cannes. Get there on the train from Cannes.
How Much? Train fare, plus museum entry (variable).
Time requirement? Full day.

the ultimate travelling companion

Book two in the Festival Virgin's Guide series is for filmmakers, film fans, and film industry professionals looking to attend America's most important film festival.

At over 200 pages, this book is one of the most detailed Sundance resources available!

Created with the assistance of the
Sundance Institute

Available now from Amazon.com, Amazon.co.uk, abebooks.com or ask your local bookstore. Alternatively, buy online from Cinemagine Media Publishing.

www.sundanceguide.net

the festival

the festival

For 12 days in May the city of Cannes is transformed from a quiet seaside resort into the entire focus of the international film industry. Over 200,000 people – filmmakers, film fans, and star-gazers alike – descend on the Croisette to take part in the Cannes Film Festival (or more correctly, the Festival de Cannes). During these two weeks thousands of films are screened, careers are made (and ruined), and stars from all over the world gather to bask in the limelight.

Ever since the early 1950s, when a bikini-clad Brigitte Bardot frolicked on the beach for the cameras, Cannes has grown to embody two of the world's favourite pastimes: sex and cinema. Now easily the most famous film festival of them all, the mere mention of Cannes conjures up images of red carpets, palm trees, scantily-clad starlets, the blinding flashes of a million paparazzi cameras, and of course, celebrity parties.

history

On the surface, a city such as Cannes perhaps might not strike you as the place to host the world's most famous film festival. It's not a capital city, or even near one. Yes, cinema was invented in France – but that was in Paris, not Cannes. And sure, the weather in Cannes may be nice, but that certainly isn't a unique selling point. So just how did a reasonably small resort town end up hosting the most prestigious film festival there is?

Like much of the world as we know it today, the Cannes Film Festival exists as an indirect result of the rise of the fascist regimes in Europe during the 1930s. Its roots date back to 1932 when the first competitive international film festival was held in Venice. In those days, the Mostra di Venezia – and chiefly its awards – was as much about the national prestige of the participating countries as it was about the films. As the decade marched on, both the official selection and the prize-winners began to noticeably favour the countries of the fascist alliance, particularly Germany and Italy.

Matters came to a head in 1938 when Jean Renoir's "La Grande Illusion" was overlooked for the festival's top prize – known back then as the Coppa Mussolini ("Mussolini Cup") – despite being the clear favourite amongst both festivalgoers and jury members. Instead, the Coppa was jointly-awarded to a two-part German film called "Olympia", commissioned by Joseph Goebbels to document Nazi successes at the 1938 Berlin Olympics; and "Luciano Serra, Pilota", made under the supervision of Il Duce's own son. When the results were announced, the French were of course outranged and withdrew from the festival. Both the British and American jury members also resigned in protest at the idea that politics and ideology were able to stamp all over artistic appreciation. "La Grande Illusion" – a largely anti-war film – was subsequently banned in Germany and Italy; Goebbels himself labelling it "Cinematographic Enemy No.1".

But Venice's folly turned out to be Cannes' triumph. Later that same year, a group of critics and filmmakers got together to petition the French Government to underwrite the cost of running an alternative international film festival in France – one where films could be shown and compete without bias or political censorship. Afraid of upsetting Mussolini, the French government was initially lukewarm to the idea, but the powerful lobby group wasn't going to be easily dissuaded. Headed by Philippe Erlanger (head of Action Artistique Française), Robert Favre Le Bret (who would become the festival's longest serving president), and Louis Lumière (the co-inventor of cinema), the group put intense pressure on the government, which eventually caved in and gave the event the green light.

Several locations were initially considered for the festival, but the final choice came down to either Biarritz on the Atlantic coast or Cannes on the Mediterranean. Officially, it was the city's "sunny and enchanting location" which clinched it for Cannes, however most people acknowledge that the real reason for its selection was the fact that the municipal authorities agreed to cough up the dough to build a dedicated venue for the event.

The inaugural *Festival International du Film* was slated to kick-off on 1 September 1939; that month chosen by shrewd city officials who realised that such an event could be used to extend the summer tourist season by an extra two weeks. But the fledgling festival only managed its opening night before being closed down following the outbreak of World War II the following day.

The festival remained in hiatus during the war, re-emerging for a second attempt on 20 September 1946 under the joint aegis of the French ministries of Foreign Affairs and Education. As the City of Cannes had yet to make good on its promise of a dedicated venue, the first festival-proper took place in the old winter casino with the 82-year-old Loius Lumière taking on the duties of inaugural jury president. Films presented for the first festival included Billy Wilder's "Lost Weekend, David Lean's "Brief Encounter", Roberto Rossellini's "Rome Open City", George Cukor's "Gaslight", Walt Disney's "Make Mine Music", Alfred Hitchcock's "Notorious", and Jean Cocteau's "Beauty and the Beast". Films from Charles Laughton, Howard Hawks, and Cecil B. De Mille were also screened out of competition.

The first festival was generally regarded as a success by all and sundry, so for its sophomore outing in 1947, it was moved under the wing of the newly-formed Centre National de la Cinématographie (CNC), a government body charged with supporting and promoting the cinematic arts, and preserving France's screen history. Amongst its general organisational responsibilities, the CNC also took over the co-ordination of the submissions and selection process for the event.

Indeed, in the early days, films were nominated by their respective countries rather than the festival itself, with the number of berths available to a given country being proportionate to the volume of its cinematic output. As a result, Cannes in the early days was more of a "film forum" than a competitive event – with the CNC trying very hard to ensure that every film screened went home with some kind of award.

Although the 1947 festival had also been successful by most measures, budget problems in 1948 saw the event go dark for a second time. Financial woes also prevented the 1950 festival from going ahead, but in between the 1949 festival managed to secure an impressive line-up of international cinema, including Fred Zinnemann's "Act of Violence", Michelangelo Antonioni's "L'Amorosa Menzogna", Joseoph L. Mankiewicz's "House of Strangers", David Lean's "The Passionate Friends", and Carol Reed's "The Third Man" (the top prize-winner for that year). 1949 also saw the City of Cannes finally make good on its promise of a dedicated venue for the event. Built on the present site of the Noga Hilton hotel, and completed in 1952, the brand new *Palais Croisette* was to be the festival's home for the next 30-odd years.

By the early 1950s, the festival had experienced significant growth in scope and renown so it was decided to change the dates from September to April. The reason for the move was two-fold: firstly, many observers noted that competing festivals, such as Berlin and Venice, took place earlier in the year and consequently Cannes was missing out on a good deal of world premieres. Secondly, many in the local tourist industry questioned the value of holding such a large event at the end of the season when things were naturally winding down.

With the move to spring, Cannes was able to lay the foundations for its "King of Festivals" crown. After the 1950 wobble the next few festivals burst out of the gate with a range of films from the cream of international cinema. Between 1951 and 1953 over 105 feature films were presented in competition, including George Stevens' "A Place in the Sun", Alfred Hitchcock's "I Confess", Orson Welles' screen adaptation of "Othello", John Ford's "The Sun Shines Bright", Raj Kapoor's "Awara", and a back-to-back triple play from Luis Buñel ("Subida al Cielo", "Los Olividados", and "El").

In 1954 two things happened which would change the image of Cannes forever. The first involved an idea, put forward by Parisian jeweller Suzanne Lazon, that the festival award trophies should incorporate a palm leaf motif (as the trees had long since become an icon of the city). The initial concept was sketched out by legendary director Jean Cocteau – a friend of Lazon – and went down so well with the festival brass that the top prize, the Grand Prix, was renamed the Palme d'Or the following year.

The second change experienced in 1954 was the introduction of "sex" to the festival's image. During a photo call for Robert Mitchum, French starlet Simone Sylva started the now infamous tradition of "getting one's boobs out" on the beach for the cameras. A bemused Mitchum stood by as Miss Sylva's assets hit the international news wires, and with them, a lasting image of Cannes was cast in the world's mind. And as the decade progressed this image was only boosted by the presence of a bikini-clad Bridgette Bardot, who, by the end of 1950s, had become almost a permanent fixture on the beach during the festival.

Despite the attention generated by the off-screen antics of its attendees, the festival continued to present a range of films from top international directors. Indeed, the 1950s saw the selection of films starting to read like a list of usual suspects (albeit talented ones) as Cannes alumni were invited back with their next films – a practice which continues to this day. Highlights from the remainder of the decade included Fred Zinnemann's "From Here to Eternity", Walt Disney's "The Living Desert", Satyajit Ray's "Pather Pantchali" and "Parash Pathar", Federico Fellini's "Nights of Cabiria", Louis Malle's "Le Monde du Silence", Stanley Donen's "Funny Face", and a trio from Ingmar Bergman, " Smiles of a Summer Night", " The Seventh Seal", and "So Close to Life".

In the early days Cannes had largely been an event for tourists and socialites who were often more interested in attending the many parties in the expensive hotels and luxury villas than they were in watching the films. However, as the festival's popularity increased, it gradually became a place for the international film industry to gather, do business, and discuss future projects. In 1959, ten participants and a canvas screen on the roof of the Palais Croisette kicked

of the first Marché du Film, with the event becoming an official part of the festival in 1961.

Whist the arrival of the 1960s found many western countries in the midst of large scale social and economic change, the festival was building on the success of the previous decade and had begun to hit its stride. In 1965, the festival appointed its first female jury president, Olivia de Havilland (followed the next year by Sophia Loren), and the decade saw a wide variety of films presented including Fellini's "La Dolce Vita", Buñuel's "Viridiana", John Fankenheimer's "All Fall Down", Sidney Lumet's "Long Day's Journey into Night", Robert Mulligan's "To Kill a Mockingbird", François Truffaut's "Le Peau Douce", Masaki Kobayashi's "Kwaidan", David Lean's "Doctor Zhivago", Orson Welles' "Chimes at Midnight", Michelangelo Antonioni's "Blow Up", Costa-Gavras' "Z", and Dennis Hopper's "Easy Rider".

However, while the official selection witnessed many of the Cannes alumni present some of their most seminal films, there was a feeling in some quarters that it was becoming increasingly difficult for newer filmmakers to get their films shown at the festival. It was this sentiment which led to the creation of the world's first festival "sidebar", the Semaine Internationale de la Critique ("International Critics' Week"), founded in 1962 as a parallel section focussed on presenting the work of first and second time directors.

Although by the time the 1960s had rolled around, the festival was pretty much over its shaky past, there was to be one more hiccup in 1968. Amidst an undercurrent of general discontent in France, the culture minister André Malraux tried to fire the co-founder and head of the Cinématèque Française, Henri Langois, over a long-running budget dispute. Langois was an extremely popular and respected figure, particularly with the French "new wave" directors, so when the news of the sacking hit Cannes towards the middle of the 1968 festival, all hell broke loose. Louis Malle and Roman Polanski both immediately resigned from the festival jury, joining the call from François Truffaut, Jean-Luc Godard and a host of other French filmmakers, for the festival to be closed down as a sign of protest. The feelings ran so hot that on 19 May 1968 the directors burst into the noon screening and literally hung from the curtains to prevent the festival from continuing. The festival was cancelled shortly after with many foreign filmmakers finding themselves trapped in France for several days in the face of the nationwide strikes that had brought the country to a standstill.

The French authorities eventually brokered a deal to end the strikes, and the filmmakers successfully forced Malraux to reinstate Henri Langois, but it was too late to resume the festival. However, the events of 1968 did leave an impression on another group of French filmmakers, amongst them Robert Enrico and Jacques Doniol-Valcroze, who were appalled that the festival had been used as a political platform by Truffaut, Godard et al. Together with a group of colleagues they formed the Société des Réalisateurs de Films and gave birth to the second festival sidebar, Quinzaine des Réalisateurs ("Directors' Fortnight"). The Quinzaine was intended to be a forum where films could be presented free from "... all forms of censorship and diplomatic considerations." Its spirit was immortalised by a mildly Orwellian quote from French director Pierre Kast: "All films are born free and equal: we must help them to remain so."

The 1970s brought with them profound change, both in the world of filmmaking and within the festival itself. In the early days festival films had been chosen and submitted by officially appointed representatives from their country of origin. But in 1972 the board of directors decided that from that point on the festival itself would look after the process of choosing films for inclusion in the official selection, thus setting the blueprint for the selection format which is used by most modern international film festivals today.

As far as the films went, the 1970s was largely dominated by the new "golden boys" of American cinema. With Hollywood in a transitional phase (the studio system was long dead, but the corporations had yet to become interested in movies), directors such as Martin Scorcese, Francis Ford Coppola, and Robert Altman, were at the forefront of cinema in the 1970s – in effect, America's answer to the French new wave of the 60s. And Cannes certainly approved. Over the course of the decade American new wave films screened included Robert Altman's "M.A.S.H" and "3 Women", Francis Ford Coppola's "The Conversation" and an unfinished "Apocalypse Now" (which still managed to clinch the Palme d'Or), Martin Scorsese's "Alice Doesn't Live Here Anymore" and "Taxi Driver", and Steven Spielberg's "The Sugarland Express".

But the 1970s in Cannes wasn't only about American movies. Filmmakers from Europe and further a field were well represented by films including John Boorman's "Leo the Last", Louis Malle's "Murmur of the Heart", Milos Forman's "Taking Off", Andreï Tarkovski's "Solaris", Ken Russell's "Mahler", Rainer Werner Fassbinder's "Fear Eats the Soul" and "Despair", Wim Wenders' "Kings of the Road" and "The American Friend", Roman Polanski's "The Tenant", Ridley Scott's "The Duellists", Alan Parker's "Midnight Express", and Werner Herzog's "Woyzeck".

In 1975, festival boss Maurice Bessey decided to expand the scope of the event further by introducing three new out of competition sidebars to the official selection: *Les Yeux Fertiles* ("Fertile Eyes"), *l'Air du Temps* ("Spirit of the Time"), and *Le Passé Compose* ("The Perfect Past"). While this seemed like a good idea at the time, it became quick apparent that the addition of these sidebars overly complicated the official selection, so in 1978 new Delegate Générale Gilles Jacob (now festival president) rolled up these events into a single sidebar: *Un Certain Regard*. That same year Jacob also introduced the *Camera d'Or*, an award for the best first-time feature film in any section of the festival.

The arrival of the 1980s saw the festival facing the reasonably serious problem of having outgrown its home in the Palais Croisette. Not wanting to lose the lucrative event, the City of Cannes commissioned a new *Palais des Festivals et des Congrès* on the site of the old winter casino. Completed in December 1982 as a dual festival and conference venue (and quickly dubbed "The Bunker" by Cannes regulars), the new Palais hosted its first festival in 1983. To celebrate the opening, the City of Cannes invited many stars of past and present to leave their hand prints in clay outside the building on Esplanade Georges Pompidou.

Moviewise the 1980s were heralded by the comeback film from legendary Japanese director, Akira Kurosawa. Financed by George Lucas and Francis Ford Coppola, Kurosawa's "Kagemusha" shared the 1980 Palme d'Or with Bob Fosse's "All That Jazz". Other key films screened at Cannes during the 80s included, Bruce Beresford's "Breaker Morant", Bernardo Bertolucci's "Tragedy of a Ridiculous Man", Michael Mann's "Violent Streets", Costa-Gavras' "Missing", Jean-Luc Godard's "Passion", Terry Jones' "Monty Python – The Meaning of Life", Peter Weir's "The Year of Living Dangerously", Win Wenders' "Paris, Texas" and "Wings of Desire", Alan Parker's "Birdy", Peter Bogdanovich's "Mask", Roland Joffe's "The Mission", Peter Greenaway's "Drowning By Numbers", Krzysztof Kieslowski's "A Short Film About Killing", Jane Campion's "Sweetie", and Steven Soderbergh's "Sex, Lies, and Videotape" (the surprise Palme d'Or winner in 1989).

The 1990s kicked off with a continuation of the independent theme set by

Soderbergh the year before. During the early part of the decade films such as David Lynch's "Wild at Heart", Ken Loach's "Hidden Agenda", the Coen Brothers' "Barton Fink", Lars von Trier's "Europa", and Spike Lee's "Jungle Fever" all grabbing attention on the Croisette. Other notable films included James Ivory's "Howard's End", Robert Altman's "The Player", Joel Schumacher's "Falling Down", Mike Leigh's "Naked", and of course Quentin Tarantino's "Pulp Fiction". In 1993, New Zealander Jane Campion also made festival history, becoming the first female director to win the Palme d'Or (for "The Piano").

Although most of the action during the 90s took place on screen, the festival did pause in 1997 to celebrate its 50th anniversary. To mark the occasion a host of previous Palme d'Or winners were invited back to the festival for photo opportunities and to pay tribute to 50 years of film in Cannes. The festival also presented legendary Swedish director Ingmar Bergman with a special award – the *Palme des Palmes* ("Palm of Palms") – in recognition of his status as a true master of the cinematic medium. The following year, the festival also finally acknowledged the importance of the role played by film schools in developing new talent with the creation of Cinéfondation, a new sidebar dedicated to showcasing the best work from training institutions around the world.

The remainder of the decade continued to be focussed on an eclectic mix of films from across the globe. Highlights included Emir Kusturica's "Underground", Larry Clark's "Kids", Lars von Trier's "Breaking

the Waves", the Coen Brothers' "Fargo", Ang Lee's "Ice Storm", Curtis Hanson's "LA Confidential", Thomas Vinterberg's Dogme 95 offering, "Festen", Terry Gilliam's "Fear and Loathing in Las Vegas", Pedro Almodovar's "All About My Mother", and Takeshi Kitano's "Kikukiro".

As the clocks ticked over to the year 2000, Cannes was busy putting together an official selection which would highlight the importance of digital technology to the future of filmmaking. The first palm of the new millennium went to Lars von Trier's DV-shot "Dancer in the Dark", and since then a whole host of digitally-shot films have appeared in every part of the official selection. But aside from the revolution seen in the way festival films were being made, several other key changes occurred at Cannes during the first half of the decade. In 2002, the festival got an image make-over, losing its somewhat lengthy title to simply becoming known as the "Festival de Cannes". Two years later the Cannes Classics sidebar was inaugurated to present films of archival importance from previous festivals and further a field. And in 2005, a new world cinema section – Tous les Cinémas du Monde – was added to help showcase films from countries with a historically-low cinematic output.

As far as the official selection has gone, key films presented at Cannes since 2000 have included Wong Kar-Wai's "In the Mood for Love", the Coen Brothers' "The Man Who Wasn't There", Baz Luhrmann's "Moulin Rouge", Michael Winterbottom's "24 Hour Party People", Roman Polanski's "The Pianist", Michael Moore's

"Bowling for Columbine" (the first documentary film ever accepted in competition), Lars von Trier's "Dogville", Gus van Sant's "Elephant", Walter Salles "The Motorcycle Diaries", Robert Rodriguez and Frank Miller's "Sin City", and Atom Egoyan's "Where the Truth Lies".

Today, Cannes is the most famous of all film festivals and one of the largest media events on the planet. The festival has an annual budget of around €20m, half of which comes from the French Ministry of Culture and Communications (through the Centre National du Cinéma), with the rest from the City of Cannes, various regional authorities, and a large group of corporate sponsors. Each year more than 1,500 films from over 100 countries are submitted to be considered for a very limited number of berths in the official selection. The stars still show up to bask in the limelight, the crowds still gather to watch, and Cannes' reputation as the king of film festivals just gets stronger each year.

structure

"In Competition", "Out of Competition", "Official Selection", "Critics' Week", "Directors' Fortnight", "the Market"... having been the first film festival to develop sidebar events, to the casual observer Cannes now appears to be a bit of a confusing mess. In reality, there are actually four organisations overseeing ten major sections that comprise what is commonly referred to as the "Cannes Film Festival".

Festival de Cannes

Officially, the Festival de Cannes is a film festival hosted by Association Française du Festival International du Film (however the name has also become the de facto collective "brand" for all of the events which comprise the festival). Within the Festival de Cannes itself, there are seven sections in which films are presented (all of which qualify the film for promoting itself as having gained "Official Selection" at Cannes):

Compétition

The competition is the festival's main event and this is where you'll find all the glamour and glory. Films screening in this section are referred to as being "in competition" and vie for an assortment of awards. The Holy Grail is of course the *Palme d'Or* (Golden Palm) for best picture, one of the most prestigious film awards on the planet. Winning the Palme d'Or generally gives the film a massive lift: for art-house films, it can bring in millions of extra dollars at the international box-office, for foreign films it means worldwide distribution. Historically, the competition has only been open to narrative films, although occasionally a documentary is slipped in (such as Michael Moore's "Fahrenheit 9/11" which won the top prize in 2004). The competition welcomes both features and shorts, and there are different awards in each category.

Hors Compétition

"Out of Competition". Not strictly an official section per se, the festival's practice of screening films out of the competition line-up has been around since the very beginning. Over the years, films screened have tended to be special events or films which did not necessarily meet the criteria for entering the competition. More recently, the festival has also found that this practice enables them to screen films which bolster the big-name presence in Cannes without compromising the artistic values of the main competition.

Films that have screened out of competition in recent years include: George Lucas' "Star Wars Episode III: Revenge of the Sith" (world premiere), Woody Allen's "Match Point", Shane Black's "Kiss Kiss, Bang Bang", Francis Ford Coppola's "Apocalypse Now Redux", Quentin Tarantino's "Kill Bill Vol.2", and James Cameron's "Ghosts of the Abyss". Occasionally, the festival also uses the out of competition section to screen footage of works in progress from well-respected filmmakers. Previous screenings have included scenes from Kenneth Branagh's "Hamlet", Peter Jackson's "Lord of the Rings" trilogy, and Martin Scorsese's "Gangs of New York".

Un Certain Regard

Created in 1978 to absorb several ambiguous sidebars, Un Certain Regard is now the main showcase section of the festival and is intended to be a "survey of current world cinema". Historically there were no awards attached to Un Certain Regard, but in recent years the festival has created the Prix Un Certain Regard to help the best film in the sidebar achieve distribution in France. Occasionally other awards are made in this section as well.

Cinéfondation

Added in 1998, Cinéfondation is the festival's competition for short and medium-length films made at film schools around the world. The Cinéfondation sidebar has its own jury and there are three awards (which include a cash prize) for the best films in this section.

Cannes Classics

Inaugurated in 2004, the Cannes Classics sidebar is a showcase section which centres on screening a selection of new or restored prints of classic films, tributes to foreign cinema, documentaries on filmmaking, and occasionally rare or rediscovered footage of from days gone by.

Tous les Cinémas du Monde

Literally, "All Cinemas of the World", this new sidebar was added in 2005 as a showcase section to present a programme of films from selected countries which have historically had a low cinema output. Each day during the festival, Tous Les Cinéma du Monde focuses on one country, presenting a range of films which "reflect its cultural identity and the uniqueness of expression". Films are screened in the 170-seat temporary Cinéma du Monde theatre, located in the Village International Pantiero.

The Sidebars

By the time the 1960s rolled around Cannes had already established itself as one of the world's premiere film festivals. It was probably inevitable that other groups would want to run parallel events in the city at the same time, however the two sidebars which emerged were formed for vastly different reasons.

Semaine Internationale de la Critique (SIC)
"International Critics' Week". Founded in 1962 by the Syndicat Français de la Critique de Cinéma to focus on the work of new filmmakers, the Critics' Week is the oldest of the festival sidebars. The International Critic's Week comprises a competition for around 14 features and shorts from first and second-time filmmakers, and a programme of special screenings. Films are selected by a panel of international film critics, appointed by the SIC, and cash prizes are awarded for the best film in each category. The award for best feature film is the *Grand Prix de la Semaine de la Critique* (Critics' Week Grand Prize).

The Critics' Week has always been a great launching pad for talented international filmmakers. Famous directors including Bernardo Bertolucci, Barbet Schroeder, Ken Loach, Neil Jordan, John Sayles, and Kevin Smith have all had films shown in this section. Although it works closely with the Festival de Cannes, the Critics' Week is run autonomously by the Syndicat Français de la Critique de Cinéma.

Quinzaine des Réalisateurs
"The Directors' Fortnight". Created in 1968 by a group of French filmmakers to present films in a forum which was free from politics, censorship and elitism, the first Directors' Fortnight kicked off along side the festival in 1969, and the two events have co-existed for nearly 40 years. Today the sidebar occupies a slightly-higher profile at the festival than the Critics' Week, due mainly to a larger selection of films (the 2005 programme included 23 features and 14 shorts). Once the festival closes the Quinzaine also goes on tour in Europe, with repeat screenings of the films in Paris, Rome, Milan, and Brussels.

The alumni of the Directors' Fortnight participants reads like a who's who of world cinema, but surely the best anecdote has to be from 1974. Following the screening of a little-known American film that year, none of the journalists stayed to talk to the filmmakers. Fortnight boss, Jacques Doniol-Valcroze, found he had his work cut out for him keeping the dejected filmmakers' spirits high by reassuring them that the film was indeed great. The filmmakers were Martin Scorsese and Robert De Niro, and the film was "Mean Streets".

As with the International Critic's Week, The Directors' Fortnight is run autonomously by a separate organisation – the Société des Réalisateurs de Films (SRF) – but collaborates closely with the Festival de Cannes.

Marché du Film
"The Film Market" or simply, the "Cannes Market", is the largest event of its type in the world. As the name suggests, it's the nuts and bolts end of the festival in which the movie industry gets together to do business: primarily the buying and selling of films. The Market is not prestigious – it's a tradeshow open to anyone who is looking to buy or has something to sell – and it's attended by around 10,000 film industry professional each year.

To compliment the traditional film sales and networking arena, the Marché du Film launched two new initiatives in 2004: *Le Réseau des Producteurs* (The Producers' Network) – a special initiative to provide a series of services and events to help producers do business; and the *Marché du Courts Métrages* (Short Film Corner) – a forum for buying and selling short films.

Like the Festival de Cannes, the Marché du Film is also run by the Association Française du Festival International du Film, however it has a completely separate management structure.

other festival events

In addition to the film programmes, the Festival de Cannes hosts a range of other events for the enjoyment of festivalgoers each year. Some are permanent fixtures on the Cannes calendar while others are tied to a single year only. Full details regarding the special events for the next festival are always available from the official web site (www.festival-cannes.org).

Masterclasses

Since 1991, the festival has run a series of masterclasses (in reality, lectures), given by established and respected film practitioners. There are now three different masterclasses held during the event: La Leçon de Cinéma (directors), La Leçon d'Acteur (actors), and La Leçon de Musique (film composers). Previous speakers in the various categories have included Oliver Stone, Stephen Frears, Kar-Wai Wong, Catherine Deneuve, Max von Sydow, and Patrick Doyle.

Exhibitions

From as far back as the early 90s, the festival has included a programme of exhibitions with themes that are strongly linked to cinema; such as tributes to the work of a particular filmmaker, or a collection of items relating to a single cinematic theme. Exhibitions take place in various locations around the city.

Tributes

Each year at an evening gala, the festival pays tribute to one or more internationally-renowned artists from the film industry. Recipients are presented with a special festival trophy and a selection of their work is screened for the audience. Recent tributees include, Luis Buñel, Melanie Griffith, Raj Kapoor, and Billy Wilder, Morgan Freeman, and Liza Minnelli.

L'Atelier du Festival

Launched at the 2005 festival as part of the Cinéfondation sidebar, L'Atelier du Festival is a special programme to help young filmmakers bring their projects to the screen. Projects submissions are accepted in the period leading up to the festival, of which around 18 are selected for participation in the programme. Successful filmmakers are brought to Cannes for a series of meetings with industry professionals who may be able to help them get their projects off the ground.

La Résidence du Festival

Outside of the festival itself, the Festival de Cannes runs two six-month film development programmes for young and new filmmakers. The residences take place in Paris and there are two sessions each year, one running October – February, and the other, February – July. During the residences, filmmakers are provided with a range of financial and professional support functions to help support the development of their projects, while also offering cultural opportunities to broaden their horizons.

submission & selection

In the old days getting a film submitted to Cannes was a murky affair: your chances of selection increased if you were favoured director, had the right connections within the organisation, or a strong lobby from your national film organisation behind you. Over the past few years, the festival has become increasingly open and receptive to a wider variety of films.

While the Festival de Cannes doesn't receive as many submissions as some other A-list events (notably Sundance), competition for a place at the world's most famous film festival is still incredibly fierce. In 2005, 1,540 feature films from 97 countries were put before the selection committee for a total of 53 places (a success rate of around 3%). And this is off the back of a steady rise in submissions over the past few years, with no equivalent increase in the number of films accepted.

Eligibility and Selection Criteria

These days, submitting a film for Cannes consideration is a relatively straight-forward process. Entries for the official selection (Competition, Out of Competition, Un Certain Regard, Cinéfondation, Tous les Cinémas du Monde) are managed by the Festival de Cannes, with the SIC and SRF looking after submissions for their respective events. While each of the three organisations also

sets its own eligibility criteria, the core regulations tend to share the following themes:

Prior Screenings – being the most prestigious film festival there is means you can insist on having world premieres. To be eligible for selection in any of the sections of the festival (including the International Critics' Week and Directors' Fortnight), a film must not have been exhibited in any other festival or event, must not have been broadcast on the Internet, and must not have had release outside its country of origin.

Completion Dates – to be eligible for any of the festival sections, the film must have been completed in the 12 months prior to the festival (18 months in the case of Directors' Fortnight and Cinéfondation films).

Running Times – for a film to be considered a "feature" in any of the festival sections its running time must be at least 60 minutes. Films under 60 minutes are considered to be "shorts" by the International Critics' Week and Directors' Fortnight, but for the short film competition films must not exceed 15 minutes. The maximum running time for Cinéfondation films is 60 minutes.

Screening Prints – there are no requirements regarding a film's shooting format, but if it makes it into the official selection, two 35mm prints must be available (one screening print, one stand-by print). For the International Critics' Week and Cinéfondation sections, 16mm prints are also accepted. All printing costs are at the producer's expense.

Subtitles – if the film is given a festival berth, subtitles must be applied according to the following rules: if the original language of the film is French, then subtitles must be in English; for all other films, the subtitles must be in French, however if the original language of the film is something other than English, a set of English subtitles must also be supplied (as these will be projected digitally during the screening). With the exception of Cinéfondation films, all subtitling must be done at the producer's expense.

Films submitted for Festival de Cannes consideration (except Cinéfondation) must also respect Article 1 of the festival rules and regulations, which states:

"The spirit of the Festival de Cannes is one of friendship and universal cooperation. Its aim is to reveal and focus attention on works of quality in order to contribute to the evolution of motion picture arts and to encourage development of the film industry throughout the world."

The Cinéfondation sidebar requires that films submitted respect its own Article 1:

"The object of the Cinéfondation, official selection of the Cannes Film Festival, is to present and highlight films from film schools, fiction or animation, showing talent deserving encouragement."

Historically, the official selection has focussed on fictional film (although the definition of what constituted "fiction" has always been very loose). However, in recent years several documentaries have made it into the festival line-up; most notably, Michael Moore's "Fahrenheit 9/11", which won the Palme d'Or in 2004. There is no separate entry procedure for documentary films – they can be submitted in the same manner as fiction films, but must also meet the same eligibility rules.

The only part of the Festival de Cannes which does not have any submission criteria is of course the Marché du Film – it's a commercial enterprise, so any film can be presented as long as the registration fees are paid. The Short Film Corner does, however, impose a maximum running time of 90 minutes.

Submission Process

Submissions for all sections of the Festival de Cannes are now managed online by the respective organisations. To enter a film for consideration you will need to visit the relevant official web site. Each provides detailed information on the submission rules, plus the relevant application forms (either for completion online or for download):

Festival de Cannes
www.festival-cannes.org

International Critics' Week
www.semainedelacritique.com

Directors' Fortnight
www.quinzaine-realisateurs.com

Although there are no rules preventing you from submitting to all three organisations, it's normally best to work with your sales and publicity team to determine which section is most-suited to your film. It is of course only possible for a film to be selected for one section, but there is a large degree of cooperation between the Festival de Cannes, the SRF, and SIC, so they will often collectively decide which part of the festival is most suitable for your film.

Once you have completed the entry form, you will need to send a preview copy of the film to the address provided with the submission materials. There is also a fee to pay, which is based on the format of your preview copy, and varies between the three organisations;

Festival de Cannes
VHS/DVD: 25€
Beta SP/DigiBeta: 130€
35mm print: 300€

International Critics' Week
VHS, DVD, Beta SP, 16mm or 35mm print: 100€

Director's Fortnight
VHS, DVD, Beta SP, 16mm or 35mm print: 100€

Entry fees are waived for short films (under 60 minutes) in any of the sections (excluding films in the Short Film Corner of the Marché du Film).

For preview copies the various selection committees will accept films without subtitles if the original language is French or English. All other original languages must be subtitled in either French or English. The Festival de Cannes selection committee will also decide which section of the festival (i.e. Competition, Out of Competition, Un Certain Regard etc) that the film is best suited for.

To screen films in the Marché du Film, there is no submission or selection process. You simply register to attend, pay the registration fee, then make use of the various market facilities to show your film. The fees for screening your film in the Market will vary depending on the size of the venue you require, the time of day, and the number of screenings. For more information on the Market, see "The Biz" section later in this book.

Dates and Deadlines
Submissions for the various sections of the festival normally open at the beginning of the year, with deadlines varying between the three different organisations. You should check the respective official web sites at the beginning of the year for the next set of dates, but in general the deadlines tend to be as follows:

Cinéfondation: Mid-February
Festival de Cannes: Mid-March
Int. Critics' Week: Early April
Directors' Fortnight: Mid-April

Once the submission process has closed, the Festival de Cannes spends a few weeks compiling the final list of films before announcing the official selection at a press conference in mid-April. The International Critic's Week normally announces its line-up several days later, and the Directors' Fortnight, the following week.

juries and awards

Prior each year's event the festival's board of directors appoints four juries who will hold responsibility for selecting films from the official selection which will receive the blessing of a Cannes award. Jurors are chosen from all walks of the film industry, based on their previous body of work and respect from their peers. In many cases, jury membership (especially the presidency) is bestowed on a kind of "lifetime achievement award" basis.

Feature Films Jury

The Feature Films Jury is comprised of nine members and holds the unenviable task of selecting the award-winners from the films screened in the festival's Compétition section. The jury is headed up by a president who is normally a leading and accomplished figure from the international film industry. Previous presidents have included Quentin Tarantino, David Lynch, Martin Scorsese, Francis Ford Coppola, Clint Eastwood, Luc Besson, Kirk Douglas, Sophia Loren, Ingrid Bergman, Louis Malle, Olivia de Havilland, Fritz Lang, and Tennessee Williams.

Over the course of the festival, the jurors view all of the features in competition before casting their vote for the film they feel deserves each award. Voting is conducted by secret ballot and the winners are determined on an absolute majority basis. The President and Artistic Director of the Festival de Cannes are present during the jury's deliberations, but do not take part in the voting process.

The festival rules oblige the Feature Film Jury to bestow the following awards:

Palme d'Or
For best feature film of the festival.

Grand Prix
For the film which shows the most originality, a kind of "runner up" award.

Prix d'Interprétation Féminine
For the best performance by an actress in a competition film.

Prix d'Interprétation Masculine
For the best performance by an actor in a competition film

Prix de la Mise en Scène
For best director

Prix du Scénario
For best original or adapted screenplay

In addition to the obligatory awards the jury also has the power to confer one or more *Prix du Jury* (Special Jury Prize) awards to films they feel deserve particular recognition.

Where there is a tied ballot, most of the awards can be split equally between two recipients, although the festival only allows one shared award per year. The Palme d'Or cannot be awarded jointly, although the Festival President has the power to make exceptions to any of the festival's awards criteria. Indeed, the Palme d'Or has been shared at least three times during the festival's history: in 1979 between Völker Schlondorff's "Die Blechtrommel" ("The Tin Drum") and Francis Ford Coppola's "Apocalypse Now"; in 1980 between Bob Fosse's "All That Jazz" and Akira Kurosawa's "Kagemusha"; and in 1997 between Shohei Imamura's "Unagi" ("The Eel") and Abbas Kiarostami's "Ta'm e Guilass" ("The Taste of Cherry").

Cinéfondation/Short Film Jury

A five-member jury is appointed to take responsibility for handing out the awards in the short film competition and the Cinéfondation sidebar. As with the Feature Film Jury, voting is conducted by secret ballot and the winners are determined by absolute majority.

The Cinéfondation/Short Film Jury is obliged to bestow the following awards:

Palme d'Or du Court Métage
For best short film in competition

Mention Spéciale, Court Métage
Up to two special jury prizes for short films in competition

Premier Prix de la Cinéfondation
First prize in the Cinéfondation sidebar

Deuxième Prix de la Cinéfondation
Second prize in the Cinéfondation sidebar

Troisième Prix de la Cinéfondation
Third prize in the Cinéfondation sidebar

The Cinéfondation/Short Film Jury also has the power to confer joint awards, however a special waiver must be grated by the Festival President for a tied Palme d'Or du Court Métage or Premier Prix de la Cinéfondation.

The winner of the Palme d'Or du Court Métage is also presented with the Norman McLaren Prize by the National Film Board of Canada (NFB). The award includes a cash prize of 3,000€ for the director along with an offer from the NFB to take care of international distribution for the film and to co-produce the winner's next short.

All of the Cinéfondation awards come with cash prizes attached: 15,000€ (for first place), 11,250€ (for second place), and 7,500€ (for third place). The winner of the Premier Prix de la Cinéfondation is also guaranteed that their first feature film will be presented at a future Festival de Cannes.

Un Certain Regard Jury

A president heads up a seven-member jury which makes a small number of awards to films being showcased in the Un Certain Regard section:

Prix Un Certain Regard
For the best film in the section

Prix de l'Intimité
Prize for Intimacy

Prix de l'Espoir
Prize for Hope

The winner of the Prix Un Certain Regard also receives a cash prize to aid the film's distribution in France.

Caméra d'Or Jury

Introduced in 1978, the *Prix de la Caméra d'Or* is a prize presented to the best feature film by a first-time director in any section of the festival (including the International Critics' Week and Directors' Fortnight). The task of selecting the winner of this prestigious award is handed to a special nine-member jury appointed by the Festival de Cannes. The jury is made up of seven industry professionals and two film fans, one of which is nominated by the City of Cannes.

For a film to be eligible for the Caméra d'Or, it must not only be the director's first feature, but it must also respect Article 1 of the award's regulations:

> "The aim of the Caméra d'Or award is to reveal and to assist a first film shown in the Cannes Film Festival, whose qualities seem to be of a nature to encourage his or her director to undertake a second film."

The winner of the Caméra d'Or also receives a cash prize from the award's patron, Eastman Kodak, as well as grant money from other sponsors to aid distribution of the film in France, Spain, Italy, and Belgium.

International Critics' Week Awards
Films selected for the International Critics' Week vie for a selection of awards from both SIC itself and also from the sidebar's various sponsors.

Grand Prix de la
Semaine de la Critique
The Critics' Week Grand Prize. After each screening, journalists and film critics are asked to cast their votes, and at the end of the week, the film with the most popular film is presented with the Grand Prize. In addition to the award the winner also receives a cash prize of around 5,000€ and a three-month residence at Moulin d'André, a workshop for writers and directors.

Prix SACD
A jury appointed by the Société des Auteurs et Compositeurs

Dramatiques (SACD) bestows this award for best screenwriting to one of the feature films screening in the sidebar. The winner also receives a cash prize of around 2,500€.

Prix ACID
A jury appointed by Agence du Cinéma Indépendant pour sa Diffusion (ACID) bestows a special prize for the best feature film in the section. The prize includes financial support from ACID to aid the film's distribution.

Prix Canal+ du
Meilleur Court Métrage
The Canal+ Award for Best Short Film. Presented by the French mini-major to the best short film in the sidebar. In addition to the award, Canal+ makes a guarantee to buy the rights to the film for broadcast on its network and the director is also invited to a one-month workshop at Moulin d'André.

Prix Découverte Kodak
du Court Métrage
The Kodak Discovery Award for Best Short Film. A jury of different professionals involved in short filmmaking is appointed by Kodak to bestow the discovery award for the most innovative short film in the sidebar. Kodak also provides an in-kind donation of stock for the director's next film

Prix TV5 de la (Toute)
Jeune Critique
The TV5 (Very) Young Critic Awards. Each year, the International Critics' Week invites a selection of French and German

high school students to attend the screenings in the sidebar. During the course of the festival the students asked to view and write a review for each film. At the end of the week, the students vote for the best feature film (*Prix TV5 de la (Toute) Jeune Critique pour le Court Métrage*) and best short film (*Prix TV5 de la (Toute) Jeune Critique pour le Long Métrage*) in the section. A special prize – the *Prix TV5 de la Meilleure Critique* – is also awarded by SIC to the best young French and German critics.

Rails d'Or
Since 1995, a group of rail worker film enthusiasts have attended the International Critics' Week screenings. The group presents two "golden rail" awards to films in the sidebar: Petit Rail d'Or for best short film, and Grand Rail d'Or for best feature.

Prix Regards Jeunes
The SIC and Directors' Fortnight collaborate to appoint a five-member jury comprised of young French-speaking film fans. The jury makes two awards for films in either of the sidebars: one for best feature film, one for best short.

Feature films in the International Critics' Week from first-time directors also qualify for the Caméra d'Or award.

Directors Fortnight Awards
The core sponsors of the Directors' Fortnight – the Société des Auteurs et Compositeurs Dramatiques (SACD), Kodak, and Gras Savoye – appoint a small jury to hold responsibility for

awarding the various prizes for the best films in the sidebar.

Prix SACD du Court Métrage
For best short film in the sidebar.

Carrosse d'Or
The Golden Cart. A peer-awarded prize made by the SACD for the best screenplay in the sidebar.

3ème Label Europa Cinemas
An award made to recognise and support the best European film in the sidebar.

3ème Prix Regards Jeunes
Two awards, made by a special jury of young film enthusiasts, for the best feature and short film in the sidebar. The jury is appointed by the French Ministry for Youth, Sport, and Community.

Prix Gras Savoye – sponsor's prize for best film in the sidebar.

Films in the Directors' Fortnight are also eligible for the Prix Regards Jeunes, and features from first-time directors also qualify for Caméra d'Or consideration.

attending

Unlike most festivals around the world, Cannes is an event reserved predominantly for film industry professionals and the press. Accreditation, entry to screenings, and admission to official venues is strictly controlled, with public access to the vast majority of the festival virtually non-existent. The International Critics' Week and

Directors' Fortnight sidebars do offer some consolation via a small public ticket allocation, and educational groups and French film enthusiasts can gain limited access through the Cannes Cinéphiles programme. But in most cases, non-industry types just have to be happy star-gazing and enjoying what the south of France has to offer.

If you're a filmmaker, attending the festival for the first time will probably be one of the most valuable things you do for your career. Twelve days in Cannes will teach you more about how the international film industry works than several years at film school. You will realise pretty quickly that films are simply a commodity to be bought and sold, and like everything else, the market is governed by the age-old rules of commerce.

For this reason, the people who tend to get the most value out of attending the festival are producers, those involved with buying and selling films (i.e. sales companies and distributors), financiers, and quasi-industry types – such as film lawyers – for whom networking is an essential business tool. Those of a more directly creative nature – writers, directors, actors etc – may find the in-your-face business activities and commoditisation of films somewhat unpalatable, but this is the nature of the beast. Attending the festival will still be an immensely-valuable experience because it provides the opportunity to make loads of new contacts (particularly outside your own local industry).

Of course against the backdrop of this monster film industry get-together there is the little matter of that famous film festival which also happens to be taking place in town. As well as meeting your peers you also get the chance to attend world premieres of the latest films from big name directors, get exposed to the best new cinema from across the globe, and last, but not least, get to enjoy a stay on the French Riviera and call it a business trip!

Who Can Attend

Accreditation for the Festival de Cannes is open to a wide variety of practicing industry professionals. In addition to those directly involved in filmmaking – producers, directors, writers, technicians, composers, actors etc – a range of associated professions are also eligible to attend. These include: civil servants from Arts Ministries and the like, embassy staff, artistic and press agents, film lawyers, film librarians/archivists, film commission staff, distributors, film school staff, music publishers, employees of organisations involved in film financing, cinema owners, film festival staff, and employees of companies which produce videos and DVDs. And of course, there's the press.

Due to the diverse needs of vetting all the various industry professions there are around 22 different organisations which have been given the power to accredit attendees by the Festival de Cannes. In the past, it was necessary to deal directly with the relevant organisation for your specific area of "professionalism", however thankfully the festival has moved to an online system which automatically routes your accreditation request to the appropriate organisation for your discipline.

So do you need accreditation? If you're simply heading to the festival for business, obtaining accreditation isn't strictly necessary per se. However, doing Cannes sans accreditation will introduce a fairly large degree of hassle to your visit as you won't be able get into most of the key business areas – the Palais, Riviera, or Village International – nor the big hotels (unless you're staying in one).

Different Types of Accreditation

There are six different types of accreditation available for Cannes and each has different rules, fees, and eligibility criteria.

Festival Accreditation

Previously known as "professional accreditation", this is basically your bog-standard credentials for entry to the Cannes' screenings and official activities. Festival Accreditation is available to all of the professions outlined under "Who Can Attend" and provides access to all festival venues (the Palais, Riviera, Village International and the major hotels) and to screenings in the official selection and sidebars.

Festival Accreditation is free, but there's a catch – you will be asked to provide proof of your eligibility for accreditation in the discipline you select. In previous years, the festival simply asked for you to name three feature films that you had worked on, but in these days of heightened security threats and ever-increasing crowds, the rules have been tightened up significantly.

For filmmakers (producers, writers, directors, composers, technicians etc), you will be expected to show evidence of work in your chosen discipline on one or more feature films in the last three years. The guidelines for what constitutes "evidence" is fairly opaque, but the festival often makes mention of things such as marketing materials (posters, flyers etc), contracts (employment, distribution etc), or membership of any approved professional organisation. A large amount of emphasis is also placed on your listing in major industry databases (particularly the Internet Movie Database, www.imdb.com), so make sure your credits list is up-to-date. Having a professionally-designed company web site which shows that you operate in the film industry will also help support your application.

Ironically, those seeking accreditation in disciplines that aren't directly-related to filmmaking will perhaps have an easier time, so long as the organisation you work for has a reasonable profile and clearly operates in a space which is related to film. The type of evidence needed will vary depending on the individual requirements of the accrediting body and will be mentioned during the online application process. However, things such as a professionally-designed company web site and marketing materials showing your activities relating to film will also be paramount.

Applications for Festival Accreditation normally open mid-January and are now submitted online via the official Festival de Cannes web site (www.festival-cannes.org). If you were accredited for the previous year it's normally possible to retrieve your last set of details to save some time.

The festival is, however, notorious for having badly-designed web sites with poor usability, so working your way through the information and forms does tend to take a little longer than it really should, but it isn't overly complex.

Once you've completed your details online, you'll need to send any supporting materials to the relevant accreditation body (address details will be provided during the registration process). You'll normally be notified via email of the status of your request within a few days of the accrediting body receiving your application. They will also contact you if there are any queries regarding your supporting materials. The deadline for all Festival Accreditation requests is normally the beginning of April.

Market Accreditation

Each year nearly 10,000 industry professionals attend the Marché du Film. Market Accreditation is available to the board members and employees of:

• companies whose main activity is the production, distribution, exploitation or international broadcasting of cinema films,

• companies providing related services, including technical, business, financial or legal services

• institutions, associations and professional organisations whose principal work is in relation to the film industry

Unlike Festival Accreditation, there are fees involved in obtaining Market Accreditation, but it can be a good option if you're planning on doing a lot of business in Cannes, or if your recent feature credits aren't quite up to scratch. In addition to providing all of the same privileges as the Festival flavour, Market Accreditation provides access to market screenings and a whole range of additional benefits (including listing in and a free copy of the film sales Bible – The Market Guide; priority invitations to Competition and Out of Competition screenings; and access to the online facilities at the official Market web site, www.cannesmarket.com).

The registration process for Market Accreditation is fairly straight-forward. The first step is to nominate one person from your company to be the main contact for accreditation purposes. That person then points their web browser to the official Market site and completes the online registration process for themselves and your organisation.

Once the Market had validated your company's registration, the main contact can return to the site to add additional participants as required. The fees for Market Accreditation are around 299€ per person, however the fee is discounted to 250€ for participants who are registered before the beginning of March. All fees can be paid online via credit card.

Access to add and amend details for each participant is available via the web site until around 10 April. After this time, registration closes for approximately one week while the Market Guide is prepared. The final registration deadline is normally the end of April, however, after the 10th any additional participants added will not appear in the Market Guide.

Producers Network

Created in 2004, *Le Réseau des Producteurs* is a special type of accreditation within the Marché du Film aimed at producers. The intention of the Producers Network is to provide a collection of services and events to help producers develop their projects and to encourage international co-productions. Services include, a programme of daily networking breakfasts, hosted by a moderator and with a range of special guest speakers from across the industry, a special catalogue profiling each Producers Network participant which is distributed to all producers, distributors and sales companies in the Market and series of exclusive online tools to help producers get their projects off the ground. In addition to these benefits Producers Network accreditation provides all the privileges available under Market Accreditation.

The Producers Network is reserved for filmmakers with at least one producer credit on a feature film that's been commercially released in the last three years. A credit of "Producer", "Executive Producer", and "Co-Producer" is accepted on a qualifying film; "Line Producer" or "Associate Producer" credits are not eligible. A film is deemed to have had a commercial release if it's been screened for at least one week in cinema open to the public.

Producers Network accreditation comes with a fee of around 335€ per participant and there is a limited of two producers per company. A discounted free of 299€ is available for registrations received before the beginning of March. To sign up for the Producers Network visit the official Market web site.

Short Film Corner

Launched in 2004 alongside the Producers Network, the Short Film Corner is a programme within the Marché du Film dedicated to providing a marketplace for professionals interested in buying and selling short films. Located on the lower level of the Palais the Short Film Corner has its own screen room and all of the participating films are available to watch on interactive screens.

Because the Short Film Corner is a market, there are no selection criteria other than a requirement that the film must be less than 90 minutes in length to be considered a short. Registration operates on a per film basis. Each film entered entitles two representatives (normally the producer and director) to take part in the Short Film Corner activities and provides 12 months access to the exclusive Short Film Corner web site. Those registering also receive a Short Film Corner badge which provides entry to all official venues and to screenings in the official selection (excluding films in Competition or Out of Competition).

If you don't qualify for Festival Accreditation, but have been busy making shorts, then the Short Film Corner represents your best option for getting access to Cannes. And if you're films are good enough you may even pick up a small sale or two in the process! The fee for entering a film in the Short Film Corner is around 75€ for films under 30 minutes, and 125€ for films between 30 and 90 minutes. You can also enter more than one film, in which case the additional fee is based on the total running time of the films submitted after the first, and calculated at 2.50€ per minute.

The deadline for Short Film Corner registration is normally around the first week of April. Register online at the official Market web site from mid-January.

Press Accreditation

Cannes is one of the largest media events in the world and is attended by around 4,000 journalists, representing 1,500 media outlets in over 75 countries. Media access is managed directly by the Festival de Cannes via its "Press Accreditation Commission". Press credentials come in a range of flavours for different audience levels and media types– in other words, the higher the press outlet's profile, and the more people it reaches, the better the access that will be provided.

The Press Accreditation Commission maintains a database of previous accreditees, so if you've held press accreditation for the previous year, and your situation hasn't changed (i.e. a change of company or media type), then it's fairly straightforward to gain entry to the next festival. For new requests, or where there's been a change, the accreditation process simply involves supplying more samples of your work.

The various media types eligible for press accreditation are:

- Written Press
- Television
- Radio
- Press Photographers*
- Press Agencies
- Photo Agencies
- Audio-Visual Press Agencies
- Online Press

* Press photographers must be assigned by a media company - it isn't possible for unassigned freelancers to get accreditation.

There are two main steps required for press accreditation. Firstly, you need to prepare the various supporting materials for your application. The nature and volume of material required depends on whether or not you are applying for accreditation for the first time, and which of the media types you would like to be accredited for (you can only be registered for one). Once you've collected all of the necessary materials, they must be sent via regular post to the Press Accreditation Commission (note that email submissions and web links are not accepted). Information regarding the various requirements for each media type can be found in the Press section of the official festival web site (www.festival-cannes.org).

On receipt and validation of your materials, the press office will provide you with a unique reference and an address for the pre-registration web site where you'll need to complete the accreditation application forms (step two). Once you've submitted your application you can monitor its progress at the same site.

Applications for press accreditation open in mid-January and the deadline is normally the end of March.

Cinéphiles Accreditation

Organised by the City of Cannes, in association with the Festival, Cinéphiles accreditation enables local residents to see films from the official selection and sidebars in several cinemas around Cannes, and some screenings in the Palais. Cinéphiles accreditation is also open to film enthusiast and education groups (both French and foreign).

Requests for Cinéphiles accreditation from groups within the PACA region of France should be sent to:

L'OMACC
La Malmaison
47 la Croisette
06400 Cannes
Tel. 04 97 06 44 90
Fax. 04 93 68 34 49

All other requests for Cinéphiles accreditation should be sent to:

Festival de Cannes
Service des accréditations
3 Rue Amélie
75007 Paris
Tel. +33 (0)1 53 59 61 19
Fax. +33 (0)1 53 59 61 17
cinephiles@festival-cannes.fr

Requests for Cinéphiles accreditation must be accompanied by documentation certifying membership of a group which is either resident in the PACA region or a recognised film enthusiast or educational group. Cinéphiles accreditation opens in mid-January and closes early March.

Public Access

Admission to festival screenings and official venues without any form of accreditation is limited to the films showing at the Cinéma de la Plage (beach cinema), and some screenings in the International Critics Week and Directors' Fortnight sidebars.

For non-accredited festivalgoers an invitation is required to attend screenings in the Cinéma de la Plage (unless you just want to sit on the wall and watch). Invitations are free and handed out on a first come, first served basis from the tourist office in the Palais on the day of the screening.

A limited number of public tickets are also available for screenings in the International Critics' Week and Directors Fortnight sidebars. These can be purchased from the respective ticket offices:

International Critics' Week
Espace Miramar
35 rue Pasteur

Directors' Fortnight
La Malmaison
47 Boulevard de la Croisette

Tickets are around 6€ each and discounts are available for students or multiple bookings.

Late Registration

If you've managed to miss the various deadlines, it's still possible to obtain Festival or Market accreditation once you arrive in Cannes. Presumably because there's money in it for them, the Market tends to be more laid back towards late accreditation (although it's not possible to join the Producers Network or Short Film Corner after the deadlines). However, obtaining

Festival Accreditation in Cannes can be a real pain in the arse.

To discourage late registration the Festival uses language such as "subject to severe restrictions" and "only accepted in very exceptional cases" in the information it provides. The reality is, if you show up with your supporting materials, an up-to-date IMDB listing, a professional company web site, and a good deal of patience, you should be able to get yourself accredited.

Unfortunately, late Festival Accreditation is not free – there's an 85€ fee to cover the "administration costs" incurred by making you wait around. For last minute Market Accreditation there are fewer questions, but the standard fees apply. You can find the late registration desk at the Accreditation Centre in the Palais (Level 0).

Day Passes
If you're only popping into Cannes for a couple of days on business, it is possible to obtain a day pass which provides access to the Palais, Riviera, and Village International areas (but not the screenings). Day passes cost around 20€ per day and come in one, two, and three-day flavours. You will still need to prove that you work in the film industry or a related area, although an official invitation from a company which is exhibiting in the Palais, Riviera, or Village International will should also secure you a pass.

Picking Up Your Badge
On arrival in Cannes, one of the first things you should do is collect your badge. The Accreditation Centre is located in the Palais (Level 0) –

enter to the left of the blue Théâtre Debussy steps – and is open from the day before the festival starts through the remainder of the event.

To collect your badge and accreditation pack, you'll need to line up with your passport or other photo ID, but queues move quickly and the multi-lingual hostesses are friendly and helpful. Your badge is your most important festival possession – carry it day and night, but guard it with your life. If you're unfortunate enough to lose it, contact the Accreditation Centre immediately.

screenings

Despite the presence of the international film industry and the hyperactive Market, Cannes is of course, first and foremost, a film festival. During the 12 day event, over 120 films are screened in the official selection and festival sidebars. And being the world's most prestigious festival means that this crop will definitely include some of the best new cinema from across the globe so you'll probably want to see a couple of films while you're in town.

Venues
Cannes as a festival location has come a long way since the first films were shown in the old winter casino. Most of the official selection is screened in the various cinemas within the Palais, however the size of the event and the presence of the various sidebars (not to mention the needs of the Market) mean that the event spills over into most of the cinemas across town. Fortunately, almost all of the festival screening

venues are located within, or walking distance of the Centre Ville area.

Palais des Festivals

The Palais is located at Esplanade Georges Pompidou on the seafront in the middle of town. As well as being the centre of the Market it is also the main screening venue for the festival. In the Palais, you'll find the following cinemas and screening rooms:

Grand Théâtre Lumière

The Lumière is unmistakable due to the large amount of red shag pile carpet out the front. This massive 2,246-seat cinema has state of the art projection and sound, superb eye-lines, and is the flagship screening venue for the festival.

Théâtre Claude Debussy

With 1,061 seats, Debussy is the second largest theatre in Cannes. During the festival, its steps decked out in a less audacious blue.

Théâtre Buñuel

Located on level 5 inside the Palais.

Théâtre Bazin

Also known as "Auditorium A", this 280 seat cinema is the main press screening venue for films in the official selection. The theatre is located inside the Palais (level 3) and press accreditation is normally required for entry.

Théâtre Bory

A 147-seat theatre located inside the Palais. Bory is used mainly for Market screenings, and is sometimes referred to as "Auditorium K".

Auditoriums B – J, L, M

The various rooms within the Palais used for marketing screenings during the festival. The capacities of Auditoriums L and M are 80 seats; the remaining rooms have 40 seats each.

Riviera 1–8

Located upstairs in the Riviera building behind the Palais, these rooms are used for market screenings.

Cinéma de la Plage

Located at Plage Macé in front of the Majestic Hotel, the beach cinema is hard to miss due to the large scaffold sitting in the water. During the day, the screen is packed away and the beach is used by sunbathers and swimmers. Once night falls, the screen is rolled out and various films from the official selection are shown over the water. Screenings tend of kick-off around 8.45pm.

Cinéma du Monde

Located in the Village International – Pantiero, this temporary cinema houses the Tous les Cinéma du Monde sidebar of the official selection.

Espace Miramar

35 Rue Pasteur (near the corner with the Croisette). The Miramar is the main screening venue for films in the International Critics' Week sidebar.

Théâtre Noga Croisette

50 Boulevard de la Croisette (enter off Rue Frédéric Amouretti). Sometimes referred to as "Théâtre Palais Croisette", "Salle Doniol-Valcroze", or simply the "Noga", this cinema is the main screening venue for films in the Directors' Fortnight sidebar.

Les Arcades
77 Rue Félix Faure (near the corner with Rue Rouguière). Screens some re-runs of films in the official selection or sidebars, plus some market and press screenings.

Olympia
18 Rue de la Pompe. Houses some market screenings and special events, but also continues to function as a normal cinema for the public with current release films (mainly dubbed in French).

Star
98 Rue d'Antibes. Used mainly for market and press screenings.

Théâtre de la Licorne
25 Avenue Francis Tonnor. The main venue for Cinéphiles screenings.

Studio 13
23 Avenue Docteur Picaud (near Chemin de la Nadine). Located outside of the Centre Ville area, Studio 13 is used mainly for Cinéphiles and repeat screenings of films in the International Critics' Week and Directors' Fortnight sidebars.

It's worth noting that cinemas in Cannes are sometimes referred to using the French word *salle* (room) as in "Salle Lumière".

Finding Out What's on Where
Because the festival it managed by several different organisations, there doesn't tend to be a single official list of all the screenings taking place in Cannes on any given day. Around a week or so ahead of the festival the schedule for films screening in official selection is normally posted on the Festival de Cannes web site.

In Cannes, your accreditation pack includes a printed version of the same information. The International Critics' Week and Directors' Fortnight look after their own respective schedules – again, with information posted on the web just ahead of the festival, which is also available in a printed format from the screening venues in Cannes.

The best place to get the lowdown on what's shown in Cannes on any given day is from one of the major industry trade magazines: Screen International, Variety, and The Hollywood Reporter. During the festival, all three (festival regulars will note that Moving Pictures ceased production of its Cannes daily in 2004) publish free daily editions in Cannes which contain information about the screening schedule for the next 24 hours (across sections of the festival) plus festival news, reviews of the previous day's films, and special features on key industry topics.

You can pick up copies of the daily trades from inside the Palais and Riviera buildings, but also from many other locations across the city such as lobbies of the major hotels, pavilions in the Village International, and of course from the Cannes offices of the magazines themselves (see Appendix II). Screen International provides the most comprehensive and well-organised screening schedule, while the American trades generally focus more heavily on reviews and industry news. Regardless of which magazine you prefer, make sure you pick up your copies first thing in the morning – by early afternoon the free supply has usually dried up.

Fortunately, each section of the festival has a standard screening schedule and venue in Cannes. These are:

Competition (In or Out)

Each day two feature films from the competition crop screen in the Théâtre Lumière. Both films normally screen twice: once during the day and once at an evening gala. Films in competition also generally screen once the following day in either the Debussy or Bazin theatres, and the whole official selection is screened again in the Palais during the closing weekend of the festival.

Un Certain Regard

Screenings of films in this sidebar take place in the Théâtre Debussy. Press screenings of films in this section also take place in Théâtre Bazin the following day.

Competition Shorts

Short films in competition are screened in the Théâtre Debussy, with repeat screenings in the Théâtre Buñuel.

Cinéfondation/Cannes Classics

Screenings in these sidebars take place in Théâtre Buñuel.

Tous les Cinéma du Monde

Films in this programme screen in the high-tech temporary Cinéma du Monde.

International Critics' Week

The main screening venue for the International Critics' Week is the Espace Miramar theatre in the Hotel Martinez. The entrance to the Miramar is on Rue Pasteur. The Critics' Week also conducts repeat screenings in Théâtre Buñel, Studio 13, and Théâtre de la Licorne. The latter two venues are mainly targeted at the public so access to festivalgoers can be limited.

Directors' Fortnight Screenings

The Théâtre Palais Croisette at the Noga Hilton is home to the Directors' Fortnight screenings during the festival. Repeat screenings are also held at Les Arcades and Studio 13, although these are more for the benefit of the general public.

Market Screenings

The official selection tends to dominate everyone's attention, however there are literally thousands of other films screening in Cannes during the festival. Most of these are shown as part of the Market – where sellers (sales agents and/or producers) are presenting their product in the hope of attracting the attention of a buyer (distributor).

Access to market screenings varies according to a range of factors, but predominantly the type of accreditation you hold and the size of the screening venue which will determine whether you can get in or not. As the primary focus of the Market is to sell films, festivalgoers with the "revered" buyer type Market badges are welcomed with all the zeal of a long lost relative, but others with regular Market accreditation (including Producers Network) are often also admitted. For holders of press accreditation it's normally 50/50 as sometimes the sales agent and/or producer isn't prepared to risk an early bad review in case it puts off potential buyers.

Market screenings are usually off-limits to those with Festival or Short Film Corner accreditation (although holders of the latter can of course take part in screenings which are part of that event). However, if there is a film you are particularly intent on seeing it's sometimes possible to blag your way in. The ushers working these screenings are generally pretty bored and will often let you in if you give them a smile and a half-decent excuse – but be prepared to part with a business card on entry. In saying that, you shouldn't blag you way into a busy Market screening at the expense of a legitimate buyer. It's not fair to the filmmakers and you would certainly expect the same in return.

Most of the Market screenings take place in the myriad of rooms that honeycomb the Palais and Riviera buildings. Films in the Short Film Corner are available to view on interactive screens in a dedicated area of the Palais.

Ticketing

Cannes is a rather unusual film festival in that, other than for films screening in the Competition and Out of Competition programmes, you do not need a ticket to see a film if you're an accredited festival attendee. In most cases, entry is free on a first come, first served basis – you simply line up outside of the venue with your badge around an hour or so before the scheduled start time (sometimes earlier for highly-anticipated films). For competition films, *invitations* (tickets) are required to attend any screening in the Théâtre Lumière (although tickets are not required for screenings during the last weekend of

the festival, or for repeat screenings in Debussy or Bazin).

Unfortunately, the ticketing system is the single largest area of complaint from most festivalgoers – it's overly complex, badly organised, full of favouritism, and in a constant state of flux. In the past getting tickets for gala screenings meant playing the waiting game. But so long as you were patient (and an earlier riser) getting your hands on a ticket was a fairly straightforward affair. Not any more. In the last couple of years, the festival has moved to a more mechanical system of dealing with ticketing for the competition screenings.

To see a film in competition you must obtain a ticket from your "allocated ticketing office". For most festivalgoers this means Billetterie Centrale (the central ticket office), but you should check the specific instructions which are provided when you collect your accreditation pack. To use the Billetterie Centrale system you either need to jump online and head to:

ticket.cannesinteractive.com (NB. There's no "www" in this address)

Alternatively, you can call the ticket hotline on the number provided with your accreditation details (calls cost around 0.15€ per minute). The festival also provides a number of interactive kiosk terminals where you can access the ticketing web site. These can be found in Hall Méditerranée which is located on the ground floor inside the Palais (directly "behind" the red carpet stairs).

As with all of the festival's online endeavours the usability of the ticketing web site has a lot to be desired (and may well morph again for the next festival). To access the system you need your badge number and the unique personal identification number which was supplied when you collected your accreditation pack. After you've logged in you are presented with an indication of ticket availability for a list of films screening within the next 24 hours or so.

Tickets are normally released about 12 hours before the screening is due to take place, so you need to be online virtually the minute ticketing opens to ensure that you get a seat. Once you've successfully made your reservation (one ticket per badge), you can then collect it from the Billetterie Centrale in Hall Méditerranée at least two hours before the scheduled screening time. The central ticket office is open 9am – 6pm every day during the festival. Tickets are also non-transferable and information on the terms and conditions of entry is provided on the reverse (the main condition being that you agree to be filmed and/or photographed at any time while you're entering or sitting in the Palais).

On the day of the screening you should line-up outside the Palais about 30 – 60 minutes before the scheduled start time. You'll need both the invitation and your badge. Your ticket will indicate the area in the Théâtre Lumière in which you will be sitting – Orchestre, Corbeille, or Balcon – so make sure you join the correct line. The various entry points are usually well sign-posted and an access map for the Palais is normally included in your accreditation pack. Seating is not reserved and most screenings are "oversold" so being fashionably late is a privilege reserved only for the famous.

Ticket Return System

Given the demand, the festival is quite keen that you only obtain invitations for screenings you're actually going to attend so a return system is in operation for you to offload any unneeded tickets. Tickets should be returned to your specific office (see your accreditation documentation) or Billetterie Centrale by 3pm for evening screenings, or by 5pm the previous day for day-time screenings. All tickets are tracked electronically on issue and at the door of the screening. If have a ticket which you don't use, the system will note this, and as punishment for your heinous crime, may prevent you from obtaining tickets for future screenings.

Last Minute Access

Aka *Accès de Dernière Minute* or "Access without Invitation". If you don't have a ticket for a screening, but are burning to attend, you can try your luck with last minute access line. Five minutes before the scheduled start time any available seats are given away to accredited festivalgoers on a first come, first served basis at the *Entrée Personnaltés et Protocole* (Personalities and Protocol Entrance) of the Palais. Successful attendees are then whisked inside to fill the spare seats. Last minute access doesn't allow you to climb the red carpet, but it can sometimes provide access to a screening you otherwise couldn't see.

If you're going to give it a shot make sure you're at the entrance at least an hour before the screening time. You should also be dressed appropriately (black tie) and don't forget your badge.

Subtitles

All films in official selection at Cannes are screened in their original language, with subtitles according to the festival's official policy (mimicked by the International Critics' Week and Directors' Fortnight). If the original language is French, the film will be subtitled in English; if the original language of the film is English, it will be subtitled in French. For films in other languages, French subtitles will be added to the print and English subtitles will normally be electronically projected under the screen.

Dress Code

During the day, the dress requirements for festival screenings are pretty lax. Neat casual should suffice, but don't forget to bring your badge. Evening screenings (after 6pm) are a completely different story – it's black tie and it's strictly observed. This means a tux for the blokes, although you can often get away with a black

suit and dress shirt (with bow tie). Tuxedo rental is available from Air de Fête (16 Rue Gazagnaire. Tel. 04 93 39 15 97), but be prepared to pay for the privilege. You can save a little money by supplying your own shirt and tie. As always, the dress code for women is a little looser; you don't have to wear a ball gown but you must dress for a swanky evening out.

The dress requirements for non-official screenings tend to vary according to the time of day, the nature of the event, and the desires of the venue management or hirers. It's always a good idea to dress up for evening screenings, regardless of what's playing, as your Sunday best will undoubtedly pale in comparison to some of the other wardrobes on display in Cannes at night.

parties and hanging out

"But what about the parties?" If I had a dollar for every... well, you know how that one goes. Parties are the lifeblood of Cannes and consequently, pretty high up on most festival agendas. At these events you can meet people, have a few

paparazzi fodder

You can always tell when someone famous enters a screening: the steps of the Palais suddenly erupt in a blinding array of paparazzi flashes. It would be nice to think that a couple of the photographers lined up along the red carpet might be interested in taking a photo of you. The reality is, they're more interested than you think for two reasons: firstly, because shots of noticeable non-famous people easily fill last minute gaps in the press; and secondly, because the photographers know that many festivalgoers are happy to buy a shot of themselves walking up the red carpet at Cannes. So dress to impress, get snapped, and if you don't appear in someone's magazine, you can always have the picture for your own album (purchase them from the official photography tent in the Village International).

free drinks, and sort out that annoying problem of having to eat – all in one go!

The party scene in Cannes involves a kind of unofficial two-step process. From about 6pm to 9pm you have the low-key corporate and organisational cocktail parties. These are intended to allow people to wind down from the day's work, catch up with colleagues or contacts in a more relaxed environment, and lay the foundations for the night ahead. The next round of parties doesn't normally kick-off until at least 10.30pm in order to allow people leaving the cocktail soirees to have dinner, and also to wait for the early evening screenings in the Palais to finish. The later parties tend to be the bigger, brasher affairs, run by publicists for large companies or high-profile films, with fancy locations, corporate sponsors, private guest lists, and heavy security. Many take place in the villas in the hills behind Cannes, with free shuttle buses laid on for invited guests.

So how do you get to rub shoulders with the Cannes in-crowd? Simple. You either work your contact network to find out who's throwing a bash and see if they can orchestrate you an invite; or you make new friends in Cannes, discretely pump them for party information, and most importantly, ways of getting on the guest list. Alternatively, you can try contacting the event organisers directly and using your boundless wit and creativity, explain why you should be allowed to come to their shindig. Likely candidates to hit up for party invites would be national or regional film commissions, large production companies or distributors, unions, and even big media accounting or law firms. Failing that, you can always try crashing.

Party-crashing is of course an art form unto itself and a bit like a career in filmmaking: there is no single route in, but if you are dedicated, talented, lucky, and smart, you'll probably find a way. Blag your way in by pretending you're famous, delivering a very important package for [insert important-sounding executive name], busting to go to the loo, suddenly remembering your little-used stage name after an illicit glance at the door list, insisting that the producer/ chief executive/company honcho personally invited you, or undertaking a little bit of fancy footwork. Indeed, many a partygoer has been known to kick off their shoes, roll up their trousers or hitch up their dress, and literally wade into the beachfront soirée of their desire.

Regardless of whether you're invited or not always remember that unless you're famous, there's no such thing as "fashionably late" in Cannes. Party space is limited and sponsored booze finite, so it's important to make sure you arrive on time. No-one wants to host an empty party, so most organisers hand out many more tickets than the venue will hold. After capacity has been reached you may be barred from entry even if you do have a ticket.

Once you're in keep in mind that while this may look and feel like a party, it is in reality work. Doing parties in Cannes always involves walking that fine between having a good time and meeting your business objectives so make sure you network as hard as you can. Parties offer a great opportunity to meet people in a relaxed setting, and indeed, people whom you otherwise would find it difficult to see. It's therefore important that you spend your party time being friendly and outgoing. Don't just simply hang out in a big group with your mates. Be bold and introduce yourself to people whenever the opportunity presents itself.

It's also a good idea to make an effort to take most people you meet seriously. Inevitably, you will encounter some people who seem to be just wasting space on this planet, but you never really know how important they might be (either now or in the future). Consequently, you should be polite, steer clear of conversation that might provoke strong reaction – religion, politics, or, from personal experience, how crap the film you saw today was – and be careful with jokes as not everyone may have the same appreciation of your razor-sharp wit. Finally, remember to take it easy on the alcohol, since you'll want to stay astute and coherent in case you meet anyone important.

Although the party scene in Cannes can be a load of fun, you shouldn't get too obsessed with trying to get into every single party, nor get depressed if your invite haul feels a tad light. There are plenty of other ways to network in Cannes and in many cases, the most valuable contacts are not made at the biggest parties (where the ratio of blaggers to useful contacts can be over 100:1), but rather at bars, cafes, waiting in line, or at various pavilions in the Village International.

Daytime Hanging Out

There will be times during your stay in Cannes when simply kicking back will be just what the doctor ordered (particularly if your business agenda and party schedule have been rather intense). Most festivalgoers tend to hangout at the beachfront restaurants or in the various national pavilions in the Village International. Popular pavilions include:

The American Pavilion

For over 16 years the American Pavilion has provided the "home away from home" environment that those of a stateside origin tend to like when they travel overseas. It offers a bar and restaurant, free internet access (terminals and wireless), and free daily trade magazines and US newspapers. The AmPav, as it's sometimes known, also hosts a range of free seminars throughout the festival and has a special programme for bringing student filmmakers to Cannes. Much to the annoyance of many festival regulars the American Pavilion went "members-only" for 2005 (and presumably beyond). Accredited festivalgoers are now asked to pay a once-off membership fee of around USD $25 to secure access for the duration of the festival. The fee can be paid in advance via the American Pavilion web site (www.ampav.com) or at the door in Cannes.

The UK Film Centre

Set-up under the aegis of the UK Film Council, the UK Film Centre is the hub of British activity in Cannes, but is also an unofficial meeting/hang-out out place for Brits and other English speakers (including fee refugees from the American Pavilion). Like its

US neighbour, the UK Film Centre has bar and snack facilities, provides free Internet access, and hosts a range of seminars.

The Irish Pavilion

Run jointly by the Irish Film Board and the Northern Ireland Film Commission, the Irish Pavilion is the focus for the business, information and social elements of the Irish presence in Cannes. Historically there have been less facilities on offer than at the American Pavilion or UK Film Centre, but the staff are normally friendly and it can be a good if the others are crowded or hosting a private function.

Kodak Pavilion

For many years Kodak has run a pavilion in the Village International, hosting a range of events throughout the festival (some public, some invitation-only). The pavilion is normally open to all during the day, attracting range of visitors off the back of beach access, Internet access, and free refreshments.

Variety Beach Club

The trade magazine's presence in Cannes has moved about over the past few years. Most recently, Variety have opted to pitch their tent on the beach outside the Carlton Hotel. Dubbed the "Variety Beach Club", like most of the pavilions it offers free Internet access and basic catering services. Variety also run an excellent programme of free seminars throughout the festival.

Other Pavilions

A host of other countries and organisations also pitch their tents in the Village International during the festival. Although the primary focus of the national pavilions tends to be about promoting their country as a centre for filmmaking, most also offer a degree of hospitality services such as Internet access, cafes, or simply just a quiet(er) place to sit.

Other than the pavilions you have a whole city at your disposal for daytime hanging out. There is of course the official festival lounge, Le Club, located on Level 4 of the Palais. Otherwise most of the restaurants and cafes in town are happy to let you sit at a table with a coffee, particularly outside of peak dining times.

After Dark

If your blagging skills are not fired up one night, you're in need of something a little less intensely "industry", or it's simply beer-o'clock, then there are many options available. Like its Riviera neighbours Cannes has a many a little nightspot for you to take part in some fascinating people-watching, strut your funky stuff, or simply enjoy a quiet after-hours beverage. And although there is a tendency to think that most of these places cater towards people with a lot more money than you (and many do), your wallet needn't have a coronary when you decide it's time to head out.

For years, the unofficial hang-outs for English speakers in Cannes were always the Petit Majestic and the Petit Carlton bars (nothing to do with the hotels of the same names). Sadly, the Petit Carlton, always the better of the two, closed down several years ago and although recently resurrected by the original owners, its new location means it doesn't attract the old crowd. In saying that, it's still a great venue for a quiet drink or cheap meal – but make sure any Cannes veterans you arrange to meet there know the new location! The Petit Carlton is now at 4 Place de la Gare (next to Monoprix).

The closure of its main competitor has meant that all of the crowds now flock to the Petit Majestic, making it the undisputed late-night hangout for those not attending parties or other events. Early in the evening the bar is generally pretty empty, but from about 10.30pm onwards it starts to fill up. By midnight, the crowds get so large that they actually have to cordon off the street every evening for the duration of the festival. While the Petit Majestic has all the charm of a student keg party, it's a great place to meet both friends and new contacts, and is normally a requisite stop for anyone heading home. Indeed, "just swinging by to see if anyone's there" are often famous last words preceding a big night and a cracking hangover, for many people where the Petit Majestic is concerned. You can find this bar behind the Grand Hotel (a good option for toilets!) on the corner of Rue Tony Allard and Rue Victor Cousin.

Other cool places to hang out include: Saint Georges (at the front of the Grand Hotel), an evening socialising venue run by the team who provided the British Pavilion until it was taken over by the UK Film Council; the Havana Room, on the corner of the Croisette and Rue du Commandant André, which has an excellent terrace; and Les Coulisses, a cosy little bar with chilled tunes, also on Rue du Commandant André

(No. 29). There's also normally plenty of action in the various temporary beach-front restaurants/cafes, although it is common to need an invite or a clever cover story to get in.

If something more frenetic is your style, clubbing is on offer at Loft on Rue du Docteur Gérard Monod, and at Le Légend Café (9 Rue d'Oran) which plays chilled music early on before cranking up the techno later in the evening. Janes, inside the Hotel Gray D'Albion on Rue des Serbes, caters to a slightly older crowd, but can also be a lot of fun (although take care as some drinks can be a little pricey). If you are in the mood for music and dancing, then La Chunga (24 Rue Latour Maubourg) serves up a dish of Spanish flamenco and up-beat piano tunes. Those in search of rock and blues should drop by Midnight Blues on Avenue Georges Clémenceau for live music on Wednesdays and sometimes other nights. Live music also abounds at Cannes' authentic Irish pub, Morrisons (10 Rue Teissiere). It's usually traditional Irish tunes on Wednesdays, and rock, blues, or jazz on Thursdays.

Big Hotels
It's unlikely you'll get away with being in Cannes and not visiting one of the big hotels at least once during your stay. Cannes vets tend to prefer the bar at the Majestic and the Carlton terrace for their hobnobbing, although the Gray d'Albion is also a popular choice with the cashed-up indie set. Although slightly more down market the lively alfresco atmosphere of the terrace at the Grand Hotel has also a regular favourite, but if you're meeting someone you're

trying to impress the more laidback environment of the Martiez might be just up your alley. Finally, if you're looking to rub shoulders with the A-list then you need to take yourself and a wad of cash out to the Cap d'Antibes and spent an evening in one of the various bars in the Hotel du Cap complex. The Eden Roc terrace is the top of most people's lists here.

Regardless of which hotel takes your fancy, make sure you're prepared for the drinks to be considerably more expensive than at other places in town. If you're travelling on an expense account, then it probably won't be too much of a concern, but if you're a cash-strapped indie it's worth taking care to make sure you're not the poor sod left picking up the tab. You'd be amazed at how many "friends" seem to pop out of the woodwork when it's time for a trip to the bar, and before you know it you will have blown the budget of your next film on a single round.

the biz

the biz

Red carpets, cinema auteurs, and the flashes of the Paparazzo's cameras aside, each year more film business is done in Cannes than in all but a handful of other places on the planet. Behind all the glitz and glamour lurks the world's largest film market – the Marché du Film – and for 12 days a year virtually the entire international film industry is jammed into a few square blocks of this small Riviera city.

From humble beginnings in 1959 when a small group of distributors hung a white sheet on the roof of the old winter casino to show films to potential buyers, Cannes is responsible for inventing the festival-market relationship which is now emulated by a range of major international events such as Berlin, Toronto, Rotterdam, and increasingly, even Sundance. For those new to the film industry, 12 days in Cannes will teach you more about how the international business operates than most books or courses.

The official structure for business in Cannes is of course the Marché, which in 2005 was attended by nearly 10,000 cinema professionals from 83 countries. However, the concentration of film industry people in Cannes during the festival far exceeds this number as these figures don't take into account those who opt for Festival Accreditation or those who come to Cannes to do business, but do not formally register with any of the official organisations. Estimates put the total number of industry attendees well north of 30,000.

Aside from the press corps (which at Cannes is a good 4,000 strong), the largest single contingent of industry people in town during the festival are those who work directly in sales and acquisitions or in other sectors which directly support sales (i.e. publicity). Typically, industry people who are not involved in these areas tend to be filmmakers (predominantly producers, directors, and writers), equipment vendors, facilities providers, and of course agents. For these people the business side of the festival is mainly about meetings and networking, although some filmmakers may of course be involved in selling their films as well.

business at cannes

Cannes is the daddy of film business events and perhaps the single most important date on the international film industry calendar. On the whole business for most attendees can be a pretty intense affair - virtually everyone in town is peddling something, either formally (i.e. a film or film-related service) or informally (i.e. themselves). People's schedules tend to be very hectic and a high level of energy is required to keep on top of long days and late nights which normally involve too much alcohol. It's quite common for many attending Cannes for business reasons to not see a single film in the official selection or sidebars, and some sales agents have even been heard to complain of seeing very little daylight (which is no mean feat given the physical environment the city offers).

Business at Cannes tends to fall into three main areas and if you're heading to town with a business agenda it's important to understand how each of these areas work.

Sales & Acquisitions

The idea of an international film market was born in Cannes when the first Marché du Film was held in 1961. It was used as the principle marketplace for American companies selling the foreign distribution and ancillary rights for their films. These days the market's focus has shifted to sales and acquisitions activities of all kinds – sales agents show up in town with a slate of projects under their arm and spent 12 days courting foreign and domestic distributors in an effort to flog their merchandise. While the festival is about toasting the cream of filmmaking, the Marché is about selling everything else. Glamour is pushed aside for profit, and art takes a distant second place to genre.

The Marché du Film is the single largest event of its type in the world (ahead of the American Film Market (AFM) in Los Angeles, and MIFED in Milan). Each day hundreds of films are screened and millions of dollars change hands as films are bought and sold with all the vigour of a busy day on Wall Street. The main Market action is centred in the Palais and Riviera buildings, with the former honeycombed with small offices which are used by visiting companies and media outlets as a base for their operations and the latter hosting your standard tradeshow floor filled with companies peddling their wares.

Activity within the formalised market structure tends to focus mainly on small to mid-sized companies selling films made outside of North America or strong genre products such as action, horror, soft porn, and anything else that is selling well at the time. Larger players are normally less inclined to directly participate in the market, opting instead to take a suite in one of the large hotels or apartment blocks along the Croisette and conducting business from there.

Meetings & Networking

For those outside of the sales and acquisitions arena Cannes is about primarily about meeting with people who are likely to be able to help get your next project off the ground, but it's also about seeing movies, catching up with friends, and generally increasing your contact network. During the festival the city is literally crawling with film industry people, from PAs to studio bosses, so it's a great opportunity to bolster that little black book.

Meetings in Cannes tend to be less formal than at home – usually taking place over a meal or in a hotel suite which has been commandeered by a company for the duration of the event – and more focussed on discussion than action. Indeed meetings are often the primer or first step in a larger process, with the real business being done once everyone gets back home.

Networking also takes up a big chunk of most people's Cannes business agenda and is really about making new contacts that might perhaps be useful in the future. Of course some networking is also about generating new business opportunities, particularly where agents or equipment/service vendors are concerned, but even that can have its uses. Most of the networking in Cannes tends to get done after hours, while the daytime is reserved for more formal discussions.

Development & Financing

Given the presence of the world's largest film market it shouldn't really be that surprising to learn that Cannes is predominantly a "finished product" event. For sales agents and distributors – a good chunk of the people you want to talk to about development and financing – the intensity of either selling or acquiring films at the festival tends to leave little time to contemplate films which haven't been made yet. This is particularly true where a project doesn't come strongly packaged (i.e. with named talent attached) or isn't an official international co-production. Certainly discussions may take place between filmmakers and financiers, sales agents, and/or acquisitions executives regarding upcoming projects, but most of the serious talking (and all of the deal-making) will normally be completed away from the festival.

preparing for cannes

If you are planning on hitting Cannes for anything other than and an education and some interesting R&R it's essential to prepare your game plan well ahead of time. You need to have a clear idea about why you're attending and what you want to achieve. Without it you run the risk of wasting your time in Cannes and possibly quite a bit of money in the process. But perhaps the biggest risk of heading to the festival sans plan is that of inadvertently messing people around. For a global industry the film business is very insular; people tend to hold grudges and if you mess someone about you might find it's much harder to make things happen in the future.

The first part of your Cannes preparation should therefore involve thinking about why you actually want to go to the festival in the first place. Are you going to see films, make contacts, sell your movie, pick up new clients, or even all of the above? Each of these reasons alone requires comprehensive planning and if you're considering all of them then extensive preparation is even more important.

Seeing Films

Although seeing films may not be the main focus of a business agenda per se, it's an important consideration if you're coming to town with any kind of business objectives in mind. Once you're in Cannes surrounded by all that is the world's most famous film festival you will definitely feel the temptation to catch a couple of movies.

For those who are heading to the festival with a slate of business objectives it's really important to make sure that attending screenings is an activity built into your overall schedule, not just a last minute decision. Once you've taken into account the queuing time, the possibility of the screening starting late, watching the film itself, and finally any post-show Q&A sessions, attending movies can take big chunks out of your day. During much of this time your mobile phone will be off (well, it should be) and being out of contact for so long can make doing business that much more difficult. In a nutshell it's essential to make sure you've thought about how all of this impacts your business agenda. That way you can get to see some cool films, but also get your work done.

Most of the veterans either catch the first screening of the day (bleary-eyed at 8:30am) or head on to an evening screening before hitting a party or a bar. Seeing films at the beginning or the end of the day is a good strategy since it leaves the most important hours free for you to get on with your work.

Meeting People

Heading to Cannes is an excellent way to expand your contact network and also to see people from places which might normally require a plane ticket to get you to their front door. Meeting people usually happens in one of two ways: either you've made an appointment with someone prior to arriving in town (or perhaps while you're there), or you bump into someone along the way and, for whatever reason, you hit it off.

When it comes to pre-arranged meetings a big part of your preparation for the festival should involve taking the time to set them up before you get to Cannes. Many people who are working during the festival can be extremely busy so pre-

arranging meetings not only helps with your own planning, but having it in someone's diary ahead of time dramatically increases the chance of the meeting actually happening. In saying that, you should only pre-arrange a meeting with someone if you actually have a reason to meet. Discussing projects, pitching ideas, and talking finance are all good reasons to meet. Meetings to introduce yourself or to find out more about what someone does are bar-room or party conversations, not formal meetings.

The second way of meeting people is obviously a little more serendipitous – you have to be in the right place at the right time. However, the way the festival operates you often can't help but meet people in Cannes. But you can boost your chances of meeting more appropriate kinds of people by hanging out at the various pavilions in the Village International, Le Club in the Palais, or well-known socialising venues like the Petit Majestic. Networking and meeting people is of course also a major part of attending parties and you also shouldn't discount the value of chatting to people when you're standing in line for anything from a coffee to a screening. While it's difficult to specifically prepare for these types of meetings, you can help your chances by building in some "hang out" time into your Cannes schedule and picking venues where the concentration of the type of people you would like to meet should be reasonably high.

One of the beauties of Cannes is that during the festival there is an "accessibility" in people that often doesn't exist anywhere else. Maybe it's the change of scenery that makes everyone more open than they are at home, or that some of the normal barriers are dropped because everyone is a foreigner in a foreign land, suddenly having at least one piece of common ground. You should use this Cannes accessibility to your advantage as much as possible, but it's also important not to come off looking and sounding like a chump. Prepare your "story" ahead of the festival, ideally in short, medium, and long versions. You should be able to effortlessly answer questions like "What do you do?" "What are you trying to do?" "What does your company do?" "What have you done?" without hesitation. Depending on the situation and the audience you must be ready to roll out the short, medium, or long story at any time.

Selling Films

Of all the business activities undertaken at Cannes selling films is by far the hardest and most intense. To achieve success in this area your preparation will need to meticulous, your execution flawless, and your enthusiasm boundless (with a good deal of luck thrown in on top). The first stage of your preparation for selling a film should be to seek professional representation. This means getting a sales agent onboard and if your budget can stretch it, a publicist as well.

There are several reasons why having at least a sales agent for your film is absolutely essential. Firstly, a reputable sales agent should know the marketplace and will have the necessary contacts to get the right people into your screening. Without these contacts you are really fighting an uphill battle to get distributors to see your film. Secondly, when it comes to making a deal, having the negotiations done by a third-party who's familiar with the shape of distribution agreements, and is as keen as you are to sell the film (since their commission depends on it), is essential to ensure you get the best possible arrangement. Finally, if you've approached a large number of sales agents and they've all decided to pass, then there's a good chance that your film just isn't up to scratch. As harsh as that sounds, finding out that your film has little or no commercial value before you blow a load of your own money on a trip to Cannes is certainly better than coming home empty-handed with a lighter wallet.

So how do you go about finding a sales agent for your film? A common strategy employed by many filmmakers who are starting out involves getting your hands on a copy of a "product guide" from Cannes or one of the other big international markets such as MIFED or AFM. Produced by the markets themselves and also by trade magazines such as Variety, The Hollywood Reporter, and Screen International, the product guides are in effect directories of buyers and sellers attending each event (note that the trades often refer to these as "market previews"). The best of the bunch is the official Cannes Market Guide, produced by the Marché du Film and provided free to accredited Market attendees. This tome is about five inches thick and comprised of pure informational gold. It lists everyone who has registered for the Market, grouped by country along with their contact details, role in Cannes (i.e. buyer, seller, etc) and a mug shot so you know who to sidle up to at a party.

Copies of the various product guides can be picked up by getting in touch with the markets or trade magazines themselves (see Appendix II) or by working your contact network to see if anyone you know has a copy you can borrow. Even if you can only lay your hands on last year's copy - that will do fine. The major players don't change that often so you shouldn't be overly concerned if you can't obtain a product guide for the most recent event.

Once you have your guide(s) devour them in every detail, searching for companies that seem to be selling films which are similar to your own. It's important to pick the right type of sales agent since there's no point taking your quirky Gen-X comedy to someone who seems to specialise in period drama. Using the details in the guide, compile your hit list and start approaching these companies to see if they're interested in taking on your film. You'll get plenty of rejections, but that's part of the game so you just have to keep plugging away. It's always best to start the process of locating suitable representation as far ahead of the festival as you possibly can. Your sales agent and publicist will then be able to work with you to formulate the most effective strategy for selling your film and also help you prepare fully before you arrive in Cannes.

Although it's far better to have your team in place ahead of the festival, it is possible (although considerably harder) to seek representation once you're in Cannes. If you're going to try this route, you'll still need to prepare your hit list and as many meetings as possible before you arrive. You should also put together a basic "sales kit" for your film which at minimum contains a synopsis of the film (short, medium, and long), a complete cast and crew list highlighting recognisable credits and biographies of the key crew members.

You will of course also need a copy of the film itself. Don't waste your time with trailers or clips – if you're going to get people interested in your movie it's the finished product that you should be showing. If people are too busy to watch the film in its entirety in Cannes (which is quite likely) you should arrange a full screening for another time. Trailers are a marketing tool used to market films to the general public. Most distributors know that it's very easy to misrepresent a film with a trailer so they would rather see the whole thing.

Projects in Development
With the industry largely focussed on completed films pushing your project in development in Cannes most likely doesn't represent a worthwhile investment of your time or money, unless it is well-packaged or an official international co-production. It's probably better to consider other events in less expensive surrounds which have a more formalised development structure in place.

If you're hell-bent on pitching your project in Cannes the overriding piece of advice is: keep it brief. Most of the people you want to talk to will be extremely busy and if you do manage to get someone's attention you'll need to make the best use of it. Don't bother bringing clips or trailers you've put together for a film that isn't made yet – these often do more harm than good. Also, don't bring scripts for people in Cannes as no-one has time to read them, nor wants the excess baggage on the way back. Your script will be the first thing binned to save space in someone's return luggage. When someone wants to see your script they will normally ask you to send it to their offices.

at the festival

Once you've arrived in Cannes you should make an effort to familiarise yourself with the locations of key festival venues and more importantly, how far they are from each other. Figuring this out ahead of time means that you'll be better prepared when you need to meet someone as you'll know how long to allow in order to get there on time. It's also worth remembering that as the day draws on the crowds around the Palais get bigger (particularly on the weekends) and it can be difficult to get from one side to the other. Normally it's quicker to scoot through the inside of the Palais (although bag searches can also slow this down), but you can also go around the back where there are virtually no crowds.

Meetings

Meetings are one of the most important activities you'll undertake in Cannes, so it's important to allow plenty of time to get to any you've arranged. It's always better to have time to kill than to be late and

have to apologise. Before you get to your meeting make sure you've prepared yourself so that when you walk through the door you are calm and confident, and can blind them with your ability to get to the point in an interesting, but speedy manner. Know what you're going to say but don't work from a script. You will be most effective where you come across naturally and with a personal touch.

Most formal meetings in Cannes will be fairly brief, so it's vital that you are focussed (because it's quite likely the other person won't be). Remember to turn off your mobile phone for the duration of the meeting, or if you're reasonably friendly with the person, decide at the beginning whether it's a "phones on" or "phones off" meeting. If you're meeting someone for the first time don't be offended if they take calls during the meeting. However, your position in the grand pecking order of the film industry means that you probably shouldn't take calls yourself.

After you've finished take a few minutes to make some notes about what was discussed and follow-up any successful meetings one to two weeks after the festival.

Networking

If you're at Cannes with any form of business agenda, then you should be networking as much as you can. This means being forward (but friendly) and striking up a conversation wherever the opportunity presents itself – at a party, waiting in line, in the pavilions, at the Petit Majestic, wherever! It's also a good idea to never be dismissive of someone's ultimate worth. Just because they're a wannabe now, doesn't mean that they won't be in a position of power a few years down the track. It's often the people you least expect who end up being the most important to your future.

If you do meet someone interesting make sure you swap business cards. It's quite common to collect a wad of cards over the course of the festival so a neat trick is to jot down a note about who the person was on the back of the card. This is particularly useful for people you meet at parties or other events where the alcohol might be flowing freely. That way the following morning when you're staring at some dude's business card you won't be scratching your head thinking, "Who the hell was that?"

Networking opportunities abound throughout Cannes during the festival, however your best bet is to congregate around areas where the types of people you would like to meet will be. Generally the various pavilions in the Village International are a good place start making connections and the early evening cocktail parties are often a networking bonanza. To get invited make sure you contact the various national and regional film commissions as well as relevant companies, and even the trade magazines if you have contacts there or are of a generally jammy nature.

The Market

The formal Marché du Film is centred in the Riviera and the bowels of the Palais. Here you will find the standard tradeshow floor housing a whole bunch of companies peddling their wares. It's important to remember that you don't need to register for a Market stand in order to sell your film in Cannes. If you've done your preparation ahead of the festival and have your team in place they will be able to advise you on the best way to approach selling the film in Cannes. Market stands are most suitable for companies with a slate of projects or an established name and customer base.

If you haven't managed to get a sales agent on board prior to the festival then you should be trying to meet them while you're in Cannes and again, you don't need to be signed up for the Market to do this. It's worth remembering the most decent sales agents will be extremely busy in Cannes so don't be surprised if people prove difficult to see. You can generally increase your chances by trying to arrange meetings either before you arrive or during the second week of the festival (when things are starting to wind down a little). If you're looking to meet sales agents in Cannes it's best to focus on those who are based outside of your home country (you can visit the local ones anytime!). Film sales is a very international business so just because a sales company is based somewhere other than your home country doesn't mean they aren't a viable option. For example, a Dutch sales company may be very interested in looking at pictures from American indies or an Australian company may have a tendency to pick up UK films.

screening a film

Screening a film in town during a major festival has become a bit of a dream for many independent filmmakers. Even though the concept was around long before, it was probably the various "alternative events" that sprung up on the coattails of the Sundance Film Festival that popularised the idea. And many filmmakers have since taken the DIY approach.

Of all the world's film festivals Cannes is probably the hardest event at which to screen an unknown film outside the formalised structures. There is so much attention focussed on the official selection and sidebars and so much noise generated by the Market (both official and unofficial) that it's virtually impossible for films screened independently to get any attention whatsoever. Unless you've made it into official selection Cannes isn't really the right festival to premiere your film to anyone other than potential buyers. Getting a screening in space that even vaguely resembles a cinema is nigh on impossible and shouting load enough to be heard amongst the noise of multi-million dollar marketing campaigns is sadly beyond the reach of most first-time filmmakers.

If you still think you want to take a crack at screening a film independently during the festival, you probably have two realistic options. The first, and perhaps the easier of the two, is to sign up for the Market and use the screening facilities available to those with accreditation. The Market has a range of screening options on offer from small preview theatres through to full-size cinemas. The fees for hiring a screen will vary depending on the time of day and the size of the venue.

The second option is probably harder to achieve, but not out of the realms of possibility. Cannes has three main cinema complexes outside of the Palais: Les Arcades, Olympia, and Star. Although these venues do show various films from the sidebars and Market screenings it is sometimes possible to make a deal directly with the proprietors for a screening slot (particularly at the Olympia).

Promoting Your Screening

If you've managed to secure a venue in Cannes the next major obstacle will be promoting your screening to the right people. If you're taking the DIY approach then it's likely that your pockets are not going to be flush with advertising dosh so whatever you do to promote the screening, it needs to deliver maximum bang for the buck. Prior to spending a cent on any form of marketing you should stop and take a moment to think about who exactly you want to come to your screening. The first rule of marketing is: know your audience. If you want to have any success in Cannes you need to figure out who you're going to be talking to.

If your main aim is to try to get your film acquired then you should be thinking of ways to market to acquisitions executives and the press, not to the general public. Marketing to buyers is a very different affair to marketing for a cinema-going audience. If acquisition is the name of the game then putting a huge amount effort into getting a posse of cinema-lovers to show up for your screening is largely a waste of time. Even if the audience likes your film the chances of such a small number of people creating enough buzz to prick up the ears of buyers is rather remote to say the least. On the other hand, if your idea is to hold a screening that will go down in Cannes history then you're going to need to develop a good deal of interest ahead of time in order to get people to show up. You'll therefore want to focus your energies on building the anticipation amongst your audience and having them spread the word before your premiere.

Strategies for hyping your screening are as limitless as your creativity, however "unique" and "memorable" should be the two keywords that govern everything that you do. Remember that the second law of marketing applies to hyping films as well: it's all in the mix. In other words, there's no one sure-fire thing to do that will result in hundreds of people showing up, rather it's the combination of a bunch of activities which will hopefully achieve the desired results. Some suggestions include:

Hire Professionals
At a minimum a sales agent, and ideally a publicist as well. Sales agents will take their fees from selling your film, and publicists aren't as expensive as you might think - particularly if they like your film.

Talk to Journalists
Browse the trade magazines, local newspapers, and any other publications that cover the festival. Find the names of journalists who seem to have a style appropriate to your movie, then contact them via their magazines to see if they're interested. You will probably be ignored by many of them, but all you need is one or two onboard and you're in business.

Invite People Personally
Once you have your screening in place and understand your target audience, do your research and invite the necessary people personally.

Make it a Premiere
Don't show your film to anyone ahead of the first screening. Once you let the cat out the bag you will lose a major advantage.

Postcards
Make sure you always carry a bundle of postcards which have your film's screening time(s) and venue(s) printed on the back. That way, when you meet people in lines, at the Pavilions, or around town, and tell them about your film, you have something to give them to help them remember when and where they can see it.

These are just a few ideas. The finer points of festival marketing are beyond the scope of this book - there are complete volumes dedicated to the art of getting films noticed at festivals. For more on this subject check out, "Marketing & Selling Your Film Around the World: A Guide for Independent Filmmakers," by John

Durie et al, or "The Ultimate Film Festival Survival Guide," by Chris Gore. Both books are available from the CFVG Shop at the official companion web site for this book (www.cannesguide.com).

final words of wisdom

Before we finish, here a couple of final snippets of Cannes advice that will go a long way to making your festival experience successful and that much more valuable.

Receipts
Make sure you get one for everything you pay for. This is one of the only times you'll be able to claim a holiday on the French Riviera a legitimate business expense.

Film Commissions
Get friendly with your national and/or regional film commissions in Cannes. They are a source of party invites, free faxing/photocopying, and introductions to a whole range of people and events. Most of all, they are there to help you.

Free Lectures/Seminars
Many of the pavilions in the Village International, including the American Pavilion, Variety Beach Club, and UK Film Centre, run a series of seminars and lectures during the festival. Most of these are free and open to all accredited festivalgoers. Drop in to the various pavilions early in the festival to pick up a schedule and remember that space is limited so make sure you arrive early for anything you want to see.

Broaden Your Horizons
With over 30,000 film industry professionals in Cannes for the festival the potential for meeting new and interesting contacts is greater than ever. You should resist the temptation to spend your whole time in Cannes hanging out with your cast and crew or people from your home country. There's no point in making the trek to Cannes simply to hang out with the people you could hang out with at home. Broaden your horizons and meet people who would otherwise be difficult or impossible to see.

Eyes on the Road
While walking down the street your attention may be temporarily distracted by a weird piece of publicity or a fine specimen of the opposite sex. However, it's very important to keep your eyes on the road at all times for one simple reason: small "rat on string" -type dogs abound in Cannes... and no-one has ever heard of a pooper scooper.

Spotting Famous People
Cannes is literally crawling with celebs during the festival so if you're around town you will most likely see at least someone recognisable. If you get excited by such things the best place for guaranteed celeb-spotting is of course the steps of the Palais prior to an evening screening. Get there early and stand behind the white barriers on the road looking straight up the steps. The sides might look enticing early on, but you'll be disappointed later when all you can see is the backs of a hundred cameramen and photographers.

Take Time Out

If you're planning to stay in Cannes for more than a few days, it's a really good idea to take some time out. The festival can be very intense, with long days and very late nights – if you're not careful it will burn you out quicker than you'd think. And besides, you're in the South of France! Take a bit of time to see it.

"People who go to bed early lose out"

Words of wisdom from Stephan Elliott, director of "Priscilla: Queen of the Desert". He says he's done his "best work at night... well, early morning." You can sleep when you get home.

Keep It Real

It's a good idea to make sure you keep your expectations in check if you're trying to pitch your project or sell a film at Cannes. The reality is that only a small number of independent films get picked up by distributors at the festival and these tend to be films which have recognisable names involved (either in front of or behind the camera). Some films will go on to be picked up at other events later in the year – even if deals were talked about in Cannes – but sadly a good deal will simply fade into the annals of festival history, never to be heard of again. All of these scenarios are possibilities you should be prepared to deal with.

Cannes – A Festival Virgin's Guide... out.

the lowdown

Dennis Davidson

Chairman
Dennis Davidson Associates

Dennis Davidson's first introduction to Public Relations came when he was recruited to the TV-Radio publicity department at the Associated British Picture Corporation (ABPC); the TV-radio publicity department serviced the exhibition, distribution and production interests of the ABPC in London. These included the ABC Theatre Circuit, Warner-Pathe Film Distributors, and Elstree Film Studios. Following the restructuring of the distribution interests into MGM-EMI, Davidson resigned this position to form Davidson Dalling Associates, a specialist entertainment PR consultancy in August 1970. Since that time, DDA (the name was changed to Dennis Davidson Associates in 1975) has become the most successful entertainment industry public relations consultancy operating on a global basis, with offices in London, Los Angeles, Cannes, and Sydney, and affiliates in Paris, Berlin, Madrid and Johannesburg. DDA associated companies are involved with publishing, events management, market and creative services and television production.

Since 1997 DDA has produced the European Film Awards under a contract with the European Film Academy. Davidson also served on one of the six committees that formed New Labour's Film Policy Review. He is a Fellow of the Institute of Public Relations, and a member of the Academy of Motion Picture Arts & Sciences, of BAFTA, the Institute of Directors, and the Variety Club of Great Britain.

BC: When did you lose your 'Cannes virginity' and what were your impressions of the city and the festival?

DD: I started DDA in 1970 and in 1972, really to celebrate surviving for 18 months, my partner and I decided that we would go and look at this thing called the Cannes Film Festival. We were total virgins and had no idea what to expect. We booked a British Airways Sovereign Holiday and shared a twin-bedded room in the Sofitel Hotel, which was about as cheap as you can go. I'm sure you can't get packages like that anymore - it was very cheap. I was absolutely astonished at the level of activity in Cannes... and it was much lower key then than it is now. I was brought up in the English-language world and I suddenly found myself in the world of auteurs and people who respected film, respected film directors and filmmakers. It was a stunning place.

I think very soon after that first trip we realised that there was quite a lot of business to be done in Cannes. We were doing a really tiny bit of work for [British movie mogul] Lew Grade's company at the time, just brochures and flyers and so on. Between 1972 and 1975, we had taken over Lew Grade's account, starting off really with a couple of crumbs off the table, and then moved up to organising their Cannes activities. We set up the first office in 1975 and took an apartment at the Palais d'Orsay. That eventually became three apartments in the same building, but then they threw us out because we were too busy.

There was an old Palais where the Noga Hilton is now and after we were thrown out of the apartment, we weren't able to get anything in our first choice, the Carlton Hotel, which was close to the old Palais. They just wouldn't give us a room. So we moved to this then backwater, called the Majestic, where all the Europeans stayed. The US studios stayed at the Carlton, the major British players stayed at the Carlton or the Martinez, and the Europeans stayed at the Majestic. So we moved into the Majestic and set up some offices. We were perhaps handling Goldcrest by then and we launched Richard Attenborough's "Gandhi" down in Cannes before they started shooting the film. There was lots of activity, but we did it all at Majestic because we were not allowed into the Carlton. Then in the early 80s, they knocked the old Palais down and built a new one right opposite the Majestic. Suddenly I'm a hero because all my clients are now adjacent to the Palais.

BC: So these days, what sort of preparation do you do before you arrive in Cannes?

DD: We have two sides to the company. There's a logistic side which literally starts working on the following year's festival the day after Cannes finishes. We have a permanent representative in Cannes and they're locking in all the logistical stuff for the following year. They are paying the hotels, paying the cinemas, paying all the vendors, and at the same time, reconfirming for the following year. And that's a continuing process.

From a PR point of view, there are two or three stages. Cannes is multi-layered... far too many layers to even describe, but the principal one from an independent filmmaker's point of view is selling. That's the marketplace and it can either be the Marché du Film, or in the streets independently, or in the various strands of the festival and the Quinzaine [Directors' Fortnight]. For the market part, we know what's going on with our producer clients so we can pre-plan that two, three, four months out. The process really starts in January/February.

The strands of the festival obviously come into play much later because, although the Festival keeps you up-to-date as time goes by, often you don't know the final selection until the middle of April. Then it's a mad scramble because you've got to get the talent, you've got to get the hotels, and you've got to work with the protocol of the Festival or the Quinzaine, which have totally separate management. You've got to work with the French press attaché, you've got to work with the French film distributor, the sales agent, and that's usually a four-week scramble at the end. But our logistics people will have held back some rooms for key talent; they are prepared for that eventuality.

BC: How does a typical day in Cannes pan out for you these days?

DD: Well, we still have this sort of rather nasty regime... with eight o'clock staff meetings every morning. Although everybody is usually on call at quarter to eight, I actually get in at about seven to try and clear my head from the revelry the night before. So quarter to eight, it's general assembly and then eight o'clock we start - that is running through everything, arrivals, departures, screenings, trade press, junkets, staffing, tickets, fireworks, whatever it is that day. After that, it breaks into groups... account teams and the press office, which will start their meetings when we open the office at about 9.00 - 9.15.

From there, my day can be anything. Generally in the morning I spend a couple of hours troubleshooting or meeting with clients, just making sure that everything is working. If there is an important movie screening that night, then I'll be involved with the filmmaker, or not, depending on which filmmaker. The afternoon is pretty much the same... there are a lot of events and if we're doing an event then I normally would pass by. And there's always a crisis. There's always something that happens... somebody's bag has gone on the wrong plane, or someone doesn't have a dress to wear, or the tickets

haven't arrived, or any of those things that could happen in the chaos of a major convention. So I often end up troubleshooting that as well.

BC: What about the evenings? There seems to be two camps in that respect, the party crowd and the wind-down crowd.

DD: I rarely go to the big parties. I will usually go to a few of the dinners, such as the AmFAR [American Foundation for AIDS Research] dinner because it's a nice, big glamorous occasion and my people do all the work. I go to the Vanity Fair dinner because again, most of my clients, most of the key people are going to be there. We did that "Lord of the Rings" huge event down in Cannes a couple of years ago I went to that, but in general I don't do parties... OK, one night, some time during Cannes, and hopefully towards the end, I will do a party, when the adrenalin is still there and I can actually keep my eyes open.

BC: How does a publicist work with a producer leading up to and during a festival?

DD: Again, in several ways. If we are involved with the producer from the start of production we will normally have a timeline and a strategy of what can be done based on the post-production schedule and whether that film is realistically able to get to a strand of the festival. Or if that isn't going to happen, no matter what the producer and director believe they've made, we'll be figuring out plan B. We're also looking at which sales company will be responsible for taking it to the market place. You will work with the producer and sales agent to try and find a way to move that particular film above the other 600 that are going to be available at Cannes... and that can be pretty much anything. The whole point is that there is no hard and fast rules; if there was a hard and fast rule, you wouldn't need companies like mine.

To give you some examples, we built a hill on the beach one year for "The Englishman Who Went Up a Hill But Came Down a Mountain" - the Hugh Grant film - and the stars climbed up on the top of this hill for a photo call. We had "My Little Pony" there another year so we converted the merry-go-round by the beach and put little ponies all over the thing for a photo call. So we manipulated it so that Elizabeth Taylor met Stallone at the top of the stairs for "Cliffhanger"... it was an AmFAR event, the first and only time there's been a charity event in the Palais. If you've got a piece of talent, you might try and do a red carpet at one of the back street cinemas... basically, you're trying to get someone important in to see a film and say, "Why hasn't this great gem been recognised?"

But the reality is, it's really difficult, particularly if you're going in to Cannes with the finished movie, with no distributors, no budget, no recognisable names! You've really got to think, "Can I find somebody to champion this?" And you've got to get people in to see this somehow. You see people doing it and they go up and down with flyers and faces painted, there's a million different things, motorcycles going up and down, but it really is very difficult to

get attention in an environment like Cannes. But then, people do, you know, and it's a multi-layered thing.

I think when we work with producers, you first of all have to define who your audience is going to be. There's no reason to go for mass publicity when you know that there's only seven distributors that are going to take this film, you're not going to be able to sell it to Japan, and in the US you'll be lucky if it goes on cable. So you define who your audience is and you define who the consumer is. Is this a multiplex, is this straight art? Are we looking for a media sale in European cinemas, or are we looking for Warner multiplexes? I think it's a discipline. One of the main problems is filmmakers are too close to what they have created and they don't want to hear realism. Before they green-light a film they should hear realism.

BC: How far ahead would you start planning the campaign if you were going to do something for Cannes with a film and the producer?

DD: If we haven't been there from the start, probably about two months, but most producers don't think, "Cannes is happening in two months, we've got a finished movie, we'd better get a publicist onboard." Most of the time it is much later than that, if at all.

BC: Assuming that they haven't engaged a publicist earlier on, what sort of materials would you expect the producer to come with if they would like to work with you?

DD: Once the film is made, there are lots of things that are very difficult to recreate. Yes, you can get stills off the film digitally, you can shoot interviews afterwards, but they're never as good. In an ideal world, when you come to us you'll have some great, emblematic stills - digital images, slides and black & white - that you can really see being on the front cover of the Sunday Times colour supplement or at least on the inside page of Time Out. And they need to be professional. Most people do it in an amateurish way and you suddenly find you've only got something that looks very nice in a 10x8, very artistic, but it won't work in a newspaper or a magazine.

I think that people should shoot some B-roll during principal photography... they don't have to finish the B-roll, just that they shoot it and it's in the can, then if they do get distribution, they can hand it over for completion, which is the expensive part. I'm also amazed at how badly written and amateurish production notes can be. It's like "My Personal Odyssey." Who cares?! Is anyone going to be interested in reading this? If they're not interested in reading it, they sure as hell aren't going to go and see the film. So it's just basic materials I think, although unfortunately in this day and age, sexy young actors are also going do a lot better than a 60-year-old unknown character actor... but I guess the most important thing of all is to have a good film! If you've got a good film, then you'll find a way to get an audience.

BC: Cannes, particularly the market, is renowned for the enormous volumes or marketing and publicity. Are there any general strategies for getting heard above the noise, particularly for lower-budget/independent films?

DD: It depends on what you've got. There is the Critics' Week, Un Certain Regard, the Festival, and out of competition. You've also got the Marché du Film, you've got the Quinzaine, you've got the back street stuff, you've got the national film bodies doing their thing, you've got the Espace DVD, you've now got a video library - there are 600 or more titles in Cannes during the festival. So you need to invite people to your screening before Cannes, you need to identify the distributors. Most people in the position you're talking about are going to Cannes without distribution or have distribution in their home country and nothing else. There are only 200 buyers, that's all there are, so do your prep-work, write to them, or email them, and say, "At two o'clock on Friday afternoon on May whatever it is, there will be a screening of my film and it's going to be worth 15 minutes of your time. Come see it! I expect you're going to be there 90 minutes later." You've got to tell people what you've got. But there's no point in going to Warner Brothers with a little film shot on DV. Do your research and find the right person who will identify with what you've got.

BC: Do you have any particularly memorable experiences from the many festivals you been to?

DD: There's a lot of them over 30 years... I actually got married there [laughs].

We did a huge party for Carolco a number of years ago, which is sort of legendary now, where Stallone and Arnold Schwarzenegger just pretended to waltz. The photograph is still used. It was in the middle of a junket and it was just one of those incredible moments where you know that this is going to play forever.

We took Madonna to Cannes for her docu-thing, "In Bed with Madonna", and we played it in the Palais at midnight. It was a huge event. Madonna... she does what she does, she was at the top of Palais steps... the coat came off and the bustier was there, and you know... one of the most memorable Cannes photos ever was produced.

We took "To Die For" to Cannes a few years ago - it was the first time Nicole Kidman was there as a star in her own right, as opposed to being a spouse. It was a Gus van Sant film; it was just a magical moment.

I remember going to a party which had nothing to do with me - a nice change - for "The Blues Brothers". I popped in because it was some friends of mine literally thinking that I'd just drop in, do a quick beer and leave. I was still there four hours later because it was such a great gig.

We had the AmFAR dinner, which is the annual charity thing we organise. We got Victoria's Secret to be one of their key sponsors and Victoria's Secret did their fashion show which web-cast almost all over the world. I went down to a few rehearsals, and... I don't know how to describe it... just beautiful, beautiful half-naked women all over the place. I needed to get back to reality after that.

Jack Nicholson has been to Cannes many times and we took "The Postman Always Rings Twice" there, many many years ago. Jack used to go out from the Majestic Hotel and just walk through the market, walk through the streets, totally unmolested and undisturbed. One particular morning I was driving... I didn't stay at the Majestic in those days... I was driving in for my morning meeting and I knew he had a breakfast with 12 Italian journalists at eight o'clock. I was driving in, I was late that morning it was about twenty to eight, and he was just walking back to the hotel. I went upstairs and I thought, "Oh shit! How am I going to explain that Jack is not going to make the breakfast?" But I went downstairs and arrived in the room to find Jack already holding court with the journalists, looking like he'd just come off a good night's sleep.

I've been using that story about Jack's walks for years, telling people, "You know, you couldn't do that anymore, that just doesn't happen anymore." Well, we had "About Schmidt" in Cannes last year and most mornings, Jack would get up from the Majestic Hotel and go for a walk through the markets and the old town, exactly the same, no bodyguards, just by himself.

BC: Do you have a favourite place to eat in Cannes?

DD: I'm very lucky now that I'm back in the Majestic - I have a balcony, so one of my favourite places is to sit and eat a pizza on my own balcony and watch. You can see the Palais from there, and I know it's not far to my bed.

But there are lots of restaurants... I love Le Maschou; you eat there so well because it's really, really simple and pretty good value. I also like Le Festival, to which a lot of people turn their nose up and go, "Oh, The Festival?!" But I think their food and their wine list is pretty good and pretty fair. I also love the Hotel du Cap... the terrace at the Eden Roc. I have to go there for lunch, at least once every festival.

But there are really so many places to choose from. When we go, we just walk in the back streets and just try out luck. We used to love the Petit Carlton before it closed [Ed - now reopened!] and there's nothing like that, because the Petit Majestic doesn't do it for me. I use Morrisons, the Irish pub a bit. I go in there, two or three or four times... I was about to say "a night," but during the festival of course!

I do think it's tough to do Cannes on a budget and I don't envy an individual without a 'home' in Cannes, you know, without a sale's agent or a PR company... some home. I think one of the problems you have in Cannes is you see all the Brits together, all the Australians together, and all the Scandinavians together. It's really silly... you could do that here in London or wherever. It's so much better to meet people who are not from your home country.

BC: Do you have any favourite socialising/networking venues?

DD: I think it's really quite tough because most parties are relatively exclusive. If you're a party-organiser spending £100 per head, or even £20 per head, you don't really want 100 great unwashed people you've never met in your life before flooding in. We have turned significant sums of money over the years from wealthy people who want to "facilitate" being invited to parties and dinners, or get tickets in to the Palais. We don't ever do it... we don't even do it for our clients and we certainly don't do it for people off the street.

A lot of people gravitate to parties and I don't know how, even when you're networking, you can make a judgment about whether you're talking to some loser who is fooling you, or whether they are legit. If you sit at table almost everywhere in Cannes you'll hear such incredible bullshit, which hopefully even the most virgin of virgins will recognise as such. However, sorting the wheat from the chaff I think is very difficult in a place like Cannes. I suspect that it would be more productive to be going to places at breakfast time and going to the Blue Bar and those kinds of places for coffee in the mornings, and also making a point of going to the various pavilions as opposed to just sticking with your national one. I suspect that networking after dark is just total crap.

BC: Do you have any specific advice for Cannes virgins, particularly producers looking to bring an unrepresented film to Cannes with a view to sell it?

DD: I think they need to seek representation. We're living in a real capitalist business and sales agents are desperate for new product. Therefore, if you are unable to get a sales agent on board, then there's something wrong with the product. You should be able to entice at least a local indigenous distributor to take your home territory. If you have a film which you've shown to half a dozen sales agents and they've all said "pass," then you probably have to re-evaluate the situation. And I'm not talking about major deals here... I'm not talking about them giving you loads of money, but maybe them paying the freight to take you down there, maybe putting a proper press kit together, putting a sales team together, paying for a couple of screenings, you know... if they're not willing to invest 10, 20, 30,000 dollars, euros, whatever in at least taking the film down there, then there's something wrong. It's different if you turn and say, "I want a million euros in advance", but generally, most sales agents are looking for new hooks, even if they think they're only going to sell it on DVD, so there's something seriously wrong if you can't attach a sales rep.

So I think representation is essential, but I think it is sales representation - it's not an agent, it's not a PR company, it's someone who believes enough in your film that they are willing to invest a minimum amount of money in it, to buy a couple of ads and take you down there and do the stuff. You can go to their office and drive them crazy and somebody's paying for a couple of screenings. Without that, it's really, really tough.

Simon Franks
Chief Executive
Redbus Film Distribution

Simon Franks is co-founder and Chief Executive of Redbus. After graduating from Manchester University, Simon worked for five years as an investment banker with JP Morgan and then BNP Paribas. He left banking in November 1997 to co-found Redbus as a mainstream distribution and production company. In October 2000, he sold a stake in the business to Helkon Media AG, a German publicly quoted company, for $23 million.
Redbus' credits include Gurinder Chadha's "Bend it Like Beckham", Sam Raimi's "The Gift", David Cronenberg's "Spider", and Victor Salva's "Jeepers Creepers".
Redbus is now one of the largest independent film businesses in Europe, and currently has in excess of 20 projects in development.

BC: When did you lose your 'Cannes virginity'?

SF: I went to Cannes for the first time on business in 1996. At that point I was still working in the City [of London] and was just in the process of leaving to set up Redbus, so I went to Cannes as someone trying to learn about what goes on. I did know some people there, not from the film industry, but from my time in banking, so I used the Soho House boat [run by the London media club of the same name], I got an apartment in Cannes and spent probably three or four days there, just getting to grips with what it's all about.

On that trip I came to the view that there's two sides to Cannes and that I only had access to one of these sides. I think it's probably only in the last two or three years that I've seen the other side to Cannes.

BC: So what was your first impression of the city and the festival?

SF: Well, it's an incredible place and it's an incredible festival. The city is probably Southend-on-Sea with sunshine. The hotels aren't that great and they're overcrowded, but the shopping's lovely. I think that France has got a certain feel about it, better than Southend, but it's incredibly busy. I remember, I used to be amazed at how many American film students you could fit into one town, and I found that a bit of a pain because when you're there trying to do business, the whole razzmatazz just gets in the way. One of the problems is there's a market attached to the festival and people confuse them; they're totally distinct things, they just happen to be at the same time. We're there for the film market and the festival side of things just gets in the way. However, it is of course the festival that adds all the glamour and don't get me wrong, we do leverage off the festival, but it can also be a real pain. The crowds are there to see famous people and you can't get into a bar because there are thousands of people sitting around and all the tables are full. It can be really annoying.

I also remember being amazed just how many people were there. It was crazy. Oh, and loads of blaggers... people trying to get into parties. You see, I have this view that any party that other people are trying to blag their way into is a party that you don't want to go to, and any party where no one is blagging, that's the party you want to go to because no one knows about it. And no one knowing about it means the invite list is very small. The big parties are really for tourists. The MTV party for example... there's lots of famous people around you, but they're not going to talk to you. It's just thousands of people blagging it, trying to get drunk on free alcohol.

BC: How do you prepare ahead of Cannes?

SF: Preparation is quite important for us from an acquisition's point of view. In our company there are two primary acquisition groups. One is the development group, which takes onboard scripts and works with writers and books, and tries to develop those into movies. The other side is straight acquisitions - acquisitions of other people's films. We can sometimes have a crossover where we acquire something and we say, "Listen, we think you should develop it for a couple of months, then we can take it a bit further".

But Cannes is a market and for us, it is mainly about acquisitions of other people's films. As such we're on it year-round, tracking all the movies that are getting made. We can then have target lists of movies we want to see in Cannes and all sorts of data on every single movie screening. This will include who made it, when it was shot, who's in it, and industry gossip on it and any contact we've had to date. For movies that are of specific interest to us we will usually have had some contact with the production companies so we're not going in blind.

Often, if you're a big enough company, you get shown stuff early anyway. To be a big enough company, you need to be one of the top few distributors in a large territory like France, Germany, Japan or UK. So a big part of our preparation is about seeing films in advance. You're looking for that gem that no one has spotted, however in all honesty, movies that are made without distribution... they're just so unlikely to be any good.

Of course, the majority of what goes on in Cannes really is meetings with producers and sales agents who are pitching scripts, not completed movies. For this, we would have a look at the package and the script, and we would probably get the scripts three weeks before most markets. So we already know the scripts we're interested in and what we want to talk about with the various sales agents.

The reality is that for a company like Redbus, we're not trying to do that many movies, but the movies we do take on, we want to be doing $4m to $6m minimum box office in the UK. There are very few sales agents that handle movies which have got the calibre to do that sort of business. So really, there are probably only five meetings that count, and there are 25 other meetings with companies that are largely a waste of time. But you never know in this business, someone, even a very small sales agent with no track record, can just have that one great script. You never know. So we cover that as well.

BC: So do you mostly deal with sales agents in Cannes, or with producers as well?

SF: Our acquisitions group would probably only deal with sales agents in Cannes, but for me personally I deal with a few sales agents and a few producers, but those would be American studio kind of producer. I won't really see any independent producers - a first-time producer is very unlikely to get to see me. I don't mean to sound arrogant, but it would only be by mistake that I would see them because if I did, I wouldn't be able to run my business - I would be inundated all day. I can't even put my mobile number or my email address on my business card because I would get so much grief.

So I guess it would only be established, mainly American producers we'd talk to about co-financing on some project. In terms of other producers, it's unlikely that a first-time producer is going to have anything that would make me want to see them; unless it's

a first-time producer who happens to be best friends with Tom Cruise, and then obviously I will want to see them. I'm not saying that Redbus won't see first-time producers as a company, it just wouldn't be me, it would be the acquisitions group, and it wouldn't be in Cannes because they're really busy there.

In most cases we won't see British-based companies or producers in Cannes. Obviously they're in the UK, so why see them in Cannes? It's ridiculous... it's like the guy next door, who doesn't try to see me the whole year, but when we're in Cannes, he drives me mad to see me. It's ridiculous, so I don't really tolerate that. We may see established foreign independent producers who we know and like their work. Cannes is a good place for that because they're in town, but this is really what I'm getting at when I say there are two sides of Cannes.

On one side, there's a certain circle of people you're seeing who you know and have probably been involved in many projects you have heard of, whereas the indie scene... these guys lugging around pitches, that's not really for us.

BC: What sort of things would the acquisition's groups expect to see from the producers that they are going to meet with in Cannes?

SF: Well, we won't read unsolicited scripts in Cannes, so I'm just trying to think how that would happen. The acquisition's group would probably say, "We can't meet during Cannes, however please contact us at the office and we'll talk." If the company is from out of town and they want to get to meet us in Cannes then their only chance is if, in a 30 second phone call or a short email, they can say something so exciting that someone thinks, "We really want to meet this guy." That has happened a few times before. And by "exciting" I mean something like, for example, "I'm producing a movie and I've got Quentin Tarantino to direct it." Or someone even less big, but someone very interesting: "I've got Alejandro Amenábar" or someone like that. We did Amenábar's "Abre Los Ojos" ("Open Your Eyes"), which was the film that became "Vanilla Sky", before he was a huge director. We loved his first movie, "Tesis", and even though no-one had heard of him at that point, when we got an email saying that there's this project going on called "Abre Los Ojos", we obviously responded to it.

I think there's got to be something exciting, or who you've got attached, or who you know: "I'm friendly with Brad Pitt, or I'm friendly with Matt Damon or I'm friendly with Ben Affleck or I'm friendly with Heath Ledger." And then of course our ears pick up and go, "OK, we'll listen." But again I think our acquisitions group will have 50 meetings at Cannes, out of those there will be two that will be with non-established producers.

BC: Have you heard any memorable pitches in Cannes - memorable for either the right or the wrong reasons?

SF: Yes, I've had a few. The one I'm going to tell you about was a few years ago when we were entertaining a pretty famous popstar, who I believe will be a talented actor. We were doing other business with him at the time which wasn't related to his pitch, but he and I were having a glass of wine overlooking the sea - I think we were on a boat actually - and he started telling me this idea. He said, "Listen, I want to make a movie which is about me doing something noble, changing the world and all that." I said, "Great. Do you have anything in mind?" And he goes, "Well, yeah. I was flying to America and I came up with this idea, you know, it's about this schizophrenic popstar..." and this was totally deadpan "... it's about a schizophrenic popstar, who goes to Africa to save blind people and to work with them and help them do what they can't see with their eyes." So I'm sitting there just thinking, "What?!?" And he goes - and this is the best line - he goes, "Yeah, obviously it's a comedy." And I'm like, "What?!? A schizophrenic popstar goes to Africa to help blind people and it's a comedy? I mean, what are you talking about?!"

That's one of my most memorable pitches... I'm not going to tell you who it was, but it's someone, if you heard their name you'd probably laugh and go, "Wow!"

BC: Do you have any favourite anecdotes that you like to recount when the topic of Cannes comes up over the dinner table?

SF: If you're lucky enough to be on the buying side of Cannes, and especially buying for a key territory, people, particularly young American filmmakers, basically treat you like a king. I don't feel very comfortable with that whole scene because I think there are a lot of people who make fools of themselves. A lot of these guys think they can just make friends with a film executive in a bar, and then the exec's going to give them $5 million to go and make their movie. You get that a lot.

I remember one time, which was just really funny. I was on a boat in Cannes in the main port. I don't know how this person knew who I was - it's not like I'm famous or in the papers every day - but I suppose that if you're making a film, you do the research.

Anyway, so this person had seen me on this boat and one of the hostesses came up to me and said, "Excuse me. There's a guy who wants to see you." I said, "Well, who? No-one knows I'm here. Could you go back, get a card, and find out who it is?" The hostess came back with this card saying something like 'Steve, Independent Filmmaker, Alabama' or something like that. So I say, "Listen, tell Steve, my very best regards, I'm happy to speak with him, but it's much better if he speaks with the acquisitions group. Here's their number, call them in London after the festival." She then comes back again saying, "Well, he really wants to see you," and I say, "Listen, he can't see me." So she goes away and I forget about it.

A couple of hours later, I'm getting off the boat and it just so happened that I had arrived in Cannes that morning and hadn't had a chance to get to our villa yet. I still had all of my luggage with me and I'm walking off the boat with my bags and this kid comes up to me, literally script in hand, and says, "Hi." I'm like, "Hello?" and he says,

"I'm Steve, from Alabama," as if he's my best mate. I go, "OK, hold on... you're the guy... please tell me you haven't been waiting for two hours?" And he goes, "Yeah. I really really wanted to see you." So I said, "Listen, I'm sure you're a great guy and I'm sure your film is amazing, and I'm sure I'm making the biggest mistake of my life, but I'm really tired and I really want to go home. I just don't do this. You need to contact our people. I've given you the number." And he goes, "Look. I really think that this is going to change your life. Just give me five minutes." I said, "No. If I give it to you, I'd be giving five minutes to everybody down here".

As it turned out, my car and driver were down the very front of the port and the boat was at the far end of the port. Because it was our first day in town, we hadn't got the various passes sorted out yet the car couldn't get come down to meet me, so I had to walk down to the car with all my bags, a good five-minute walk. So Steve from Alabama says, "Well, how about I carry your bags for you?" And these are like some heavy bags! And I say, "No. Don't be silly. What do you want to carry my bags for?" He says, "No, no, no. Please, I just want to talk to you." I say, "No, I don't want you to. I'd feel very uncomfortable with you carrying my bags. I'll give you my number and please, let's just leave it at that." He says, "You don't understand. I'm telling you, you're going to love this idea. What do you have to lose? All I want to do is carry your bags, and in return for me carrying your bags, you'll let me talk to you whilst I'm carrying these bags." So I thought, "It's bloody hot, my bags are heavy...

alright, 'Here are my bags.'" So he takes these big bags, and I've got this guy, script under arm, carrying my bags, pitching me! By the time we get to the car, the poor guy is dripping with sweat, panting. He's been speaking, he's a bit nervous, telling me his pitch. I literally just looked at him - it was such a terrible idea - and I turned around and said, "You know what..." And I never lie... I never have the heart, I never tell them it's not for us, but I found myself saying, "You know what? That was great. I'm not sure it is for us, but that was great. Please call us and maybe we can help you."

I think he did subsequently call and we did help him with something, but I always remember this guy, sweating his arse off, carrying my bags, just pitching me some ridiculous idea. And that is really what Cannes can be like.

BC: Do you have any particularly memorable encounters with very famous people?

SF: Not really, it's different for us as film producers. We work a lot of the time with 'famous people' and I don't think they would rush to work with us again if we went around spreading gossip. Now and then a few of what you would call 'famous people' stay at our house. One of the reasons we take a house on the Cap d'Antibes is that it's a little bit out of town, it's right on the sea, and talent often prefer to stay there than in town.

BC: Do you have any favourite places to eat in Cannes?

SF: I do, but I'm not sure I want to tell you them. My favourite restaurant in Cannes... I'm not going to tell you its name, but it's a small restaurant near the bus station... I'm not going to tell you what it's called simply because I struggle to get a table there as it is. But I would suggest that for people looking for a nice restaurant, go by the bus station, or up the steps in to Le Suquet.

BC: Do you have any specific advice for future Cannes virgins?

SF: For many independent filmmakers the key will be just getting completely lucky, bumping into the right person and them being prepared to do something to help. The chance of that happening is something like 1 in a 100,000, but literally, you have a chance of bumping into Barry Diller [former Chairman of Vivendi Universal Entertainment], him loving your idea and you're done. You have that chance in Cannes because he'll be there... so might Rupert Murdoch or the heads of most of the Studios. But although you have that chance, I wouldn't come to Cannes on the basis of that chance happening because it's extremely difficult to get near these people. And sadly, most people, even if they do get their chance, screw it up because they end up blabbing and straight away these Studio heads simply go, "Hold on. Sorry, call the office."

The thing to do, if you're going to go that route of literally camping outside the Hotel du Cap and trying your luck, is not pitch your project. Form a relationship yourself, form some kind of connection, where they think,

"Wow, this is a smart person." And that means when you then contact them later down the track you can say, "Dear Barry, I met you at the bar at the Hotel du Cap, it was very nice to have a drink with you, I wondered if you could do me a favour?" They're much more likely do you a favour, if they did like you, because you didn't get in their face straight away.

If you're going through the more mainstream route, which is pavement pounding in Cannes, then the advice would be: prepare before you arrive. Don't come with scripts... we never take scripts home, they're too bulky, we throw them away. Send your scripts to whomever you want to read them ahead of Cannes with a covering letter explaining why you want them to read it, who you've got attached, who's going to direct, how much of the financing you've got, what you need to do the project, and so on. The more you've got in the package, the more chance you've got of it being read.

You should really go to Cannes to meet people you've already spoken to, and to meet people who've already read your script and want to talk to you about it. Don't go there cold saying, "Hi I'm Steve, I'm a producer, and here's my script." Don't do that, it's an absolute waste of time. Preparation is everything.

Another thing I would say is, don't waste your time blagging to get into parties. Most independent filmmakers, no matter how much they say they love movie-making, spend more time trying to blag into parties, than they do making their films. And it is just really not worth it.

This comes back to the other side of Cannes I mentioned earlier. The other side of Cannes is a scene which probably only 300 people participate in. It is the dinners, the parties, the AmFAR [American Foundation for AIDS Research] thing, where you get to watch Shirley Bassey and George Michael performing for a dinner party for 200-300 people, or the party Elton John throws each year at his house in Nice. It's the boats, the dinner parties, the Hotel du Cap, the villas... that's the other scene in which the more important meetings take place. People come back to our villa where you can look at the sea with a glass of wine, and it's a very nice environment through which to make business relationships. And that's the other side of Cannes, and it's a whole different world. It doesn't even take place in Cannes; it probably takes place on the Cap d'Antibes. If you get into the other side, then you've got a decent chance, but as I said before, don't come on the basis that that's going to happen.

Patrick Frater
International Editor
Screen International

Patrick Frater is international editor of film business publication Screen International and Screendaily.com. Currently based in London, he is responsible for managing Screen's coverage outside North America and the UK. He was previously the paper's news editor and for six years its Paris correspondent.

Patrick has been a journalist and consultant covering film, TV and finance for over ten years was previously European editor of the Financial Times' investment and finance title Investors' Chronicle. He travels to Cannes three times a year.

BC: When did you first lose your 'Cannes virginity' and what were your first impressions of the city and the festival?

PF: It was 1991. I'd been a freelance journalist based in Paris for a few months and got myself involved in all sorts of little things, but was really looking for something a bit bigger. It was at this time that Screen International approached me and sort of said, "Would you be interested in working for us as our Paris correspondent?" I hadn't actually been interviewed by anyone at Screen, apart from over the phone, and it so turned out that my first day in the new job was to be the first day of Cannes, 1991.

So my first experience was of being thrown in completely at the deep end because Cannes is one of the four or five times a year when Screen goes daily in print, publishing ten market editions during the festival. The first day is particularly hard because the festival hasn't started, so there's absolutely no news to write. You've just got to bring something you think might interest readers on the first day of the festival, because nothing has happened that you could possibly report on.

I was very lucky on my first day. I picked up Nice Matin, which is the local paper down there, and found a story on their back page about a French film which had been invited to go into competition, but had been pulled on the eve of the festival. They were suggesting that this was only for political reasons because it was the first film to be produced by the Bouygues Group - this operation called CiBy2000. Bouygues was seen as the lowbrow end of the market because its core business was in construction and building materials and this guy with lots of money was seen as muscling into the film industry. Nice Matin was very much suggesting that this film had been kicked out for that kind of reason... that the Paris film establishment couldn't possibly bear to have this cement manufacturer on the steps at Cannes, even though he probably built the Palais. So I followed up that story and they ran it as the front-page lead on my first day, and from then on I was sailing with Screen.

BC: So what were your first impressions of the festival?

PF: It was colossal, huge, and massively confusing. I don't think that I understood until the end of that first festival what the different sections were about... the Quinzaine [Directors' Fortnight], the Critics' Week and so on. People kept asking me about films that I didn't know about. I thought I'd covered the competition and Un Certain Regard - the official sections - and they kept saying, "Well this film is here." and I thought, "But I know about all of the French films that are here?" And they kept coming up with more and more films that I didn't know were in the festival. That baffled me straight away, but also the scale of the thing and the colossal amounts of money that was swishing around Cannes being used just to impress people with really.

BC: What about the city itself... it's the French Riviera, it's supposed to be glamorous, how did you find it when you first got there?

PF: When I first got there I was blown away by the architecture along the Croisette, but I guess that pales quite quickly. It just becomes your working environment because, unlike other

festivals where they dip in for two or three days, most people who go to Cannes are there for ten days. The whole of the independent film industry goes to Cannes to work and stay there pretty much for the duration. For those of us who've got a punishing daily schedule, the glamour side rapidly shifts into the background.

BC: These days, in your capacity as a journalist for Screen International, what do you normally do to prepare ahead of Cannes?

PF: There's no short answer to that - in a way, we spend virtually the whole year preparing for Cannes. Screen International's predecessors virtually claim to have invented the Cannes market. They're not saying that they put up the buildings and organised the screenings etc, but they realised a long time ago that that a market existed. People were buying and selling films, doing deals in the corridors of the old Palais, and they were doing the same kind of things in the other screening rooms and hotels around town - it was a market in all but name. Screen was the first trade publication to do dailies at Cannes, recognising that there was something to say and that people needed somewhere to get that information, rather than just through corridor-talk where some people had it and some people didn't.

So that's how Screen got started in Cannes and it has remained ever since then pretty much the high-point of our year. Everything starts or finishes with the beginning and end of Cannes. As soon as one year's Cannes is over, we all go on holiday for a bit, but after that we're already looking at which directors and which companies have got things in production or will be in production soon that will be ready for next year. It starts straight away. At the moment we're preparing the second edition of our "Cannes 101", which is a guide we did last year for the festival and who's got deal-making power. I'm currently looking at how I'm going to put together this year's list and which people are the 100 most important deal-makers internationally. I've found myself looking at it quite a bit more cynically this year because of just how many companies from last year's top 100 have gone bust or are diminished powers.

I'm also in touch with the festival organisers year-round. I see Thierry Fremaux and Christian Jeune [the two main selectors for the Official Selection] regularly, I talk to them, I talk to the press people at the festival, and more importantly, I talk to sales agents and producers all the time. The conversations people are having all year around are, "What is going to be ready for Cannes?" That's an obsession with a certain group of people, myself included. At the end of the AFM [American Film Market], I usually publish a list of films that I think have got a good chance of being in the festival - a kind of a teaser list for our readers and for film buyers. I collate masses of information and tips, from sales agents mostly, and run them by people who may or may not be in the know, particularly other festival directors as they tend to know what's been withheld from them. If it's the Berlin people for instance, and they say that a film is suddenly not available to their festival, it can be a

good indicator that it might be going to Cannes.

I spoke to one sales agent at the end of one AFM and asked him what his tips for Cannes contenders were, and he said "I'm absolutely not helping you this time. We've got too many things that may or may not go, so I'm not going to help you. Just do your own homework." But he then added, "I can't wait to see your list."

BC: How does a typical day in Cannes during the festival pan out for you?

PF: My job tends to vary from year to year because I'm the International Editor and I don't really know what that means apart from that my responsibly is coverage for everything that is not American and not British. Some years I've found myself news editing, other years I've found myself covering particular territories where Screen hasn't got a correspondent, or other times I'm simply the floating person who's been around for a long time and can dip into any situation. So it has varied a lot. For the 2003 festival I was the French, German and Korean correspondent.

In general, my day pans out in a fairly regular fashion, but you never know what's going to come in between. We have a news meeting at nine o'clock every day and then we rush off to press conferences, meetings, breakfasts, and come back into the office with incredible regularity to try and hit various page deadlines. In Cannes, we publish up to ten pages of news each day, and each has a different deadline during the day, so you've got to just keep filing stuff.

It's a bit of a treadmill if you think about it because you can't just wait until 11am or lunchtime to file the first story because there are three or four pages which need copy before then. Our office is in the ground floor of the Carlton. It's been there for a long time and nowadays people generally know where to find us - things like that make it all a little bit easier.

Then there's the meetings... I always have a series of meetings that I set up in advance, others which I arrange more spontaneously, and of course there are the things which you can't plan - like when someone announces a press conference because a deal they did during Cannes has finally come together - nobody knew that two days ago, so off I go. I do that throughout the day typically until about four or five o'clock, when we've closed the last pages. Sometimes I'll be involved in proofing pages, re-reading stories, or helping other correspondents with their copy, again that's what my job involves. Being International Editor I'm expected to be a bit of a know-all really.

The evening tends to start with the rounds of cocktails, parties, and so on, which for us are work. It sounds ridiculous, and it sounds obscene to people who are not down in Cannes I suspect, but whenever I news edit I tell our people, "By the time we close page one, I expect you to be empty of news, by the time you get into the office at nine o'clock the next morning for the news meeting, I expect you to have a whole slate of stories you can be offering me." So you've got to work the parties, talk to everyone there... producers, distributors, directors, publicists, and come up with angles and stories to put together throughout the next day. Consequently, the day may finish at one or two or three in the morning... I prefer not to think about that.

BC: As a journalist do you find yourself attracting the attention of filmmakers who are trying to promote their films, and if so, have you had any particularly memorable experiences where a filmmaker has done something really crazy to try and attract your attention?

PF: To get me personally interested in their film, not really. I actually find filmmakers are on the whole pretty modest about their ambitions and their talent and most of them don't make a fool of themselves at all. It's some of their producers and publicists that go over the top and get wacky. Filmmakers themselves tend to be pretty responsible and in some cases, overawed by the amount of attention that is given to films that are in the festival. They can't believe that there are 120 journalists queuing up to see their film and interview them, and it's got to be done in two days. The more crazy and eccentric things tend to be done for the films which are slightly more marginal, if they've actually been made at all. Often they're the films that are still looking for finance, so they tend to try and put on a big show suggesting that they're that are going to get made. Noise breeds more noise in Cannes.

Back in the good old days when there was lots of money sloshing around, when video was very healthy and the pre-sales market was buoyant, you could get films financed in

Cannes that didn't even exist on paper even at the beginning of the festival. Someone would just say that Sylvester Stallone was attached to the film - Stallone had probably never even heard of the project, but if you created a buzz and noise around it and someone's offering to put money on the table, well... if there's $20 million on the table, Stallone will probably be there too. It used to happen like that a lot, but I've found in the last four or five years that there's much less of that 'excess for the sake of excess'. If there are people creating heat around a project it's because there is something there.

BC: It's nice to see heat where heat is due for a change.

PF: Yes. It's also a one of the signs of the difficulties in the industry that there's not as much spare cash floating around. Cash now for film finance comes more from public sources, at least in Europe, and the civil servants who are dishing that out are less impressed by 'flash' than some of the flamboyant producers who used to have all the money.

BC: Do you have a particularly memorable festival anecdote that you like to recount when the topic of Cannes comes up at the dinner table?

PF: I've got loads of anecdotes. One, which is a very journalistic experience, was during the second year that I went to Cannes in 1992. I was still in Paris and some of the other people had already gone down to Cannes. I called the editor when I heard the local news in Paris that Marlene Dietrich had died. Few

people were aware of this to start with but as soon as they were, they realised they needed photographs. This was back in the days before the Internet really had taken off so it actually meant we needed physical photographs for the front page. Fortunately my wife had tipped me off on this story because her office in Paris was opposite Marlene Dietrich's flat. So she saw funeral things going on and rang me to tell me something had happened. I then called a photo agency friend of mine who gave me loads of photos before he'd handed them out to anybody else, because he hadn't had a call from anybody else yet. So I had 200-300 pictures of Marlene Dietrich to take down to Cannes the next morning on the plane. Our deadline for pictures was very early that day because it was the first issue, and they needed the pictures to be there absolutely immediately. So I took the helicopter [from Nice airport to Cannes]. It's the only time I've expensed a helicopter to Screen, and it's the only time I'm ever likely too. So that was one journalistic thing, but nobody bats an eyelid half the time at that kind of excess... they do at Screen, but other parts of the industry... "Take the helicopter? Great."

One of my other silly things was about five or six years ago, the year that Planet Hollywood opened in Cannes for the first time and took over the ground floor of the Splendid Hotel. For some reason they were handing out various different passes to people and I got a pass which gave me breakfast for every day I wanted it, so I wore that one, and another pass which gave me all-areas access anytime, and I thought, "This is great."

One of the days, I got invited to a party there... I've forgotten which film it was promoting, but in addition to all my Planet Hollywood passes, I also had the correct party ticket. Iggy Pop was playing - he's a favourite of mine - and what I hadn't realised until I got there was that this was such a select party - either that or the bouncers had been too heavy - because there was almost nobody there. So there's Iggy Pop on stage doing a fantastic set and there were about maybe 20 or 30 people in the audience, but they were celebrities. There was Demi Moore, one of the Sheen brothers, Mick Hucknell, Kate Moss, other supermodels... and me. I have no idea what I was doing in there with this lot - it felt like a private party that Iggy Pop was playing for. He was completely over the top, everyone was off their heads, he was doing a great set in private, and he was spitting into the audience of celebrities and they were loving it... it was absurd and over the top.

But to finish off this silly anecdote, I saw this rather lonely, spiky-haired figure turn up at the velvet rope, but he was debarred by the bouncers. They told him that they didn't need him in this party, he hadn't got an invitation, and that he probably should leave. It was Pedro Almodóvar and I recognised him. I don't know him, but I went up to the bouncers and said, "Are you really, really sure you should be doing this to this guy? He's probably the most successful foreign language director working today, and did you realise that he got the Légion d'Honneur [Legion of Honour] today from the French Government?" Nothing had worked until then, but telling him that

he'd got the Légion d'Honneur that lunchtime... the bouncers opened up and in he came. I think it's the only time that pure reason has actually worked with bouncers in Cannes.

BC: Do you have any favourite places to eat when you are in Cannes?

PF: One is not really a restaurant. Near where we work at the Carlton, on one of the back roads - the Rue Rouaze - there's a Lebanese traiteur which has the best food in Cannes - I'm convinced of it. Their food is fresh, fantastically tasty and cheap, and they serve it with a kind of deliberately gruff insolence, but they recognise you year in, year out. You're made to feel welcome by them being ruder than ever to you. I kind of look forward to those lunchtimes where I don't have an organised lunch and just grab something from there and bring it back to the office. Their food is fantastic.

Real restaurants... my favourite is probably the Gaston Gastounette, which is near the old port. If you want a celebrity anecdote there... I organised a dinner for Michelle Yeoh last year - she's a friend of mine, one of the few celebrities I would call a friend - and she was on the jury last year. We'd met up at the Carlton on the terrace and I'd organised dinner for eight o'clock. With Michelle on jury duty, her time-keeping was not really of her own making. That evening, she only managed to turn up at the Carlton at eight o'clock, then had to get changed. We had drinks on the Terrace and we were running massively late. So I called the restaurant, not just once but twice to tell them that we were getting later and later. I'd warned them in advance that we had a VIP and the difference in service when you've got a VIP - "Come whenever you like" - was hilarious. But it was absolutely necessary because Michelle, who's quite athletic, decided she wanted to walk to the restaurant. So we walked from the Carlton all the way to the old town. She was on the jury, an absolutely recognisable celebrity and in high heels... it took forever to get there because, you can imagine, hundreds of people were asking for autographs all the way along the Croisette. So we got there about ten o'clock and the restaurant couldn't have been nicer.

BC: What about socialising/ networking venues?

PF: Not really. They tend to vary from year to year actually, where the hotspot is. The one place I tend to gravitate to is the terrace at the Grand Hotel, but that's kind of very British. It used to be kind of French, and as I don't cover Britain it's not really that useful to me anymore.

BC: Do you have any advice for future Cannes virgins, particularly producers who are coming to Cannes with films?

PF: Prepare and be realistic about what you want to achieve. If you expect to get your film, which is at the moment barely developed, to be fully-financed by the end of Cannes, you'll be out of pocket and disappointed. If you know what you want, if you set yourself certain realistic goals, if you set up a few meetings beforehand, then that's going to help a lot.

Also, get a couple of good people on your side, whether it's another producer who's not in competition with you or a publicist. Indeed, some of the publicists are very friendly and amenable to people who are first-timers. You'd be surprised - they are generally very stressed people who've got masses of other things to do, but some can often find time to help people who could be clients five years down the road. And they have very good advice, always, because they've been inside every venue, they've been inside every party, they've worked with other producers, distributors, and they know how the festival itself can grind people down - because the festival organisation is pretty scary sometimes. So, make a couple of good friends before you get there and stick with them.

Other practical things... good shoes, you've heard that one a hundred times before.

Stay there as long as you can, but that might mean being prepared to share rooms with people. Don't stay too far out of town, but don't necessarily try and stay on the Croisette either. Stay there as long as you can because relationships happen and can form very quickly. I often suggest to people that you can live a whole relationship with a person in a day in Cannes. You can meet them for the first time, be attracted, fall in love, fall out of love - I mean this in a professional sense of course. You can go through all that sort of thing, you can fall out, make up again, and go off into the sunset together in a day. That's probably a bit of a journalistic exaggeration, but within the twelve days that the festival is on you can achieve a lot.

Harry Hicks MA ACA CTA
Head of Film & TV
Chiltern Media Consulting

Harry Hicks is a chartered accountant and tax advisor who specialises in structuring finance for film and TV productions. He has executive produced a number of films and has extensive experience of the UK and international fiscal incentives for film production. He is a director of First Up Film, a company providing a comprehensive film development, financing and production service. His clients include some of the major UK film financing funds. Harry sits on the Committee of the Institute of Chartered Accountants Media Group and has lectured widely on film financing.

BC: When did you first lose your 'Cannes virginity' and what were your first impressions of the city and the festival?

HH: The first time I went to the film festival was only in 1999. I had done MIDEM [International Music Market] a couple of times before that, the first time in 1995, but the film festival was all very confusing. My first feeling was really, "Who does what?" Mainly I think because everything is so spread out. It's not like MIPCOM [International TV Market] or even MIDEM where everything happens in The Bunker [aka the Palais du Festivals]; everything is spread out so there's a very amorphous feel about it when you first go, certainly there was for me.

BC: These days, how to you prepare for a visit to Cannes for the film festival?

HH: Today I'm extremely focussed and I have my agenda for why I might be going worked out well ahead of the festival. For instance, the last time I went, one agenda was to make more contacts in respect of raising UK tax money, possible sources of finance, and the other one was to link up particularly with overseas sales agents and distributors in respect of those projects that we were doing through First Up Film. What I did beforehand was to make contact by fax or email with people I wanted to see and set up as many meetings as possible in advance. So my diary is very well planned before I go. I have to say, I also leave gaps in between each meeting because my experience is that meetings are always being rescheduled or running over. You have to leave those spaces to keep your schedule flexible, and also because it's all so spread out, you have to allow yourself time to get from one venue to another. You might have one meeting at the Carlton and your next meeting might be at the Palais, and your next meeting might be at the Martinez, or wherever, so it can be very very exhausting. I find leaving that space between appointments is essential.

BC: Accommodation is one of the biggest challenges for festival attendees these days. Some people get around this by staying out of town. What are your thoughts on places to stay?

HH: I prefer to stay in town these days. I have stayed outside of town in the past, but what I find is you get a taxi in first thing in the morning, then you're there all day and all night. It's just great to be in town and at some stage during the day be able to go back to where you're staying and freshen up.

BC: Once you're in Cannes, how does a typical day tend to pan out for you?

HH: It would usually be about three meetings in the morning, and some can start at 9am - it's not always necessarily a late start. Then there's almost always a lunch at one of the beach cafes, with people I want to see, or if people have invited me, and then maybe a couple of meetings in the afternoon. Then of course there's the round of cocktail parties, starting at 6pm and running through to 9pm or whenever. You could certainly go to three in an evening. Then dinner with contacts or clients. I have to say that by about midnight, and this is probably a bit disappointing, but

I'm not one of these people that goes back to the Majestic and stays up until three o'clock in the morning - I just can't do that these days. Besides, I don't know what kind of real contacts are made at the Majestic in the early hours of the morning. It may be a place for swapping business cards but I'm not sure that the cost-benefit equation stacks up really.

BC: In your capacity as a financier, do you have people pitching projects to you at the festival, and do you have any memorable pitches that spring to mind?

HH: I tend to hear a lot of pitches at Cannes, particularly independent producers pitching projects or scripts to me. One pitch that was memorable was an animation project which looked very well thought out. The financing look convincing, it was well structured and I suppose that for me is why that did impress me. The artistic or creative value of the project wouldn't really be for me to judge.

BC: Have you heard any really awful pitches where you've just thought "these guys are wasting their time"?

HH: I've had quite a few, people that are touting around a script, which is just it... it's just a script. There's all levels of projects in Cannes, everybody's hustling from one end to the other. I've even had wanna-be actors hustling because they think I might be in some way important, and I've certainly had independent producers with scripts that had not really had a 'bat in hell's chance' of going anywhere.

BC: Cannes is known as a 'finished product' festival. Is it common for financing deals to be put together there?

HH: I would be surprised if they were finalised. I personally haven't seen a financing deal locked down in Cannes. My attitude towards Cannes would be that everything is a bit too frenetic for deals to be finalised in terms of financing, but it's a good place to start the discussion. Overall, looking at it from both sides, if I had projects that wanted financing, I wouldn't be having detailed discussions about it in Cannes. I might introduce the concept and idea, and then say "we'll continue the discussion afterwards."

BC: If you were to discuss projects in development with a producer in Cannes from a financing point of view, what would you be looking for them to show you?

HH: Obviously a screenplay, and at least a wish-list of major cast, so there is an indication that thought had being given to who might take the lead roles. Also, a director, or at least thought as to who the director might be, and indicative budget. I think that's what I prefer to see as a starting point.

BC: Do you have a favourite anecdote that you like to recount at the dinner table when the topic of Cannes comes up in the conversation?

HH: Yes, it has to be Cannes 2000. I was on the plane from London with a colleague, and we were coming down into Nice into thick fog, about

an hour late or something like that. As we were coming in to land there was this almighty scaping sound - it was very scary actually. It turns out that at the last minute, the pilot realised we couldn't land because the fog was too thick and too close to the ground. We were temporarily diverted to Marseilles, and when we landed there were these two women who insisted on getting off, even though we'd been told that we would be returning to Nice as soon as the fog cleared.

Everybody on the plane was in uproar, there was nearly a riot and there was all sorts of chanting going on: "Nice, Nice, Nice." I'm amazed these women didn't get lynched. The pilot had to come out and it was absolutely amazing. All these otherwise civilised people, obviously most of them producers and the like going to the festival, got really anarchic.

I think in the end the women did get off, but it was decided to keep their luggage on the plane, because what was initially said was that if these two women get off, we're going to have to take all the luggage off the plane so we can get their bags. Of course that would have delayed us immensely. I think they got off, but it was announced that their luggage was staying on, and everyone went "Yay!!!" because that would have of course massively inconvenienced the two women. We finally got to Nice and caught a taxi from the airport to the hotel, out in La Bocca, where I was staying with a work colleague. When I got to the hotel, I was told that there was no room for me, even though I'd booked and stayed there before. This was the Friday night of the film festival. I'd arrived three hours late and I was told that there was no room for me. To cut a long story short, I had to share a small room with my colleague; not the ideal situation, but it was the only thing we could do.

BC: Do you have any favourite places to eat when you're in town?

HH: At lunch time it's usually one of the beach cafes, but I'm indiscriminate as to which one. In the evening I particularly like going up the Rue St Antoine. There's a couple of good places on there. The places I can remember having enjoyed and having a good evening... there was Le Marais, but particularly Le Mesclun - I've had some really very good meals there. It's not the cheapest, but it's not massively expensive either.

BC: Do you have any networking/ socialising venues?

HH: Well, if anywhere it would be the Carlton, but obviously when I'm on business accounts. I don't really like the Majestic. I find the Carlton more relaxed, quieter, and the Carlton Terrace is lovely. But if there was anything happening on a yacht... I think those are the best places. It's outside and it's just fun.

BC: Do you have any advice for future Cannes virgins, particularly first-time producers who are looking to come and sell their film or meet distributors/sales agents?

HH: The only thing I would say is, do some research first and have your meetings arranged before you get there. And quite honestly, there's not

a lot of point meeting people from your own country in Cannes because they'll just say, "Well, we can meet back home." I think most people see Cannes as an opportunity to see people from abroad, so I would say focus on people from long haul destinations.

Stephen Kelliher
Sales & Acquisitions Manager
Beyond Films

Stephen Kelliher joined Beyond Films in July 1998 as Sales and Acquisitions Assistant based in the London office. He quickly progressed to the position of Sales Executive and more recently the position of Sales & Acquisition Manager.

Stephen is responsible for sales to territories in Western and Central Europe, The Middle East, Latin America and Asia. In recent years Stephen has handled a range of titles including "Chopper", "Lantana", "The Business of Strangers", and "The Hard Word".

Previously, Stephen spent two years in Sales and Acquisitions at UK based sales company, Vine International Pictures.

BC: When did you lose your 'Cannes virginity'?

SK: The first time I went was eight years ago. I was working for another independent film sales company called Vine International Pictures, but I was literally the office junior and in a very lucky position to be going to Cannes at that age. I was 20 years old and it was my first time at a film festival so losing my 'Cannes virginity' was a big deal. I was there for the entire festival, running errands, making cups of tea, going to screenings, collecting business cards, and just really observing how the whole business works. Cannes and the other markets are the industry, or at least they are for a sales agent. That's where you do your business. So to see the biggest event in the film calendar for real was a very sharp learning curve and is largely responsible for making me see that this was the job I wanted to do. Previously, I thought production might be more suitable for me but experiencing Cannes first hand made me realise that I wanted to remain in international distribution.

BC: So what was your impression of the city? It's the French Riviera, it's supposed to be glamorous...?

SK: And I think it is on the surface. I mean you're walking down the Croisette and you've got all the designer shops and the imposingly lavish hotels, most of which employ security for the duration of the festival which makes them seem even more unapproachable. In saying that, from my perspective, it's never as glamorous as it appears. At the end of the day, Cannes itself is a small seaside town and, with exception of the Croisette itself, is mainly a maze of back streets which are populated by pensioners and their irritating dogs.

But jokes aside... it can be intimidating, although I think most people are like a child in a sweet shop the first time around. It is frenetic and there's 101 things happening at once and it can be difficult to take it all in. I know I certainly had to stop and ask myself whether I was really part of this. If the answer is yes, you have to embrace it and wade in, I guess.

BC: Could you provide a bit of background on how a sales agent works with a producer at a festival like Cannes?

SK: The sales agent is primarily the bridge between the producer and the international market place. As a producer, your talents tend to be creative or financial, or both. But I would argue that many independent producers don't have the time or ability to ensure that their film is seen in around the world. So it's a sales agent's job is to have those contacts, to be able to take the film - it could be a completed film or it might be a script - to distributors and be able to target the right companies in the right territory. Hopefully they will close the deal so your film has the opportunity to be seen internationally. Of course, the sales agent also plays an integral role in the financing of films whether it be through pre-sales, putting up an advance against the international rights, or by bringing a gap financing bank to a project. In this respect, their role is also key to an independent producer.

In terms of how it works day to day in Cannes, I'd say that sales agents probably have the worst wrap of everybody. It's the longest market in the film calendar, lasting 12 days...

and that's 12 days of solid work because weekends don't count when you are a sales agent. There are no lie-ins, your meetings start at nine o'clock in the morning, and they finish at seven in the evening. As a sales agent you are actually quite isolated from all the glamour that goes on around you, because you are sitting in an office day in day out, with meetings every half-hour for the duration of the festival. I think sales agents definitely have the toughest job in Cannes.

BC: So what do you do to prepare ahead of Cannes?

SK: It starts pretty much immediately after the American Film Market which ends at the beginning of March. We go straight into Cannes preparation at that point.   We've probably already sent any films that are going to be completed in time for Cannes to the official selectors, whether it's for the main competition, Un Certain Regard, the Directors' Fortnight, or the Critics' Week. Hopefully they have seen the films by then and hopefully you're on top of them, trying to get back their feedback.   Ideally, six weeks before the market we want to have our slate firmed up in terms of which projects we're going to have and which completed films will we be screening and what films are going to be in post-production. You need to get all that information out to as many people as you can, as soon as you can, because you want to get in early and avoid people coming back with: "Oh my schedules is full, but I'll drop by and see you sometime while I'm there." They never will. So it's best to get in early and make sure people know what you're up to. I've kind of summarised it all in a couple of brief sentences but it actually takes weeks to get to that point. You need to be in a position, when you get to Cannes, to be presenting your films at the highest possible level. Cannes can be the film equivalent of a cattle market, particularly if your film isn't in official selection. It's actually really tough to get those films noticed because people tend to focus on the films in official programme. In fact, I think it's important to ask yourself whether Cannes is the right place to launch a finished film because even great films can very easily be overlooked there.

In the build up to Cannes, you're working on creative publicity, with the producers and designers, coming up with visual images, trailers and that kind of thing. It's really a four-month effort to get to Cannes, and you always get there and realise you've forgotten something!

BC: So how does a typical day tend to pan out for you in Cannes?

SK: Well, as I said, meetings pretty much start at 9am... even earlier if you're unlucky enough to have a breakfast meeting in your schedule! One thing that's important to remember is that at the end of the day, you are there to do a job. You can be at whatever party until four or five in the morning, but you still have to be in the office at nine and be able to string a sentence together. Actually, the sales agent's life in Cannes can be quite unglamorous. You're meeting people from all around the world, delivering what is essentially the same pitch. And it can be hard, trying to keep it fresh, because you're not only pitching one film, you're maybe pitching six films to somebody in a half-hour period. It's extremely tiring mentally. And if you're having a successful market, or there's one title that is selling well, you'll still have to sit down at the end of each day to review the offers you've received, or the interest you have received, figure out what's the best deal, or who the best distributor is, and maybe chase people up who said they were going to see a film, or get back to you, but haven't. So you really need to spend an hour or more at the end of each day getting all that stuff clear in your head, as well as preparing a little bit for the next day. But then of course there are the infamous parties in the evening, some of which you need to go to for professional reasons and others which aren't perhaps so important from a work perspective; either way, it can be hard to find time to wind down and generally you arrive back home as something of a physical and mental wreck!

BC: How common is it for producers to pitch ideas or projects to sales agents in Cannes?

SK: The thing about Cannes is that anyone who has a project tends to be there. From a sales agent's point of view, I would say that it's not the best place for you to meet us because our primary function at a market is to sell. It is difficult to give time to someone who is thinking about shooting a film in six months time or in 12 months time, particularly if that person is based in the UK, but wants to see you in Cannes. You do try not to have an attitude about it, but it can be difficult.

Usually, the second week of the festival is the best time for us to see producers. At that point we tend to have a little more time to actually listen to what they are saying. We have recently appointed a dedicated acquisitions and development person who will come to the festival with us this year. Their job is solely to meet with producers and listen to the pitches so hopefully we will be a little more producer-friendly this year. I would say that the companies with an acquisitions person in Cannes are the ones to target. It's much easier to get to them than the sales people who need to be focused on selling.

BC: If you were going to meet a producer in Cannes, what sort of material would you expect them to be showing you?

SK: It all depends on what stage the project is at really. From our point of view, we can only become involved once a certain number of elements are in place, so it doesn't make sense for somebody to come and see us with a script and nothing else attached. We're not a financing house and we don't house a development department. So if somebody's coming to us with a project, they need to have the shooting script, they need to have a director attached, there needs to be a budget and a percentage of that budget in place, or at least working towards having a percentage of that budget in place. By it's very nature, a sales company can't be the first to commit to a project because they need to make an informed decision based on the script and the talent attached. You can't do that from a script alone.

It's different if you're going to see people about development, or you're going to see production finance people, because they are less bound by the commerciality of the project, if you like, whereas for us, that is the be all and end all. We have to know that there's a market for it and that we can market it effectively. So I would say that as much of the package as possible should be in place. Once you've got that, I wouldn't necessarily say that you need to spend a lot of money creating expensive marketing materials because I think any sales agent worth their salt will be able to pick out the good projects from a verbal presentation, a script, and a typed list of the elements attached. I don't think it's necessary to spend lots of money on that kind of thing. That's not what it's about, it's about the script and the elements attached.

BC: Do you have a particular memorable anecdote from your time in Cannes over the years?

SK: The whole thing I think is an interesting experience. I don't think I can sit here and name one thing. The first year that you go is always going to be a lasting memory. You can't believe you're walking down the street... you're not bumping into film stars, but you're seeing them at events or you walk in to a hotel lobby and there's whoever with their entourage. There are memorable people I've seen though... I think Michael Jackson was one when he had his film Ghosts screening out of competition [in 1997]. But every year it's somebody new or something new. Cannes is definitely a life experience. I would almost say that everybody should experience it once because it is so crazy.

BC: Do you have any favourite places to eat when you're in Cannes?

SK: Everybody says that Cannes is expensive, but you can do it without eating expensively. If you're going to go anywhere along the Croisette by the sea then you can expect to pay more for it. But you just take a walk in some of the less well-known places, and you can eat very reasonably. The Rue Sainte Antoine, which is in the old town, is packed with restaurants. There are a couple that are really expensive but the rest of them are priced pretty fairly. You're certainly not paying any more than you would pay in London, maybe a bit less sometimes.

For those on a very tight budget, there's always McDonald's or the fast food stall next door to the Town Hall which serves a very good horse burger - so I am reliably informed. I have never dared to try one myself though.

BC: Do you have any favourite socialising/networking places in Cannes?

SK: It is all networking really. Every night there are probably five or six cocktail parties that you could go to and those are the places where you meet people - it's one of the main reasons to go to them. For somebody who's trying to find opportunities to network, I would say get invited to as many cocktail parties as you can because that's where people talk and that's where people exchange information. There are also the international pavilions which run along the beach where there are the official film bodies for the various countries. Most of those have events and there are always interesting people to meet. I would highly recommend these as a networking exercise, just get invited to as much as you can, and speak to as many people as you can. Try not to drink as much as you can though - it's never a good look to be blind drunk when meeting a potential business partner!

BC: Any particular venues you like to hang out in or is it mainly the parties?

SK: I'm kind of over parties in Cannes at this stage. Every year I find I go to less and less because they're always such a bun-fight. It can take you an hour to get a drink at the bar, then you lose your friends and you never find them again. I would certainly never go to a party that I wasn't invited to; it's just not worth the hassle. I would much rather meet up with friends and just go for some quiet drinks around and about. Any of the bars along the Croisette or if you can get on any of the boats in the old port, that's quite nice too.

BC: Do you have any specific advice for future Cannes virgins?

SK: For first-time producers coming to Cannes to pitch their film, I think they have to be very careful about which companies they're going to target. There's a common misconception that you can just go to anyone and everyone. You should take your time and do a bit of research and see what kind of films particular companies specialise in. Ask yourself honestly whether your film is going to fit their criteria. I would also take the time to find out who the correct person to speak to is. You can look at the Cannes Market Guide and the bumper issues [of the trade magazines], and if there's someone in acquisitions or development at the company you want to talk to, contact them for a meeting. It just saves a lot of unnecessary hassle in the long run.

I suppose the only other thing I would say is: don't be daunted by it. It is a huge event. You see people who've been doing it for years and it's all like second-nature to them, but just get stuck in and enjoy it. It is something to be enjoyed, it is hard work, but just don't be too frightened by it all.

Richard Miller
Managing Director
Olsberg | SPI

Richard Miller entered the film business in 1990 after spending nine years on Wall Street where he rose to Senior Vice President in the Corporate Finance Department of Dean Witter Reynolds. Whilst acting as an independent media consultant, Richard produced several award-winning American independent films including "Heavy", the acclaimed debut feature directed by James Mangold ("Copland", "Girl, Interrupted"), starring Liv Tyler. "Heavy" won a Special Jury Prize at the 1995 Sundance Film Festival and was selected for the Directors Fortnight at Cannes the same year. In 1999 he produced "Songcatcher" directed by Maggie Greenwald ("The Ballad of Little Jo"), starring Janet McTeer and Aidan Quinn, which won a Special Jury Prize at the 2000 Sundance Film Festival. Richard also co-published Filmmaker Magazine and taught producing at New York University. He then returned to the UK and in 2000 took up a post as managing director at the specialist media consultancy, Olsberg | SPI.

BC: When did you first lose your 'Cannes virginity' and what were your first impressions of the festival?

RM: I first came to Cannes in the late 80s before I was in the film business, when I was still an investment banker. I had just taken three back-to-back red-eye flights from Hawaii to San Francisco, San Francisco to Boston, and Boston to Cannes, so I was completely burnt out. In my deranged state, Cannes seemed like this other-worldly place - seedy and strange but at the same time really beautiful and exciting.

I always say that it's really valuable that producers experience a festival before they need to deal with it professionally. So I was very lucky that I visited the festival when I had nothing at stake and could just enjoy it as a place to hang out and see films. Then later on, when I needed to work the event, I already had some understanding of how it operated. Since that first visit I've been to the festival about ten times, and in all my subsequent visits, I've probably seen half the number of films that I saw on that first visit.

BC: How did you find the city itself?

RM: Cannes is the encapsulation of the art/commerce nature of the film enterprise. Immediately everybody is overwhelmed with the massive billboards for these A and B-titles along the Croisette, but there are also a lot of dedicated cineastes and film fans queuing up to see obscure art films. Then you go behind the seafront and there's another world of French people with poodles going about the business of being glamorously French. And then you go up into the hills or out of town and there's even another world of people actually living normal suburban lives. That contrast is quite remarkable I think.

BC: What sort of preparation do you do these days before arriving in Cannes?

RM: Preparation is principally about setting up meetings. For me, both as a consultant now and when I was producing, Cannes is about meeting people that are more difficult to meet year round because they live in a different town or country. Or even meeting people that work just down the street from you, but somehow in Cannes they're there to take meetings and it's easier to get together with them. So it's all about setting up meetings - that's my preparation.

BC: So following on from that, your typical day in Cannes comprises of, surprise surprise, lots of meetings?

RM: Yes, lots of meetings, and in between the meetings, finding out where people are so that I can arrange other meetings. The great thing about Cannes is that there's a certain randomness to encountering people. You may have tried for weeks to set up a meeting through the normal channels and then at the first party you go to, you bump into somebody who says, "Oh, he's over there across the room", and takes you over and you've got your

meeting. It's important just to be out and about so that you are exposed to this serendipity that is such a big part of Cannes.

BC: How was it that "Heavy" came to be selected for the Directors Fortnight?

RM: The film had played in Sundance and had been critically acclaimed, but had not been acquired at that point. I knew the number-two man at Directors Fortnight, Olivier Jahan, from previous Cannes festivals I had attended and also knew he was coming to New York to scout for films for the sidebar. I called him ahead of time, set up a screening, and he loved the film. He called us immediately and offered us a place. We were the first American film selected that year. It was that simple.

BC: What was involved in preparing to screen the film for the Directors Fortnight?

RM: At that point we did not have a distributor anywhere, but because we had an acceptance into an official section at Cannes we were potentially quite attractive to foreign sales agents. I arranged screenings in London for foreign sales agents and had a number of discussions and ended up selecting Fortissimo, out of Amsterdam. So I was able to go into the festival with a sales agent onboard. It's pretty important to do that because without a sales agent, if there is interest among distributors, it's going to be the producer doing the deals, and it's much more difficult for a producer than for a sales agent. A producer doesn't have all those relationships with distributors in the different territories, and also doesn't know all the deal terms and comparable prices.

Fortissimo then suggested a publicity person because publicity's also a big part of Cannes. There are two different types of publicity at the festival: the French publicity and the international publicity. They work side by side, but they're kind of different worlds. Fortunately we were able to put in place a publicist who was capable of dealing with both, and with a sales agent and a publicist onboard, we were ready to take orders.

BC: Did the film actually get picked up by a distributor in Cannes?

RM: We did a number of very good foreign deals; in the UK, in Japan, and in other major territories. So it was a very good Cannes for us. We actually didn't do a US deal, principally because the US distributors wouldn't come to the screenings because they'd seen the film in Sundance and consequently felt they didn't need to. In the end we didn't do a US deal until the Toronto festival where we showed a slightly trimmed film. Off the back of that we were able to get some new companies into the screening and did a pretty good deal there too.

BC: How was "Heavy" received by audiences in Cannes?

RM: It was received very well. It's a wonderful experience to screen a film in Cannes. They have the best screening facilities you'll ever see anywhere and technicians that really care about the quality of the screening. They had the director, Jim Mangold, and I come to this test at midnight the night before our first screening, just to make sure we were perfectly happy with the presentation.

Then on the day - to be in this massive hall and have people from around the world yelling and clapping - it's a remarkable experience. And the press conference afterwards, where they ask about cinematic influences, not distribution deals.

So it was a very good experience for us. We also had a bit of glamour with the screening because it was Liv Tyler's first festival experience... her second film, first festival... and that gave us a substantial amount of press attention.

BC: Do you have a favourite Cannes anecdote that sticks in your mind?

RM: It's tough to beat that experience of walking on stage arm-in-arm with my director and my star and having thousands of people stand up and applaud.

BC: Do you have any favourite places that you like to eat when you are in Cannes?

RM: I have two favourite places in Cannes, and I'm very tempted to keep them to myself, but I'll tell you anyway although I won't give all the details. Over by the bus station there is a wonderful little bar that has beers from all around the world. You go in there and generally there's nobody wearing a Cannes badge. You can sit and have a couple of beers and just get right away from the Cannes craziness. That's one of my favourite places. Another one is called La Brouette de Grand-Mère or 'Grandmother's Wheelbarrow' and it's on a side road off the Croisette. It has really good food, but the reason I like it is that you just go in and sit down and they bring you food and drink and you have absolutely no say in what you eat or what you drink. They just keep bringing it out. You have no decisions to make, you just go to your grandmother's and she takes care of you. Sometimes at Cannes you need that.

BC: Do you have any preferred socialising/networking venues?

RM: One always goes to the parties, but for bumping into people and meeting friends, there's nothing like what used to be the Petit Carlton and Petit Majestic, but is now just the Petit Majestic in behind the Grand Hotel. It's this little bar where the crowds just spill onto the street and everyone comes by. Most evenings will find me taking a quick walk through just to see if there's anybody I know there or need to meet.

BC: Do you have any advice for future Cannes virgins, particularly first-time producers looking to either sell a film or generate interest?

RM: Well the first thing is, if you can, try to go to Cannes for the first time when you don't need to do anything so you can just work out the lay of the land. The second thing is don't just hang around your national pavilion. I talk to a lot of Americans, for example, that seem to spend most of their time in the American Pavilion. It doesn't make much sense to fly all that way and just hang out with people from home. Certainly those pavilions are handy to use as a base, but part the Cannes experience is the chance to make contacts with the industry outside your own situation. Go to other people's pavilions and hang out. The third thing is, don't go naked. Make sure that, when it's important, you have the specialist expertise in terms of film representation, publicity, the experts... the people that know how to do it, if that's at all possible. And lastly, so much of Cannes is about serendipity that you want to be open to, but can't really control. You've just got to find time to relax and enjoy it as a place, and not just be so focussed on the task in hand - because it's a very pleasant place to spend a few days.

Jonathan Olsberg
Chairman
Olsberg | SPI

Jonathan Olsberg has worked in the film industry for 20 years. Starting out as an international sales agent with Affinity Enterprises, Jonathan handled titles such as "My Beautiful Launderette" before running New York based independent distributor Spectrafilm which specialised in European directors such as Godard, Tavernier, Greenaway and Verhoeven. In 1989 Jonathan returned to London as Managing Director of international distributor and sales agent Glinwood Films ("The Last Emperor") where he oversaw acquisition and/or distribution of over 20 films with budgets totalling over $100 million.

Jonathan now splits his time between London-based consultancy firm Olsberg | SPI and running an active production company, Dakota Films. Jonathan is executive producer of the $5m feature "Me Without You",

which was nominated for a BAFTA for Best British Film in 2002. He is also a producer of the $20m "Head in the Clouds" starring Charlize Theron, Penelope Cruz, and Stuart Townsend.

BC: When did you lose your 'Cannes virginity' and how did you find the city and the festival?

JO: Mine was a baptism of fire in 1982, but not as a producer - I went there as a sales agent. I had been an investment banker in New York until six months beforehand and I'd started a small film sales company with a partner. Low and behold, in our first few months we represented a film that got selected to be in Competition in Cannes - it was a surprise and we were totally unprepared for it. The film was called "Smithereens" and was made by a student at NYU called Susan Seidelman, who later went on to make "Desperately Seeking Susan". She made it for $50,000 on Super 16mm and when it was selected, we had to find all kinds of money... to blow it up to 35mm, for a marketing campaign, to hire press agents, and so on. And it wasn't as if we'd been in business for years. We didn't actually know what we were doing, but luckily we were recommended a very good French press agent to help us handle the whole thing and they taught us what to do. So in terms of selling, we had to prepare marketing materials and send them out ahead of time. We had to start to show the film before Cannes to a few selected buyers and we did a couple of quick deals that way. Unfortunately none of these stood up and we had to sue the buyers to get paid because they saw us as neophytes and they thought that they could say they'd buy the film and wait to see how it panned out - a bit devious really. Still, we won both cases and it was a good lesson!

BC: So what were your first impressions of the festival when you arrived there?

JO: Well for us, even though we weren't neophyte producers, we were neophyte sales agents, and the first impressions were that it was incredibly disorganised. For example, there was no central directory of where people were. There are the people who register, or are invited to the festival, and if they remember to send in the information, you could find out where they are, but that's only about 20% of all the people there. And it was so spread out with all these offices in the different hotels - it was just totally chaotic but also a little thrilling.

BC: And what about the city itself?

JO: I was already familiar with the city from going on holidays there when I was younger, so I knew the area in general. Of course Cannes when it's not a big festival or market is a delightful, relatively sleepy retirement town, but during the festival it gets mobbed by literally tens of thousands of people. It's wonderful if the weather's good and it's awful if it's raining because most people have to walk around from meeting to meeting. Walking around in Cannes in the rain is not much fun because you're always late and there are so many people getting in the way, whether they are there for the festival or just members of the public hoping

to see a star. Something that is also terribly aggravating is that there are at least one or two public holidays that take place during the festival, so not only do you have the weekends where the place is mobbed, but if you have a holiday on the Thursday, it's a four-day weekend and a complete zoo. So it's an inconvenient and difficult place, but that is totally counter-balanced by the fact that if the weather's good you can have lunch on the beach with your toes in the sand and a nice bottle of wine.

BC: These days, what sort of preparation do you do ahead of Cannes?

JO: I think it depends on what I'm going to be doing there. I've been a producer in Cannes, I've sold movies, I've been a distributor buying movies, I've been a management consultant looking for other kinds of business, so I think it really depends on what hat you're wearing. If you're selling or buying films, there are certain things you have to do ahead of time.

For selling, obviously you've got to sow the seeds of your marketing campaign and make sure buyers are aware of your product. You might even start showing the film ahead of Cannes to certain people. If you're buying, you've got to be sniffing around for those sorts of opportunities to buy before the film gets to Cannes.

One essential piece of preparation is accommodation; you've got to get your hotel squared away months in advance, and you've usually got to dig deep in the pocket to do so. People going for the first time on a small budget often club together to rent an apartment somewhere close by, but nowadays if you're in a four-star hotel, by January you've got to slap down a hefty wad including various 'commissions' to people.

So accommodation has to be sorted out and then you've got to have a purpose or purposes for being there. You've got to have specific targets because otherwise you can be completely overwhelmed by some of the things that are going on. So ahead of time, you should set up your key meetings which you don't want to shift and then about two or three weeks beforehand, you email everybody who you know who might be going and let them know the dates you'll be there, how you will be contactable, and invite them to meet if there's a reason to do so.

It's generally a bad idea to completely fill your calendar with appointments before you go because you'll always be bumping into people there who you'll want to meet. You'll also be bumping into people who want to meet you, but you don't want to meet, so you've got to have enough appointments to say "Oh, sorry. I can't do it on a Thursday, how about breakfast at seven o'clock on Friday?" And inevitably they don't want to do it.

BC: How does a typical day in Cannes pan out for you these days?

JO: In my early days, when I was staying outside of Cannes, my day would start bleary eyed, getting up and getting into a rented car, heading in and finding a parking space. These days I stay at the Carlton so I usually

have a breakfast meeting and then the day will usually consist of further meetings with people. I haven't seen a film in Cannes for about three or four years, which is a shame, but I just never get the chance to do it. So in a typical day, I could have as many as 10 meetings including dinner. Sometimes I might want to take it easy, in which case I make meetings for the afternoon and just chill in the morning. That way, I've got a chance to catch up on daily trades, which are a huge volume of stuff, make calls, and also deal with what's going on back in the office, which you can't just ignore. If the festival lasts for ten or eleven days, I'll usually try and block out day seven as a free day with no meetings and just get out of town. After a week of it, you're so exhausted that you just need a little time out to recharge the batteries.

BC: Obviously you've screened films in Cannes before in a position of selling. How did you go about organising that, and what was involved in getting a non-festival/market screening?

JO: If it's in the festival in an invited section then there's an established process you have to follow, but you also want to have market screenings. If you are just a producer without a sales agent you'll really have a tough time. You need to get some help, maybe from a publicist - they might be able to book the screenings for you. Or if you've got a sales agent, it's their job to do it but you've got to push them and be on top of it so you get the best dates, times, and cinemas. You also want to have it coincide with any publicity you're doing with your stars or your director because sometimes they're only available for a small slot. With your press agent, you've got to organise interviews, and if your film is in the official program, you've got to get it subtitled. I would say if you're there screening a film for the first time as an independent producer, get help from somebody otherwise it's going to be a major headache.

BC: Did you have any interesting experiences screening your own films or films you were involved with in Cannes?

JO: My first year we were there with "Smithereens" in Competition, this tiny film with nobody in it - nobody anyone had ever heard of anyway - but it had a lot of energy to it. This was in the old Palais which doesn't exist anymore but was a beautiful old Rococo-style building. For a neophyte, my first year in Cannes, my first year in the business, walking up the red carpet with a film in competition was magic. You know, getting the limo pick us up so we could drive 100 yards and get out again further up - it was brilliant. But I have to say the biggest thrill of that first year was going to the closing night film. I'd never been to any film festival before, let alone Cannes, and the closing night film was "E.T". It was such an amazing experience that it sent shivers down my spine.

But it doesn't always go well. We had a situation when I was selling a film... a documentary called "Pumping Iron 2: The Women". This was the sequel to "Pumping Iron", the film that discovered Arnold Schwarzenegger, and this one was about female body builders. At that point we had

quite a good reputation for working festivals and for promotional ideas, so we managed to get a lot of impetus behind the screening.

The film wasn't invited into any official category, so we booked a midnight screening in the old Palais, which [prior to its demolition] was used for the Directors' Fortnight. We brought over all seven stars of the film, who were six very gorgeous muscular women and one person who I still think was really a man. We organised a fashion show for the opening night where they modelled various items, and we did a radio promotion for the first screening with a local rock station. They did a sweepstake whereby local listeners called in and got tickets and their tickets gave them a chance in a lottery for two free trips to New York for the premiere of the film.

So it was just massively over-subscribed, the hype was incredible - this film was the film that everybody knew about. The screening was a mad house; the police had to come and bar the doors because there were so many people outside the building, but the upshot of it all was we couldn't sell the film. Because we massively over-hyped it above where it sat in the market, buyers' expectations were way too high. It was an ok, interesting film but we totally screwed it up. So I learnt that in Cannes especially, you've got to make sure that you pitch your movie right. People like to 'discover' pictures there and if you're dealing with independent films, it's normally going to be a discovery, so you've got to work it so that it is a buzz film, but without overdoing it.

BC: Do you have any favourite Cannes anecdotes that you like to tell over the dinner table?

JO: Our first year at Cannes, I was there with my business partner and a friend of hers who was helping us out. We had rented a one-room apartment with a balcony overlooking part of the Croisette, for use as our office and also to sleep in. So every morning at eight o'clock we had to wake up, literally fold our beds away and stick them behind the curtain, then bring out all the posters and display materials for our office. During a meeting one day I noticed a whole pile of dirty underwear in the corner of our office (not mine I have to say) which the women had failed to remove. A little embarrassing, but Cannes is just a series of little skirmishes and battles that most of the time you get to win, but sometimes you don't.

BC: Have you ever had any memorable encounters with a big star in Cannes?

JO: I remember meeting Clint Eastwood one year at the Hotel du Cap. It's a very exclusive hotel - it's so exclusive that they only accept cash or travellers cheques. No credit cards, no personal cheques, but the big stars and big studio bosses stay out there. Punters like me can get in for lunch or dinner and I was invited by somebody who was staying there, and at a table close by was Clint Eastwood. It was actually great because at the Hotel du Cap, regardless of what you're wearing, you could be anybody. You could be a famous producer or financier or you could be a complete nothing, just someone who managed to squeeze in somewhere. But I managed to have a really good conversation with Eastwood who was very open and I explained what we'd been doing and he was very interested. So that was great.

BC: Do you have any favourite places to eat in Cannes?

JO: Unfortunately some of them have changed. You've probably heard about an old place called the Petit Carlton, which is now no longer, which is a shame [Ed - now resurrected!]. Now the late-night hang-out for the impoverished is the Petit Majestic, which is just behind the Grand Hotel. It actually caused me to no longer stay at the Grand Hotel - the noise was so great there at four o'clock in the morning I had to move.

I like to have lunch on the beach if the weather's good as they have these great restaurants that are set out directly on the beach. The food is relatively simple, but it's good enough and it's surprising how quickly a bottle of chilled rosé slips down. There's a beach restaurant called the Cannes Beach which I've just always been going to, which is great. In town, there's a restaurant called La Cave which is also good. Out of town, down the road in La Napoule is a beach restaurant called the Le Sweet which has great food and is a good place to escape to. To be honest, I think that the food in Cannes is overrated and very expensive. You can eat in London or New York or Berlin better than in Cannes, definitely.

BC: You touched a little on networking/socialising there when you mentioned the Petit Majestic. Do you have any other favourite venues in Cannes?

JO: I liked the old Carlton, which is where I used to stay. Even though it was very brash I preferred it to the Majestic. The other hotels... none particularly, but there's a place called Hotel Mondial which is a three-star hotel I used to stay in years ago which is nice, but for hanging out and networking it is the Carlton, it is the Majestic, but the terrace of the Grand Hotel is also a favourite of mine. The Grand Hotel is an old, not very impressive, but very French hotel. It's set back from the Croisette behind a little green and has a nice big terrace. It's calm and the waiters there have been there forever and they're rather eccentric. So that's a nice place and quite a few independent film folk hang out there. The Palais itself, the conference centre, is a pretty gruesome building. They call it "The Bunker" and it's a concrete monstrosity. There are loads of offices inside, but I try and avoid it as much as I can.

BC: Do you have any advice for future Cannes virgins?

JO: If you've got a finished film, there's a certain procedure; if you're trying to set up a movie, then it's about making meetings and it's much better to make your connections ahead of time. The presentation... the email that arrives on your computer, one gets so many that you've got to make it different, make it exciting. Use your connections, use your lawyer, use people you know to get those meetings and then when you get to Cannes, make sure you

figure out the lie of the land. It's a good idea to spend the first day just going everywhere and making sure you know where everything is. In fact, probably before you get there you'll want to get someone who's been there before who'll spend the time with you just to set it all out for you. There are also various pavilions that are set up just for this event on the Croisette - they're like big tents with little offices in them. And there's an American Pavilion, and a British Pavilion, and a Canadian Pavilion and these are really good places to hang out. They usually have a less-expensive little bar or a place where you can get a croissant, and lots of like-minded people will be there. It's easy to network and those are really quite good.

Another thing that's emerged in recent years is the protocol of mobile telephone usage - in a place like Cannes, a mobile is indispensable because you can never find anybody. So the thing to do is to rent a mobile locally otherwise the phone bill is going to be very expensive. If you do, make sure you know your number in advance and let people know your local number, or which number to contact you on if you're bringing your own mobile ahead of time. Then whenever you're having a meeting, agree in advance as to what the protocol is, whether or not you want to have your mobiles on or off during the meeting.

Bill Stephens
Film Sales & Marketing Consultant
Nexus

Before setting up Nexus, Bill Stephens was Director of Sales for Renaissance Films where he was one of six equity directors who re-financed and re-launched the company based in London. Prior to that, he was Director of International Sales and Marketing at Film Four, Channel Four's vertically integrated film arm.

During his career Bill has been responsible for the successful sales and marketing campaigns for films such as Mike Leigh's "Naked" and "Life Is Sweet", Ken Loach's "Riff Raff" and "Raining Stones", Danny Boyle's "Shallow Grave" and "Trainspotting", Bille August's "Best Intentions", Shekar Kapur's "Bandit Queen", and David Leland's "Wish You Were Here". Under his directorship of the sales division at Film Four, the company won every major award at The Cannes Film Festival between 1987 and 1998.

Bill has been marketing and selling films actively since 1981 before which he was in the UK film distribution business for 10 years with Walt Disney Productions, Sunn Classic Productions and Jensen Farley Pictures.

BC: When did you lose your 'Cannes virginity' and what were your impressions of the festival?

BS: I went to Cannes the first time in 1982... that was my first visit of any sort and it was a bit of a shock! If you're interested in movies, it's something you've seen... you know what it is, but I think you disassociate the glitz from the business. The glitz is what they show you on the TV programmes... you know, the Barry Normans, the Jonathan Rosses [UK film critics] running around the Croisette with all the stars and the directors, the red carpet and the premieres etc. It was still very exciting... I think it must be for everybody the first time they go. It's a big thrill because you're finally there, it's a huge eye-opener, and you cannot imagine what you're in for but you soon find out!

BC: So how did you find the city itself?

BS: Expensive... it was scarily expensive. When I first went it was as part of an American company, and I think a lot of the Americans don't understand that there's anything behind the Croisette. Everything was Mougins [Le Moulin de] dinners, Croisette bars, the Carlton, the Majestic, you know, doing the sort of typically over the top expense account thing. I was horrified by the costs, it was just extraordinary. Even in those days... 1982... it was about

£5 for a cup of coffee on the Carlton Terrace; it's probably closer to £10 now. It wasn't until after a few visits that I realised you could find very reasonable places to eat and drink.

So my first impression was, "This is hellishly expensive," but it was great to be there. You're a part of this huge buzz, and in those days it was bigger on the beach, the cameras... basically lots of paparazzi trying to get pictures of women in various stages of undress! Young girls would come from all over Europe, trying to be starlets or to hopefully be discovered. I'm not sure it's the same these days... maybe I just don't notice anymore; but it was all very exciting back then.

BC: It is quite common in independent film circles to hear the term "sales agent" used, but many people don't actually know what the job entails. Could you provide a bit of background on the role of a sales agent, particularly in relation to a festival like Cannes?

BS: A sales agent's job is essentially to represent films on behalf of independent producers or financiers because of their 'insider' knowledge of the players and the deals. Sales agents have a pretty poor reputation, in general. Producers are very disparaging about certain sales agents and you often have to "prove yourself" because everybody thinks you are on the make, you know... "sales agents don't earn their money, they simply sell something, take their commission and go home." I think when I die I will have emblazoned on my tombstone: "If the film sold well it was because it was a good film. If it sold badly, or not at all, it was because

I was a lousy sales agent!" You can't win! There's a lot of work involved in marketing films effectively, a lot of 'before and after'. You represent the film on every level. You're taking it from the point of sealing a deal with the producer or financier... let's say producer because basically they represent the front-end... you're taking the film through it's entire build, meaning the marketing build. You're creating materials like show reels, posters, flyers, stills, publicity, press packs, whatever it is, you're taking the whole thing and building an image for that film.

You then take it out into the marketplace, tailoring every move to the type of project it is. And every film is different. You try and find the right buyers and that's about getting information to those people. What should be remembered, and producers often forget this, is that we're not marketing to the public, we're marketing to buyers. That's our target audience, so when we create posters, when we create flyers, when we create anything, it's done with those guys in mind. Not the guy in the cinema, that's a different game, that's done by the distributors.

So we build a profile, a campaign, for the film and get the details to our contacts in whatever method that one uses. It could be mail-outs, it could be emails, it could be letters, it could be CDs, it could be DVDs, it could be anything you want that gets their attention. You've then started marketing the film to those buyers, and we'll talk just in terms of Cannes... Cannes is two distinct and very separate things: it's a festival and it's a market. The festival is an entirely different game to what people are doing in the market. The whole affair is around 12 days long, but in reality, the market could and should be much shorter. It should be say, a week instead of almost two weeks as with the festival. Basically, you're screening the film to the buyer in whatever way that's best for the film. The festival clearly is the most effective way to do it because the film gets a massive profile, it gets wide coverage from the world's press which can be very helpful, but it can equally be very damaging. If you're in the market, it's a much harder game because it can be difficult to get noticed. Buyers are of course watching the market screenings but the impact is very different. So you try to get your film into either Competition, Un Certain Regard, Directors' Fortnight, Critics' Week... any one of those gets massive attention on a daily basis.

If your project does make an official section, you've got about three days in Cannes per film to make a hit for yourself, and three days to make the optimum sales. If they love it, it goes crazy; if they don't, nobody even looks at you, and a film can be destroyed like that. A producer will want to be in Cannes... they all want to be in Cannes! Great, if you've got the right product for it, but just to be in Cannes for Cannes' sake can be as destructive as it can be successful. I've had both ends of that scale. I've even been involved with successful films that were ultimately a box office failure... an example was "The Best Intentions", the Bille August film for which we won the Palme d'Or and the Best Actress award in 1992. The Palme d'Or... it was the worst thing

that could have happened to us. We won, but the press didn't want us to win, so all the critics were saying, "If you want to see a boring Swedish film, this is the one to go and see." And as a result, the film didn't take a penny, anywhere in the world. So that was an example of a film that failed by succeeding. Had "The Player" or "Howard's End" [also in competition that year] won, and we just won the Best Actress award, we'd probably have been much more successful on release than we were. The support would have been more positive.

So sometimes you can go there, you get a film in, nobody pays attention - that's the worst thing that can happen, or you can get too much attention, as in this case, and the film just doesn't succeed. But essentially the sales agent's job is: "Here's my film, get attention for it, and sell the hell out of it." Then the other part of the role kicks in: doing the deals, the licensing, chasing the money, chasing the release dates, ensuring that the job is done properly, the proper title is used, the credit blocks are according to contract, that the right amount of money is spent on releasing the film, and then you have to collect the money if it makes it. So it's a whole strategy... it's a full-service agency deal. It isn't about, "Here's a movie, get the movie, take the commission, run home." You've got to work very hard to get your films noticed. From the moment you start building a marketing profile for the picture, to the moment it's released and you're out there collecting the money, there's a whole madness that goes with it. So, yes, sales agents earn their commission.

BC: These days, how far ahead, and what sort of preparation do you do for Cannes?

BS: Well, depending on which bit you're involved in, it probably begins back in November, or thereabouts, because the festival sections start looking at films around that time. You then have between November and, probably to be safe, the beginning of April, to get your films seen by whichever section you are after. It's a highly political thing because each of the different sections are not all close mates... everything has a pecking order and you have to adhere to that pecking order to do it right. It's highly political. That's the festival aspect of it and that involves an expensive build up. The costs start when you are invited to participate and very often they don't accept you immediately. They'll say: "We can't tell you now... you'll have to wait, we'll let you know". This is a horrendous time because you don't want to start spending unnecessarily on work that you will never use. Then suddenly you get the call, six weeks before the start of Cannes and all hell breaks loose because not only do you have to subtitle prints of the film in French, you have to hire publicists, you have to get hotel rooms, you have to make sure that the director and artists are available and pay for them to get there, and so on. Cannes is a hugely expensive thing to be involved with, particularly the Competition. The festival itself doesn't pay for very much: three night's accommodation for the director and the two leading artists, that's it. No flights, no per diem, nothing. So anything that you do for the artists - and very few actors will fly anything

less than first class - you have to pay for it out of the budget agreed with the producers. So you have to build a budget in keeping with the size of the film. Being a sales agent is a 'deep pockets' business because you've got to cash-flow all of these items... you'll recoup it from the sales made, but if you don't make the sales, you don't recoup the money!

If you're just in the Market section which is the screenings in the Riviera, or on the Rue d'Antibes, matters are very different because it's not dissimilar to the American Film Market or MIFED... you simply book a screening room, take an ad in a daily or a 'bumper', invite the buyers and people come or they don't. There's not the huge attendance expenses involved, there's not the whole build up involved, you probably don't need publicists, you don't have to have parties etc... but of course, you can if you want.

BC: How does a typical day pan out for you these days in Cannes?

BS: It's just meetings, meetings, meetings! It's a very long day and Cannes is a very long festival, it is extremely debilitating. You begin early... let's imagine you get up at 7am, you've probably got a breakfast, you're probably meeting someone at breakfast because there are only so many half hours in the day, or maybe you have staff meetings. So you have a breakfast at, let's say, 8am, you're in the office probably by quarter to nine. At nine o'clock the meetings start on the button. Depending on what sort of films you've got... if you've got films no-one wants it's probably not so difficult, but if you have a film that everybody's after or a slate of films that buyers are after, you are having a meeting every half an hour until around 1pm. Then with any luck, you get a break to go out for a while, but probably with a buyer or a producer. You get to leave the hotel or the stand, to eat either on the beach or you grab a sandwich somewhere, or you've got an official luncheon with someone. Back again, 2.30pm to do the whole thing again... half-hours. It can finish any time, but let's say around 6pm.

If you've got an official screening to attend, you've then got to run like crazy to get yourself dressed up because you've got to put on a tux every time you go to one of the main screenings. If you're not going to the screenings, the chances are you've got an official drinks 'do'... somebody's always having a cocktail party! Then the chances are, you've got a dinner, either official or semi-formal, with somebody. Following that, if you're not attending a film party, there's that 'thing' everybody gets into, the networking that happens after screenings and after dinner, where people sit around at the various bars, such as the Petit Majestic. In the early days of going to Cannes you probably do it until three or four in the morning, go to bed, then you're back up at seven! Strictly for the young in my opinion! So the days are very long.

I think people have a vision of, "Oh, they're all sitting around drinking gin and tonics and thoroughly enjoying themselves and getting a nice tan." For a sales agent, that just doesn't happen. You're sitting in a hotel room or an office or a villa or whatever it is, just pitching to the buyers who come and see you. Usually you know the buyers - these are people you've dealt with for years - they come around, they want to know what you've got or have coming, when are you screening and so on. The idea is that they come in, see you, collect the news, leave, see the screenings, come back, and hopefully, do the deals. It's very busy at the beginning, hopefully you're even busier at the end, but that's only a result of whether the marketing and the film has worked or not.

So the day is a conglomeration of half-hour meetings, breakfasts, lunches, dinners, screenings, and then 'network drinking'. The Petit Majestic thing is seen as a bit of a, "It's the Brits getting pissed in Cannes," but it has its importance in terms of networking, particularly meeting new independent producers, because that's where they are. They're not in the Carlton - they can't afford it. You get to meet one person who introduces you to someone else etc... it's a great networking place.

So the day is long and there are 12 of them. I don't do as much of the evening thing anymore. I'm at the age where I can't handle it... I can't do that and still get up and do a whole day's work, so something has to give.

BC: Is it common for sales agents to listen to pitches from producers in Cannes, either for projects in development or completed films?

BS: I actually try and put producers off that, for a number of different reasons. Firstly, a lot of producers from Britain go and see British sales agents. Why? They're all here. It's better to meet with a sales agent in June or July when they're not as busy - you might as well see them when they're quiet and you've got their whole attention. I try and advise producers not to do this at festivals or markets. If you are talking to a large company where they've got dedicated acquisitions people, it's probably fine because the acquisitions people sit with the producers and talk about projects, and get pitched at, leaving the sales agents to doing their selling. But if it's a small company, it's quite likely that the people who do the acquisitions are also the sellers. They haven't got the time. They're totally focussed on what they've got to sell: "These are my movies, this is what I've got to sell now, I haven't got time to talk to you and even if I have, I'm looking over your shoulder to see who's walking in the door."

It's far better to either arrange to see them before you come down, although the pre-market time can be equally busy in many cases. So it's best to think logically about when a sales agent will be the least busy. They're back from the AFM in March, so probably the whole of March they're free. They're probably also free for most of June and July. Once the 'selling' year starts, the whole marketing focus starts, most haven't got any time to give you at these events.

So actually, I think Cannes offices are the worst possible places for sales agents to hear pitches. The drinks things are different because at those events, sales agents tend to be a bit more relaxed and even though they are looking around the room trying to figure out who they need to speak to, they're away from the cliff face. If you want to see foreign companies, that's fine, but wanting to see people from your own country... that's crazy! So my advice would be: don't do it there, they're not really listening, not as much as they would be when you see them at home.

BC: Have you had any memorable pitches either at Cannes or outside of the festival; memorable for the right or the wrong reasons?

BS: I have heard some good ones, but mostly they are too apologetic. Not many people rehearse their pitch. They would do well to stand in front of a mirror and talk to themselves at home about their pitch because the apologetic approach is a bit daft given the importance of the presentation. It has to be sold to me, because I'm going to have to sell it to someone else. So it's important that you convince me... I'm feeding off the pitcher, so how can I get excited about it if they spend the whole time apologising for one element or another?

Because of the kind of background I've had... at Film Four etc, we had a commissioning structure and we didn't pick up many third party projects so pitches weren't high on my list of things to listen to. We were really only representing Film Four projects. People didn't pitch me because they knew we didn't really acquire. Similarly at Renaissance, we had acquisitions people, so I've never really devoted a huge amount of time to this. But my experience of the ones I've heard, and there've been many good ones, is that an awful lot of people are too apologetic and not enough rehearsing done.

Actually, a very important word for producers is: HOMEWORK. Do your homework on almost every level; your pitch and who you're going to pitch to, because there's no use seeing every sales agent as some of them simply don't handle your kind of project. If you've got an art house project showing it to someone who handles vampire movies is completely absurd. You've just wasted an hour of your time, and theirs. You should go through the bumper editions [of the trade magazines] at any of the markets. They've got every sales agent in them, with all the projects they're handling. You can tell what sort of films they specialise in. You've got the people, what they selling, who to approach, phone numbers, all the rest of it. But very few people do this kind of homework. They would be far better off saying to themselves "OK, I'm going to Cannes, I do want to see these people. I'm British, so I don't want to see the Brits, so what I'll do is concentrate on the Americans. So I'll get 10 American companies, and I research those guys, and I know what they sell, so when I meet them I'm able to talk about their existing catalogue." Sales agents are naturally impressed if you recognise that they've done something you approve of. Do your homework on them, know what they sell, know what their successes have been, and don't talk too much about their failures! Then pitch your movie with confidence, and really learn the pitch, learn what it is you're talking about. Don't just go in with

a bunch of, "This is going to be the best film ever made. This is a kind of cross between "Gone With The Wind" and "Spiderman"." They really don't want to hear that kind of stuff. They just want to hear about this film - they don't want it compared to anything. So, homework... a big word.

BC: Assuming you had formed a relationship with a producer and you were going to take their film to Cannes, what sort of materials would you have expected them to produce for you?

BS: Actually, none in terms of marketing. A lot of new producers think they need to produce posters and stuff. They don't because that's really the sales agent's job. As I said earlier, the sales agent is marketing to the buyer. It's a very particular kind of marketing and it's not creating a film poster in the same way as a distributor does. What you need is all the background information, you know, the credit block content, what are your arrangements with your artists, who's above whom, above titles, below titles, left of titles, who's on the front-end credits of the film itself. All the stuff which is background, the information that the sales agent needs to feed from to create their materials. It's extremely important. Many people forget things like music clearances... has this been dealt with? All of this background information should be provided to the sales agent in a form that is easily legible, in a file... "Here's my credit block, this is the music, these are the clearances, what you can do with this, what you can't," all of that is essential information.

Another thing that is terribly important for new producers, and I'm sure they've all probably had this beaten into them... is STILLS. Very few people think enough about stills. You can never have too many stills, or at least, too many of the right stills. And you need to hire a stills photographer for the production, not your brother-in-law with a camera! Other important things... unit publicity work, EPKs (electronic press kits]... fantastically important nowadays. Artists can't travel as much as they used to so you need EPKs. It's all those things and it's not a big secret - you've only got to ask a seasoned producer, "Give me three things that I should have ready?" And they'll usually say, "Stills, unit publicity, and credits." So, it's information that the sales agent will use. They don't want you second-guessing them. They don't want you producing a poster, producing a trailer, producing a show reel, because all of those things are generally done wrong... in the nicest possible way! Agents know what their buyers need. So information is the key. Leave the rest to them.

BC: Do you have a memorable Cannes anecdote you like to recount?

BS: I can't think of anything wildly memorable... there have been some great moments, and I've had some enormous fun, but they tend to be part of an overall... like the "Trainspotting" party, a fabulous experience, endlessly tiring doing it, but when it happened and it was such a huge success... that was great.

BC: Have you had any interesting encounters with a big celebrity in Cannes?

BS: A couple of years ago I was on one of the boats... I don't know whether it was the Soho House boat or someone's boat... I was having drinks and I recognised this actor, who's name has completely escaped me now... an English actor. I'd seen him on some TV commercials, but mostly I knew him from the fact that we'd done a film at Film Four called "True Blue", which was about the [Oxford vs Cambridge] Boat Race and he was in the Oxford boat. I recognised the actor, and the main reason I recognised him was because a few months before, a Japanese guy had brought me a tape of a movie that this actor was in, and he said, "Would I look at this for representation of the film?" I watched the movie and there was this same actor, speaking fluent Japanese and I thought, "This English guy's amazing, he speaks fluent Japanese!" So I saw him standing there and I went over to him, introduced myself and said, "I saw this film of yours recently. A couple of months ago, this Japanese guy brought me..." And he went, "Oh yeah," and reeled off the title. And from right out from behind him steps... Salma Heyak (who I'm a huge fan of - this is a gorgeous woman!). She steps in, puts her arm in his and says, "You saw that movie?" And I went... I just blanked. I said, "Yeah..." thinking, "What the hell's she doing with him?" They were an item... this was pre Ed Norton. We talked about this movie for about 10 or 15 minutes and I'm gazing at, what to me was one of the most gorgeous women in the world, standing with a glass of champagne in my hand thinking, "Not in my wildest dreams did I think I'd be talking to her" because I couldn't have met her any other way. I wouldn't have walked up to her on the boat and gone, "Oh, Salma Hayek. Hi!" That completely gob-smacked me... I didn't think you could tip me over that way but she did! She was just as lovely as everything I'd imagined and I'm really thrilled about Frida and all that's happened to her since. That was a great moment.

BC: Do you have any favourite places to eat when you're in Cannes?

BS: Yeah, there are lots of wonderful places that I eat at for different kinds of reasons. You know, there's casual, there's formal... I love eating on the port or in the old town on the hill. I love going up there... there's the type of restaurants up there you'd be hard pushed to find anywhere else in the world. Also on the old port itself, the pizza place, La Pizza... that I like for totally informal eating. And next door to it is Gaston Gastounette, which is a terrific seafood restaurant; the best soupe de poisson! But mostly I'm bad at going back to places. I love moving on so I'm always looking for the next one... I don't really have places where I think, "I'm going to go back there." I like to find new ones and each year when I go, I find something different that I think, "Well, this is nice," and for that year it becomes the restaurant of choice. I found a Vietnamese restaurant a few years ago near the Martinez and it was just lovely. But generally I move on.

You certainly don't need to eat in expensive places in Cannes, and if you're not on expenses, you probably don't want to! If you go back towards the railway station, three streets behind the Rue d'Antibes, you can eat there very cheaply. I've done that as an independent a lot. You can have dinner for £10, with wine... you don't have to eat this side of the bright lights. I think a lot of people don't do enough experimenting and seeking that sort of place out, but you can eat cheaply if you want to.

BC: What about places to network/socialise, you touched on the Petit Carlton and Petit Majestic earlier?

BS: Well the Petit Carlton has gone now of course [Ed - now resurrected!], but Petit Majestic... yes, it's taken over that mantle. It's just so crowded now; it's frighteningly busy these days. I suppose somebody will find somewhere else sooner or later. I think, depending on what you're looking for... the Majestic terrace is phenomenal, but you need a mortgage to buy a drink! It really depends who you're looking for because there are a lot of people there, but for networking in terms of what we do as independents, then I think the Petit Majestic is pretty much the place.

BC: Do you have any specific advice for future 'Cannes virgins', particularly producers who are coming to try and drum up interest in their completed or in-development project?

BS: Well, I do think get yourself a sales agent... I would say that wouldn't I, but I think you save yourself enormous amounts of time. I'll give you an example... I won't name names, but it involves a producer/actor/director last year at Cannes. He'd been to see me for advice but he'd never actually said, "I want to find a sales agent." He said, "We're doing this ourselves." He clearly had a bit of money behind him, from somewhere, because he'd helped to finance the film, acted in it, directed it, and helped produce it. He was down there with the writer and a producer. They spent a fortune on fly-posting, which by the way just doesn't hit the right people... you might think it does, but what it really does is hit all the other independent producers! There's no impact with that stuff. They must have spent £25,000 to go to Cannes, getting themselves there, living there, posters, flyers... and nothing happened. The film never got sold, it never went anywhere. You're wasting time, you're wasting your time AND you're ruining the prospects for the film. Get a sales agent, if you think it is good enough.

If it isn't good enough and no sales agents want it, you've got to do that stuff yourself haven't you? But if it can be avoided, avoid it. The job of the sales agent is to put up the marketing money, to market it right and to find the right buyer to buy it. Doing it guerrilla style... you might get lucky, it might work, but the chances are it won't. Not in that high-octane environment. There's lots of money there: I mean those posters you see on the Croisette cost $50,000 or more to place and I don't even notice them these days! They're there and a lot of seasoned attendees don't even notice them. To my mind it's just vanity advertising. I wouldn't dream of buying one of those things. I did it once when I first went to Cannes, I thought this was the thing to do, and then I realised, actually, there are many more effective ways of spending marketing dollars. The posters are just part of what the public sees, which isn't the point from the agent's perspective.

So I think my advice would be: think really hard about whether you want to spend this time/money. If you engage a sales agent, you won't be excluded; you just have to make yourself a part of it along with the sales agency team. You ensure they understand that you want to be included, you really do want to be involved, you want to come along and be involved in the decision-making process. But on the other hand, that doesn't mean that you can sit and watch the sales agent do their job because that's no help to anyone. Don't pester the sales agent... once you've got one, for God's sake, trust them! Going in to their offices every two minutes and asking, "Have we sold it?" doesn't actually endear you to the people in the office. If you are green, then it's hard not to do some of these things, but I would say, asking around a bit... again, homework. I would say, ask a few people about the sales agent's reputation. If you've looked in the bumpers and you've seen the films they represent, you might know one of the existing producers. Ask the producers if this particular sales agent is any good, because if the guy says, "Don't go near them, they're terrible," you don't want to waste your time... that's another one off the list.

So I think get the guys you want, the people you feel comfortable with, trust them to do the job and then let them do that job. You can be a part of it with them, you can always be involved. They'll keep you up to date... they'll only shut you out if you become a pain! I've had producers just come and sit in the office and often I've just had to say, "I'm very sorry... go have a coffee... leave. We're dealing with your movie... there's your poster, but I just can't have you sitting here watching us like a hawk! I didn't go and watch you on the set!" You have to trust pros. As a producer you hire a cameraman, an editor, you hire a soundman, they're all pros... so is the sales agent. Hire them, trust them, let them get on with it.

Jane Wright
Head of Rights & Commercial Affairs
BBC Films

Jane joined the BBC in March 1995 and currently heads the business unit responsible for the BBC's feature film activity. Jane has worked in the film and television industry for 20 years, beginning in film distribution as director of marketing and publicity where she worked on the campaigns of over 50 films.

Jane has also been a marketing consultant for a variety of organisations, including The Museum of Modern Art (New York) and Telefilm Canada. In 1992 she became the Director of New York's annual Independent Feature Film Market, a position she held for two years. In 1994 she associate-produced "Heavy", an American independent film written and directed by James Mangold.

In 1995 Jane moved to London to work for BBC Films in marketing and film investment. She then transferred back to New York to become Vice President of Co-Productions & Sales for BBC Worldwide Americas, specialising in drama and children's programs.

BC: When did you first go to Cannes and what were your impressions of the city and the festival?

JW: I first went to Cannes in 1987 when I worked for a US distribution company. I'd been to France before and I liked the city of Cannes... it was pretty and I was excited about being there again. I can't say I loved the festival. I found it huge, I found it daunting, and I had an experience there that's been repeated almost every year. For some reason it involves the Carlton Hotel: when I go in, the lobby is always full of huge posters and they all seem to have great splashes of garish red... red dresses flying up, red blood, guns, whatever, and I go into a two-day funk thinking: "What on Earth I am doing in this business?" Because my experience of the film industry, which is 20 years this year, has been mostly in art film, I tend to find the pure exploitation side of Cannes harder to take - it throws me off every single year. That's what I most remember about my first experience - being overwhelmed by the size of the industry and how many big players there are.

BC: These days, how do you prepare ahead of Cannes for the time you will be spending there?

JW: I think anyone, no matter what they're doing, needs to prepare a lot. In a sense, you are never prepared enough because our daily work lives are so busy. My own preparations have changed over the years. I first went to Cannes as part of an American distribution company, subsequently went to Cannes when I worked for the IFP [Independent Feature Project] as the Director of the Independent Feature Film Market... both had different purposes so therefore a different set of preparations. At BBC Films I'm part of an organisation that's a film financier, but we also have rights to sell, so I need to be prepared on both sides. I've also found myself at Cannes actually selling a slate of films when I was the Acting CEO at a London sales company, now called The Works.

So the preparation for each organisation and each function differs but basically, you have to know in each case what your product is and what you hope to achieve. You need to have read everything - you can't sell a project you haven't read, you can't sell a film you haven't seen. You really need to be in the know, and not just about the product you have, but how it relates to associated films, what's happened to that filmmaker in the past, and what's coming up. It's the extraneous information which is unending, but you have to gather what information and material you think is the most pertinent.

BC: So how does a typical day in Cannes during the festival tend to pan out for you?

JW: Generally I'm aware of having to get up very early. I usually start by looking through the day's activities and thinking about what I'm going to wear, particularly whether I am

going to get a chance to go back to the hotel before an evening event. I'll also ensure that I have the correct materials I'll need for the day and know whom I'm meeting for breakfast. In my job at BBC Films, I go into the office and read the trades. Ideally I like to see the 8.30 movie at the Palais at least every other day. I find that because of meetings that have been set up, it's often very hard for me to get to festival films and it's so depressing if I get through Cannes without seeing a single film. So I think it's important for people like myself who don't have to see films for acquisition purposes, to try to see movies anyway. It helps us keep a sense of being in the film business.

As the morning progresses, my life becomes dictated by new circumstances... by my boss and by my colleagues, as much as by my pre-set objectives. So I have meetings, meetings, meetings, meetings, lunches, dinners, meetings, meetings, and then maybe a cocktail party and another event afterwards where you're again meant to meet more people or be seen.

BC: 8.30 screenings... that's 8.30 in the morning, right?

JW: [smiles] Yes, but all the good acquisitions people I know are having 7.30am meetings with their teams because that's the best time for them to get organised to see all the movies they need to cover. So 'early to rise, late to bed' is the rule of Cannes.

BC: In your current capacity at BBC Films, are you hearing people pitch concepts or films requiring funding?

JW: No, that's not what my job is so I rarely hear pitches. In fact, I tend to avoid them. Certainly David Thompson, who I work for, does get pitched to at meetings, and our development team are there and hear pitches all day long.

My job involves pitching our projects to other financiers. I'm trying to meet with the key decision-makers at the major US distributors, sales agents and other funding bodies. Because I'm pitching BBC Films' projects, I'm discussing films of a pedigree that are already part funded which makes it much easier.

BC: Cannes is known largely as a finished product market. In your experience, both with BBC Films and prior to that, is it common for much in the way of development deals to be done during the festival?

JW: I think that there's a lot of it happening, but I would have to say that I think that most of the financing deals that are done are at an organisational level. I think it's very tough for independent producers who go there to try to finance their films from scratch.

The financing people are there - for example sales agents - but their primary focus is to sell. There are circumstances where they might listen to a pitch but they'll usually take the material back home for consideration. It's most likely that the deal isn't going to be tied up in Cannes. At an 'organisational level' you find that a lot of financing activity happens. A project will already be set up with one financier who then can bring others on board at Cannes.

BC: Again, in your experience with BBC Films or before that, if you were going to discuss projects in development, are there specific things that you are looking for the producer to show you?

JW: Something that sounds realistic and reasonably fully-formed even if only an idea. "I have a script, it's been written by so and so, we want to do it this year, here's why I think it's a fantastic property, I have interest from so and so." You don't have to have complete cast certainty but you do need to know who you want to cast in the main roles. What's important to avoid is pitching something that's not fully-formed, or displaying complete ignorance about the three films already out in the market place that are just like yours. Also avoid saying something which is plainly untrue. For instances, at BBC Films if we've got a particular actor already lined up in two of our movies, saying your film is going next month with this actor will not impress us. You need a compelling story and the elements you're attaching to it should be realistic.

BC: Do you have a memorable anecdote that you like to tell over the dinner table when the topic of Cannes emerges in the conversation?

JW: I think one of the nicest experiences for me was when my husband had his very first production, "Heavy", in the Directors' Fortnight, and that was lovely because we felt treated well. I had other work to do there but that experience on the filmmaking side of the business meant it was a fun year rather than hard work. That was great.

BC: Do you have any favourite places that you like to eat when you're in Cannes?

JW: Yes, Le Petite Lardon. I can't remember the street name, but I know exactly where it is. I just love it. It's a tiny little restaurant with a lovely atmosphere and I go there a lot. I have eaten at some of the finer restaurants outside of Cannes like Le Colum d'Or and Moulin des Mougins, but they are definitely not my regular haunts.

BC: Do you have any favourite socialising/networking venues in Cannes?

JW: I love the BBC Films party. That's very corporate I know, but I love our events - they're great because it does feel like family and you invite people you haven't seen for a long time. Of course the Petit Carlton is sadly missed [Ed - now resurrected!], and Le Petit Majestic is the number two. You also go to the bar at the Majestic hotel, and you go to the Carlton... but you know I have a problem with that! I'm kidding... the Carlton Terrace is absolutely fine, but it's really the parties and late night Petit Majestic that are my favourites.

BC: Lastly, do you have any specific advice for future Cannes virgins, particularly producers who are looking to sell their film in Cannes?

JW: Get a map before you go. Seriously, try to understand the layout and try to figure out where things are before you get there. Have a realistic set of expectations: worst case scenario, you go to see Cannes and only see how it operates; best case, your film gets financed. But you've got to be realistic about people's time constraints, and where you sit in the pecking order. People might see that as a little cynical and I don't mean it that way, but it's realistic. Everybody feels much the same way - you're just trying to do your own little thing which is going to be eventually a very small part of this big industry. And yes, of course we all hope we'll have hit films, whether we're with an organisation, or whether we're individuals, but if you're not approaching it with some degree of humility, then you can get psychologically crushed. That's why I believe building a realistic set of expectations for yourself is important.

A lot of people also get really upset if they're not invited to loads of parties or if they can't get tickets to the right parties. Once you've been there enough times, you can not go but tell people you did! They won't know because ultimately, it really doesn't make any difference. I think there's too much youthful anxiety over what kind of parties you can get into. Sometimes, going home and getting a decent night's sleep is actually far more worthwhile. Likewise, ending up at the Petit Majestic and just having fun can be a lot better than having tried to claw your way into some famous distributor party and not made it, where you're just going to end up feeling miserable.

Sarah McKenzie

Head of Marketing and Events,
UK Film Council

The Film Council was set up to work with the public and private sector to make film an essential part of the UK's creative economy and to create the environment for a sustainable and vibrant film culture. The Film Council aims to nurture excellence and innovation in the UK industry, and to promote innovation, diversity and social inclusion.

BC: When did you first lose your 'Cannes virginity' and what were your first impressions of the city and the festival?

SM: 1994. I went as Director of the Birmingham International Film and TV Festival (BIFTV) having been in post for just two weeks! The Festival was incredibly exciting, utterly confusing and it took me two days to see a film,

having finally deciphered the Festivals bizarre ticket allocation system.

'94 had a fantastic programme, which included "Bandit Queen" and "Pulp Fiction". The latter had its British premiere at the BIFTV and "Bandit Queen" headed the BIFTV's South Asian Programme. Cannes has its own aura and language. I soon learned that competition and other major films are not referred to by name, but by director. Many of the marketing ploys were totally outrageous, but understandable given that everyone is trying to make their film 'must-see' and 'must-buy'

The town and Croissette looked fantastic – buzzing at all hours, parties on the beach and all over town - people in bars practically all night long.

BC: Where is the Film Council usually based in Cannes during the festival?

SM: For the last two years at the Grand Hotel Residence.

BC: What services does the Film Council offer British filmmakers in Cannes?

SM: Traditionally the Film Council prioritises Cannes to develop European relationships and to promote the UK as a centre for international production. However, in 2002 we developed a wider range of initiatives to support the UK industry.

BC: In the past, has there been anything that British filmmakers expected you to offer them in Cannes, but in reality you didn't/ don't offer?

SM: In the first two years of the Film Council's existence it had to focus on international work at Cannes, so some filmmakers may have expected the organisation to be more proactive on their behalf.

BC: What does a typical day consist of for you in Cannes during the festival?

SM: Working out of the Film Council office to ensure the smooth running of activities we are producing such as seminars, lunches and receptions. Meeting with international counterparts to liaise over the production of events and marketing initiatives the BFC [British Film Commission] is producing throughout the year internationally.

BC: What's your best Cannes anecdote?

SM: Too personal to disclose!

BC: What's your best 'encounter with a famous person' story?

SM: Stalling my Peugeot 106 to avoid running Clint Eastwood over as he walked in front of the car!

BC: What are your favourite place(s) to eat in Cannes?

SM: On a budget, La Pizza down by the bus station, the Petit Majestic, Stromboli's, and with a little more money, Le Caveau.

BC: What are your favourite Cannes socialising/networking venue(s)?

SM: The Pavilions, parties (fight to get invites!!), the Rue d'Antibes, and the Croissette.

BC: Do you have any advice for future Cannes virgins (particularly first-time/independent producers coming to the festival looking to sell their film)?

SM: Preparation is essential. Research which international buyers regularly attend Cannes; check out the type of product they buy; match your film to the right buyers; try to meet with them - be persistent and tenacious; have a good oral pitch and if appropriate copies of the film on DVD or video in the appropriate territory formats.

Lise Corriveau

Manager, Festivals & Markets, International Development & Promotion Department,
Telefilm Canada

Telefilm Canada is a federal cultural agency dedicated primarily to the development and promotion of the Canadian film, television, new media and music industries. Telefilm Canada reports to the Department of Canadian Heritage.
The Corporation provides financial assistance and strategic leverage to the industry in producing high-quality works – e.g. feature films, drama series, documentaries, children's programming, variety shows and new media products - that reflect Canadian society, including its linguistic duality and cultural diversity.

BC: When did you first lose your 'Cannes virginity' and what were your first impressions of the city and the festival?

LC: I first attended the Cannes Film Festival in 1997 and was overwhelmed by the sheer size of it. It is a very glamorous affair and can be quite intimidating for a first-timer. Cannes is a very lovely city but becomes totally invaded during the festival and it is very hard to circulate anywhere close to the Croisette.

BC: Where is the Telefilm Canada usually based in Cannes during the festival? Is this always the same place or does it vary form year to year?

LC: Telefilm Canada has been attending the Cannes Film Festival for over 20 years and various venues have been tried depending on the events taking place. The year 2002 proved to be a turning point for the Canadian presence. Telefilm Canada joined the International Village and along with provincial agencies, federal departments, the producers association and a few sponsors, we launched the Canada Pavilion. And since then we have expanded our presence as well as out activities at the Festival.

BC: What services does the Telefilm Canada offer Canadian filmmakers in Cannes?

LC: We coordinate the markets registrations for the Canadian companies participating in the Marché du Film. A series of networking events, such as breakfast meetings and other small gatherings are also organized within the Canada Pavilion in order to assist the Canadian producers to develop their international contacts. We also try to connect various producers looking for co-productions partners. We are also there to act as advisers and fixers to all the Canadian participants.

BC: In the past, has there been anything that Canadian filmmakers expected you to offer them in Cannes, but in reality you don't offer?

LC: Since Canada has been participating for so long, we have constantly reviewed our services and try to adjust from year to year.

BC: What does a typical day consist of for you in Cannes during the festival?

LC: Usually my days starts around 8.30am and ends around midnight. Since I coordinate the Canada Pavilion operations, you have to be ready to react to all sorts of demands from our own industry as well as foreign partners seeking information on the Canadian industry.

BC: What is/are your favourite place(s) to eat in Cannes?

LC: I have quite a few that I like, but I have one in particular that is off the beaten track, off the tourist circuit. I really like to go there to get away from the madness of what the festival is. It is more of a local spot and I would rather keep it to myself. It is my hideaway.

BC: What is/are your favourite Cannes socialising/networking venue(s)?

LC: The Canada Pavilion being a central point of all of our operations brings in many visitors and I am lucky

to have the chance to meet very interesting and dynamic people. It is very stimulating. You really get a feel of what the industry is about.

BC: Do you have any advice for future Cannes virgins, particularly first time producers coming to the festival looking to sell their film?

LC: Before you arrive at the festival, you have to be prepared. You have to know why you are attending the festival and set some goals. Some leg-work prior to their arrival is also essential. You have to start planning your meetings at least a month ahead of the event. It is very hard to pin down people sometimes and it is best and easier if early contact has been undertaken.

I would also recommend that if you are looking for a partner, you best learn how to make a good pitch. Have good promo materials ready.

Kim Dalton
Chief Executive Officer,
Australian Film Commission

The Australian Film Commission is the Australian Government's agency for supporting the development of film, television and interactive digital media projects and their creators, particularly in the independent sector. The AFC provides resources, mainly in the form of finance and information, to people, projects, organisations and events.

BC: When did you first lose your 'Cannes virginity' and what were your first impressions of the city and the festival?

KD: My first brush with Cannes the town was in the late 1980s as an independent producer attending MIP, the annual television market held during April. I had just finished producing a four hour mini-series and was in the early stages of devel-

opment on another mini-series. The town itself was and still remains for me all these years and many festivals and markets later, slightly unreal. Provincial France but foreigners, particularly Americans, everywhere the ear can hear, working and doing deals, not on holidays. The only place to escape - and I try to get there every time - is up the hill in the surrounds of the old church.

My first film festival came quite a few years later when I was working for Beyond Films as an acquisitions executive. Attending Cannes is always a reminder - particularly for Australians - that our industry is but a tiny part of an enormous global industry overwhelmingly dominated by the US. It's exhilarating when you're with a film that for a day or two is noticed and that people want to see and buy. And just plain hard work most of the rest of the time.

BC: Where is the AFC usually based in Cannes during the festival? Is this always the same place or does it vary form year to year?

KD: The AFC has been based at the same place now for over 15 years - in the penthouse suite in the block opposite the Noga Hilton. It's a fantastic location - one of the best in Cannes - and provides us with a really flexible space.

BC: What services does the AFC offer Australian filmmakers in Cannes?

KD: We provide what is effectively a serviced office for Australian filmmakers from which they can do business. Our office also serves as a base for representatives from other Federal and State government agencies attending Cannes. It's also the place to come for anyone wanting to find out about the Australian film industry and make contact with Australian producers. And in true Cannes style, we entertain of course! We hold several larger functions which provide opportunities to Australian filmmakers to network with international sales agents and distributors and with potential co-producers. We also hold several more intimate events where we entertain key festival directors and critics.

BC: In the past, has there been anything that Australian filmmakers expected you to offer them in Cannes, but in reality you don't offer?

KD: We try to find out from filmmakers what they need from us and within our always limited budget we attempt to provide it. For the most part we have very positive feedback about the presence in Cannes.

BC: What does a typical day consist of for you in Cannes during the festival?

KD: We open the office around 9am and unless we are having a formal lunch we keep it open through to about 6pm. During the day the AFC is involved in a range of meetings with other film agencies from around the world, foreign producers making enquiries about our co-production program, Australian producers seeking assistance or advice, representatives of festivals wanting information about upcoming productions, etc.. Usually there are several functions to attend during the day and into the evening. Getting to bed before midnight is a luxury.

BC: Do you have any advice for future Cannes virgins (particularly first time producers coming to the festival looking to sell their film)?

KD: Plan, plan, plan. Research, research, research. Remind yourself regularly that most other people are having just as difficult a time as you. Keep the expectations on all fronts down to a minimum.

the appendices

appendix i

further info

This book contains a large amount of information, but that doesn't mean you should stop here. There are many excellent resources out there that will also help you with your visit to Cannes and provide useful or interesting information about the festival.

On the Web

CFVG Online
The companion web site for "Cannes - A Festival Virgin's Guide" contains a series of useful tools and wealth of additional information. Visit the site to get the latest festival news, meet other Cannes contacts, submit your own tips, and access a range of features to help you get the most out of your visit, including:

• Festival Information – updates and the latest buzz on the next festival;

• Accommodation Exchange – free message boards to find or offer festival accommodation;

• Travel Desk – good deals on flights to Cannes;

• Restaurant Guide – the lowdown on the best places to eat in Cannes for all budgets.

• Message Boards – to share information and meet new Cannes contacts.

Cannes - A Festival Virgin's Guide Online is available at www. cannesguide.com.

Official Festival Sites

Festival de Cannes
The official festival site. Film submission rules and forms, accreditation information and contacts, plus daily coverage of festival happenings, festival history, and the complete line-up (once it is announced). www. festival-cannes.org

International Critics' Week
The official site for the International Critics Week sidebar. History and details regarding the event, and online submission forms. www. semainedelacritique.com

Directors' Fortnight
The official site for the Directors Fortnight sidebar. History, information, and submission forms. www. quinzaine-realisateurs.com

Marché du Film
All of the information about the Market and attending. You can register online or download the forms. For Market attendees, a suite of online tools is available through the site. www.cannesmarket.com

Guides & Other Useful Sites

City of Cannes
The official web site for the City of Cannes has, amongst other things, one amazingly useful feature: a fully-detailed and zoomable map of the city and surrounding area. You will need the Flash plug-in to view it. www.cannes.fr

FilmFestivals.com
Covering many film festivals including Cannes, filmfestivals.com contains a huge amount of information and

has dedicated coverage leading up to and during the event. *www.filmfestivals.com*

TravLang
Essential viewing to brush up on your French and general travel information. TravLang offers a huge range of language and travel resources including online translation dictionaries (great to practice your menu-reading skills for that Croisette business brunch!) *www.travlang.com*

The American Pavilion
The official web site for the American Pavilion at Cannes provides details of activities taking place and details of services available. Membership can be purchased online via the site ahead of the festival. www.ampav.com

UK Film Centre
Provides information and an event schedule for activities taking place in the UK Film Centre in Cannes during the festival. *www.ukfilmcentre.org.uk*

News & Media Coverage

indieWIRE's Cannes
indieWIRE reporters are on the scene in Cannes throughout the festival to provide the latest news, reviews, and interviews, with an indie bias. *www.indiewire.com*

Variety
Provides extensive coverage of the festival through their web site, although to access the content in detail you need to be a subscriber. *www.variety.com*

The Hollywood Reporter
Also provides extensive coverage of the festival in a dedicated area of their web site. Access to much of the content is for subscribers only, however of all the major trades, The Hollywood Reporter has the most free content available. *www.hollywoodreporter.com.*

Screen Daily
Coverage of the festival from an international perspective. The online offering from Screen International is now a subscription service, however the rates are reasonable and the reporting extensive. *www.screendaily.com*

recommended reading

The following books provide a great way to further explore the fascinating topic of the Cannes Film Festival and the culture and history surrounding it. All of these books and more are available from the CFVG Shop at www.cannesguide.com.

Avrich, Barry. Selling the Sizzle: The Magic and Logic of Entertainment Marketing. Maxworks Publishing Group, 2002.

Dupin, Valerie, and Karen McAulay. Eyewitness Travel Phrase Book: French. London: Dorling Kindersley, 2003.

Durie, John et al. Marketing & Selling Your Film Around The World. Los Angeles: Silman-James Press, 2000.

Gore, Chris. The Ultimate Film Festival Survival Guide (3rd Edition). Los Angeles: Lone Eagle Publishing Company, 2004.

Langer, Adam. The Film Festival Guide: For Filmmakers, Film Buffs, and Industry Professionals. Chicago: Chicago Review Press, 1998.

Stolberg, Shael. International Film Festival Guide. Festival Products, 2000.

Turan, Kenneth. Sundance to Sarajevo: Film Festivals and the World They Made. Los Angeles: University of California Press, 2003.

Walker, Stephen. King of Cannes: Madness, Mayhem and the Movies. New York: Algonquin Books, 2000.

Williams, Nicola, Steve Fallon, and Miles Roddis. Lonely Planet France. Footscray: Lonely Planet Publications, 2005.

Ebert, Roger. Two Weeks in the Midday Sun. Kansas City: Andrews McMeel Publishing, 1987.

The following books are now out of print, but if you can get your hands on a copy they're also an interesting read. Try Amazon.com or second-hand specialists like abebooks.com and abrillis.com.

Bart, Peter. Cannes: Fifty Years of Sun, Sex & Celluloid. New York: Hyperion, 1997.

Beauchamp, Cari, and Henri Béhar. Hollywood on the Riviera. New York: William Morrow & Company, 1992.

appendix ii

cannes black book

Building up a little black book of Cannes contact details can be quite a time-consuming process. Thankfully, we've made a start for you...

Official Contacts

Festival de Cannes
Association Française du Festival International du Film
3 Rue Amélie
75007 Paris
France
Tel. +33 (0)1 53 59 61 00
Fax. +33 (0)1 53 59 61 10
www.festival-cannes.org

General Enquires
festival@festival-cannes.fr

Festival Accreditation
accreditationpro@festival-cannes.fr

Market Accreditation
marketbadges@festival-cannes.fr

Press Accreditation
presse@festival-cannes.fr

Cinéfondation Enquires
cinefondation@festival-cannes.fr

Marché du Film
3 Rue Amélie
75007 Paris
France
Tel. +33 (0)1 53 59 61 30
Fax. +33 (0)1 53 59 61 50
www.cannesmarket.com

General Enquires
marketinfo@festival-cannes.fr

Market Accreditation
marketbadges@festival-cannes.fr

Producers Network
network@festival-cannes.fr

Short Film Corner
sfc@festival-cannes.fr

International Critics' Week
17 Rue des Jeûneurs
75002 Paris
France
Tel. +33 (0)1 45 08 14 54
Fax. +33 (0)1 45 08 14 55
www.semainedelacritique.com

General Enquires
lasemaine@wanadoo.fr

The Directors' Fortnight
14 Rue Alexandre Parodi
75010 Paris
France

Tel. +33 (0)1 44 89 99 99
Fax. +33 (0)1 44 89 99 60
www.quinzaine-realisateurs.com

General Enquires
infos@quinzaine-realisateurs.com

Trade Magazines

The three main trade magazines, Screen International, Variety and the Hollywood Reporter, all run local offices in Cannes during the festival. While the locations tend to be the same year on year, the phone numbers are normally different for each festival. To obtain the details for the next festival either call their head office a couple of weeks beforehand or simply pick up a copy of the magazine itself in Cannes.

Screen International
33-39 Bowling Green Lane
London, EC1R 0DA
United Kingdom
Tel. +44 20 7505 8080
www.screendaily.com

In Cannes: Carlton Intercontinental Hotel, Boulevard de la Croisette

The Hollywood Reporter
5055 Wilshire Boulevard
Los Angeles, CA 90036-4396
USA
Tel. +1 323-525-2000
Fax. +1 323-525-2377
www.hollywoodreporter.com

In Cannes: Hotel Residential

Variety
5700 Wilshire Boulevard, Suite 120
Los Angeles, CA 90036
USA
Tel. +1 323-857-6600
Fax. +1 323-857-0494
www.variety.com

In Cannes: Variety Beach Club (Pavilion), 45 Boulevard de la Croisette

indieWIRE
601 West 26th Street, Suite # 1150
New York, NY 10001
USA
Tel. +1 212-320-3710
Fax. +1 212-320-3719
www.indiewire.com

Other Key Film Markets

American Film Market
10850 Wilshire Boulevard, 9th Floor
Los Angeles, CA 90024-4311, USA
Tel. +1 310 446 1000
Fax. +1 310.446 1600
AFM2005@ifta-online.org
www.americanfilmmarket.com

Audiovisual Industry Promotion (MIFED)
c/o Fiera Milano - Piazzale Giulio Cesare
1- Palazzo Cisi
20145 Milan, Italy
Tel. +39 02 48550 279
Fax +39 02 48550 420
mifed@aip-mifed.com
www.mifed.com

European Film Market
(Berlin Film Festival)
Potsdamer Straße 5
D-10785 Berlin, Germany
Tel. +49 30 259 20 666
Fax. +49 30 259 20 699
market@berlinale.de
www.berlinale.de

International Film Festival Rotterdam
(Cinemart)
Karel Doormanstraat 278b
3012 GP Rotterdam, The Netherlands
Tel. +31 10 890 90 90
Fax. +31 10 890 90 91
cinemart@filmfestivalrotterdam.com
www.filmfestivalrotterdam.com

Toronto International Film Festival
2 Carlton Street, Suite 1600
Toronto, ON M5B 1J3, Canada
Tel. +1 416 967 7371
industry@torfilmfest.ca
www.tiffg.ca

Cafes and Restaurants

Aroma Bagel Café
22 Rue du Commandant André
Tel. 04 93 99 72 03

Asian Fast Food
55 Rue Félix Faure
Tel. 04 93 38 21 00

Astoux et Brun
25 Rue Félix Faure
Tel. 04 93 39 06 33

Au Bureau
49 Rue Félix Faure
04 93 68 56 36

Auberge Provençal
10 Rue Saint Antoine
Tel. 04 93 38 52 14

Aux Bon Enfants
80 Rue Meynadier

Aux Rich-Lieu
66 Rue Maynadier
Tel. 04 93 39 98 75

Bar des Negociants
Rue Jean Jaurès
Tel. 04 93 39 06 35

Bar du Marin
13 Rue Rouguière
Tel. 04 93 39 90 00

Bistrot Le Casanova
Rue Casanova
Tel. 04 93 38 30 06

Chick 'n' Chips
Rue Jean Jaurès

Eden Roc (Antibes)
Boulevard Kennedy
Tel. 04 93 61 39 01

Gaston Gastounette
7 Quai Saint Pierre
Tel. 04 93 39 49 44

Jonathan's Snack Bar
Place Bernard Cornut Gentille

Kiosque Gambetta
Rue Chaubaud

La Brochette de Grand-Mère
Rue d'Oran
Tel. 04 93 39 12 10

La Galette de Marie
9 Rue Bivouac Napoléon
Tel. 04 93 68 15 13

La Fringale
Rue Maynadier
Tel. 04 93 39 90 79

La Marée
Boulevard Jean Hibert
Tel. 04 92 98 03 33

La Pizza
3 Quai Saint Pierre
Tel. 04 93 39 22 56

La Piazza
9 Place Cornut Gentille
Tel. 04 92 98 60 80

La Toscana
Rue Félix Faure
Tel. 04 93 68 56 36

Le Fregate
26 Boulevard Jean Hilbert
Tel. 04 93 39 45 39

Le Jardin de Bamboo
16 Rue Macé
Tel. 04 92 98 63 06

Le Merchant Loup
17 Rue Saint Antoine
Tel. 04 93 99 06 22

Le Moulin de Mougins (Mougins)
1432 Ave Notre-Dame de Vie
Tel. 04 93 75 78 24

L'Olivier
9 Rue Rouguière
Tel. 04 93 99 44 05

McDonalds
Square Lord Brougham
Tel. 04 93 38 38 11

Neat
11 Square Mérimée
Tel. 04 93 99 29 19

New Croisette
17 Rue du Commandant André
Tel. 04 92 98 62 82

Petit Carlton
4 Place de la Gare
Tel. 04 93 39 13 97

Petit Lardon
3 Rue Batéguier
Tel. 04 93 39 06 28

Restaurant Esméralda
Rue Tony Allard
Tel. 04 92 98 18 77

Restaurant Festival
52 Boulevard de la Croisette
Tel. 04 93 28 04 81

Restaurant Tovel Beth-Din
Rue Dr Monod
Tel. 04 93 39 36 25

Subway
11 Rue Hélène Vagliano
Tel. 04 93 68 53 82

Traiteur al Charq
20 Rue Rouaze
Tel. 04 93 94 01 76

Willy's Bar
144 Rue d'Antibes
Tel. 04 93 94 12 12

Tourist Offices

Cannes Tourist Office (Palais)
Palais des Festivals et des Congrès
Esplanade Georges Pompidou
06403 Cannes
Tel. +33 4 92 99 84 22
Fax. +33 4 92 99 84 23
www.cannes.fr
(open 7 days a week)

Cannes Tourist Office (Train Station)
SNCF Station - Ground Floor
06401 Cannes
Tel. +33 4 93 99 19 77
Fax. +33 4 92 59 35 11
www.cannes.fr
(closed weekends)

Cannes Reservation
(hotel reservation service)
8 Boulevard d'Alsace
06400 Cannes
Tel. +33 4 97 06 53 07
Fax. +33 4 93 99 06 60
centrale@cannes-reservation.com
www.cannes-reservation.com

Antibes Tourist Office
11 Place de Gaulle
006600 Antibes
Tel. 04 92 90 53 00
Fax. 04 92 90 53 01

Cannes La Bocca Tourist Office
1 Ave Pierre Semard
06150 Cannes La Bocca
Tel. 04 93 47 04 12
Fax. 04 93 90 99 85

Golfe-Juan Tourist Office
84 Ave de la Liberté
06220 Golfe-Juan
Tel. 04 93 63 73 12

Mougins Tourist Office
15 Ave Mallet
06250 Mougins
Tel. 04 93 75 87 67
Fax. 04 92 92 04 03

Vallauris Tourist Office
Square 8 Mai 1945
06220 Vallauris
Tel. 04 93 63 82 58

Emergency Contacts

European Emergency Call
Tel. 112

Fire Emergency
Tel. 18

Ambulance Emergency
Tel. 15

Police Emergency
Tel. 17

Doctor on Call
Tel. 0 810 850

Dental Emergencies
(SOS Dentaire)
Tel. 04 93 68 28 00

National Police
Tel. 04 93 06 22 22

Gendarmerie (Local Police)
122 Boulevard de la République
Tel. 04 93 68 01 01
Tel. 0800 117 118 (toll free)

Fire Department
(Non-Emergency)
Tel. 04 93 48 78 00

Hospitals & Pharmacies

Cannes Hospital
13 Avenue des Broussailles
Tel. 04 93 69 70 00

Pharmacie Anglo-Française
95 Rue d'Antibes
Tel. 04 93 38 53 79

Pharmacie Lienhard
36 Rue d'Antibes
Tel. 04 93 39 01 29

All-night pharmacies are open on a roster system. Call Pharmacie de Garde after 7.30pm on 04 93 06 22 22 to find the nearest open pharmacy. A list is also maintained on the official Cannes city web site: www.cannes. fr/Francais/pharmacies.html.

General Cannes Contacts

Bus Information
Tel. 04 93 39 11 39
www.busazur.com

Car Pound
Tel. 04 93 43 54 55

Central Police Station
1 Avenue de Grasse
06400 Cannes
Tel. 04 93 06 22 22

Lost & Found (City)
1 Avenue St-Louis
Tel. 04 97 06 40 00

Nice-Cote d'Azur Airport
Tel. 04 93 21 30 12
www.nice.aeroport.fr

Post Office (La Poste)
22 Rue Bivouac Napoléon
Tel. 04 93 06 26 50
www.laposte.fr

Train Station (S.N.C.F.)
Place de la Gare
Tel. 08 92 35 35 35
www.sncf.fr

Taxi Service (24 hours)
Tel. 04 92 99 27 27

Weather forecast (Météo)
08 92 6812 67

Photocopy and Fax

Business Centre
Level 01, Palais des Festivals

Buro-Copy
6 Rue Notre Dame
Tel. 04 93 39 19 49

Telecourses Bureautique
16 Rue Louis Blanc

Internet Cafes

Hopefully you should be able to get free access to the Internet through one of the pavilions or inside the Palais/Riviera. If not, try:

Asher
44 Boulevard Carnot
Open 09:30 - 19:00,
Monday – Sunday

Internet "Cyberconcept"
13 Rue Marceau

Webstation
26 Rue Hoche
Open 10:00 - 00:30,
Monday - Saturday

Computer Shops

Assistance Maintenance
Informatique
6 Boulevard Lorraine
Tel. 04 92 99 22 11

FNAC
83 Rue d'Antibes
Cannes branch of the giant electronics, books, video/DVD retailer.

Welcome Informatique
21 Boulevard de la République
Tel. 04 92 99 22 22

other organisations

You might find the following organisations useful either for help with registering for the festival, to find out more information on specific activities in your country, or even get party invites.

Australia

Australian Film Commission
Level 4
150 William Street
Woolloomooloo NSW 2011
Tel. 02 9321 6444
Fax. 02 9357 3737
info@afc.gov.au
www.afc.gov.au

Canada

Telefilm Canada
360 St. Jacques Street, Suite 700
Montréal
Quebec H2Y 4A9
Tel. 514 283 6363
Fax: 514 283 8212
info@telefilm.gc.ca
www.telefilm.gc.ca

Ireland

Irish Film Board
Rockfort House
St Augustine Street
Galway
Tel. 91 561398
Fax. 91 561405
info@filmboard.ie
www.filmboard.ie

New Zealand

New Zealand Film Commission
The Film Centre
Level 2, 119 Jervois Quay
Wellington
Tel. 04 382 7680
Fax. 04 384 9719
mail@nzfilm.co.nz
www.nzfilm.co.nz

United Kingdom

UK Film Council
10 Little Portland Street
London W1W 7JG
Tel. +44 (0)20 7861 7861
Fax. +44 (0)20 7861 7862
www.ukfilmcouncil.org.uk
info@ukfilmcouncil.org.uk

United States

Unifrance Film International
424 Madison Avenue - 8th Floor
New York, NY 1001
USA
Tel. 212 832 8860
Fax. 212 755 0629
info@frenchfilm.org
www.unifrance.org

appendix iii
a mobile phone primer

In recent years the mobile phone (AKA cell phone) has become an essential piece of kit for any professional, filmmakers among them. If you are heading to Cannes with any business objectives in mind being contactable at all times is paramount. Fortunately the pioneers of mobile phone technology had the foresight to realise that people might want to take their phones with them when they travel to new cities and even new countries.

Through a myriad of deals between national and international telecommunications companies most mobile phones can now be used in major population centres all over the world. The phone industry jargon for this ability is "roaming". In an ideal world any phone would be able to roam in any city or country without a problem, however while the vision driving the telecommunications industry was able to deliver the potential to use any phone anywhere, the economics has stopped it short of complete ubiquity. So the most important question is: will your phone work in Cannes?

For festival-goers who are heading to Cannes from another part of Europe there is little to worry about, assuming you have a digital handset and there are no operator or other bars in place. Calls will be more expensive than they are at home, since all phone companies charge you for the privilege of roaming, but other than that everything should be fine. For visitors from further a field there are several complications to add to the mix.

To understand some of these issues, we need to take a moment to examine the most common technologies which drive digital mobile phone technology today. Across the world, two (incompatible) standards dominate the market for digital phone services. These are known as CDMA ("Code Division Multiple Access") and GSM ("Global System for Mobile Communications"). While approximately 70% of the world's mobiles use the GSM standard, in North America CDMA is by far the leading system. Historically this part of the world was slower than Europe or the Far East in adopting digital mobile technologies, so market conditions as well as geography pushed the US into adopting CDMA. The coverage and user-base of networks using the GSM standard in North America is growing, but it still has a long way to go before it overtakes CDMA.

Most phones in Europe, Australasia and the Far East use the GSM standard; however there is an additional complication which stands in the way of all GSM phones working in France. For reasons which I'm sure make sense to the brain boxes that developed them, there are now three variations of the GSM standard in use across the world: GSM 900 (known as such because it uses the 900 MHz radio frequency); GSM 1800 (sometimes called PCN); and GSM 1900 (1900 MHz). Of the three standards, only GSM 900 and GSM 1800 are commonly used in France, where as GSM phones from North America almost always use the 1900 standard. So for your phone to work in Cannes it must support either the 900 or 1800 standard. Phones that do this are often referred to as "dual-band" (or "tri-band" if they support all three standards).

To find out which standards your phone supports either refer to the phone's operating manual or contact your service provider. Most mobile operators provide in depth information about international roaming on their web sites which normally includes coverage and cost details.

Cannes Coverage

The main providers of mobile phone coverage France are:

SFR
(owned by Vodafone)
www.sfr.com/en/

Bouygues
(pronounced "BWEEG")
www.bouyguestelecom.fr/
visiteurs_etrangers/index.htm

Orange France
(previously called Itineris)
www.orange.fr

Making Calls

Unless you are using a French mobile, when making calls with your own phone in France, you must dial numbers using the full international access code and country code even if the destination is local. For example, to call the weather hotline from your chair on the Croisette, you would need to dial the French international access code (00) followed by the country code for France (33), and finally the local number including the area code minus the leading zero

(8 36 68 02 06). This is instead of the local number – 08 36 68 02 06 – which you would dial from a French phone. Fortunately most handsets allow you to use the plus sign (+) in place of the international access code, so you would simply dial +33 8 36 68 02 06 from your phone.

All calls you make on your phone while roaming are charged at your phone company's international rates, regardless of the destination. This is because the host carrier you are using while roaming charges your phone company for the call, and they pass that charge, plus some of their own, on to you. Needless to say, it's probably worth keeping your calls as short as possible.

Receiving Calls

If you receive a call while roaming there is also a bit of a sting in the tail. If someone in your home country calls you, or you receive a call from another person in Cannes, they pay for the leg of the call between their location and your phone company's exchange, then you pay the remaining leg between the exchange and your location. This is of course also charged at your phone company's international rates.

To contact your phone in Cannes, people in your home country can simply dial the same number they would use to reach you when you're in town and they pay standard rates for calling mobiles. However, if someone in Cannes wants to call you, they must dial your number as if it were international, using either the international access code (00) or the plus sign, your country code (i.e. 1 for USA/Canada, 44 for the

UK, 61 for Australia etc), followed by the number minus the leading zero. They pay international rates on the call between their location and your phone company's exchange; you pay the rest as when someone calls you from home.

Keeping Your Bills Small(ish)

The moral of the story is that a mobile phone is an essential part of your Cannes arsenal, but make sure you keep the calls (both made and received) as brief as possible. Several strategies that can help reduce your post-Cannes phone bill include:

Set your phone to divert all calls to voicemail. This means that you only pay when you check your messages, a call that will inevitably be much cheaper than actually talking to someone. When using this strategy, make sure you have a message that makes it obvious to the caller than you will get back to them ASAP. You should also enable your phone's "message waiting" indicator and carry your phone at all times. When you receive notification of a message check it and return the call immediately (using a payphone of course).

It's also worth noting that the way in which you access your voicemail in France may be different than at home. Check with your mobile phone provider before you leave.

Select a different network to roam on while in Cannes. When you switch on your phone abroad most automatically connect to a default network. For some phones this is based on settings within the handset itself; for others it can be made arbitrarily based on things such as signal strength or operator coverage. But it is rarely done with an interest in keeping your bills down! Since most GSM operators are owned by a handful of giant telecommunications companies, selecting your mobile provider's "sister" company in France can often result in significant savings. For example, France's SFR network is owned by Vodafone, the largest mobile phone company on the planet. Vodafone's UK customers (and possibly those in other countries) can save around 30% on the cost of calls when roaming on SFR instead of one of the other operators.

Most handsets allow you to manually select the roaming network, so get in touch with your provider and find out if they are affiliated with any of the French networks.

Use SMS services where possible. Virtually all GSM phones can send and receive SMS text messages. Although you are limited to 160 characters per message, most mobile phone operators provide this service at a fixed price per message. SMS can be an extremely cheap way of staying in touch with friends and colleagues in Cannes, and at home.

Change from a pre-pay to contract phone. Pre-pay mobile phones may be cheap out of the box, but calls are often considerably more expensive than contract phones when roaming (if they can even roam at all). The other potential downer is the problem of getting your hands on top-up cards while you're away. If you do your research (and the sums), you may find that at the end of the day a contract phone is more flexible and cheaper to operate.

Get a local pre-pay phone or SIM card. Frequent travellers have cottoned on to the value of local pre-pay services as a way of keeping roaming bills down while remaining in full contact. You can either buy a local phone, or simply replace the SIM card in your existing handset with that from a local pre-pay operator. Once you're up and running, simply let everyone know your temporary Cannes number, and you're away. Pre-pay phones are available in many places across the city, such as large tabacs, phone shops, and electronics stores. Alternatively, try Cellular Picture+Sound at 24 Rue Jean Jaurès (opposite the train station).

Special international roaming tariffs. A few mobile phone companies have started to wise up to the fact that their customers are sick of being shafted for international roaming. Many now offer special tariffs for international travellers, so contact your own mobile provider to see if there are any options for your phone.

Rent a phone locally. As a last resort you can always hire a handset in Cannes. Prices start from around 8€ per day, plus call charges. Try:

Rentacell France
72 Rue d'Antibes
Tel. 04 93 68 18 18
Fax. 04 93 68 17 77
www.rentacell.com

Com and Call
5 Avenue du Maréchal Juin
Tel. 04 93 94 56 56
Fax. 04 93 43 50 85
www.comandcall.com

Cellhire
Tel. 06 75 37 15 55
www.cellhire.com/cannes/

More Information
The best place to start for more information on roaming is of course your phone company's web site. However, another useful site is Cellular-News. While the mobile phone industry news and statistics will probably not do much more than cure your insomnia, one extremely useful function of the site is their coverage database. This includes almost all countries and has information on phone standards and coverage maps, broken down by each operator in the selected country and region. The direct link to the coverage area is www.cellular-news.com/coverage/.

appendix iv
french 101

It's quite possible that you, like many of us, remember dipping out of high-school French, or simply putting in the minimum effort required to pass, all with the justification of "when will I ever need to know French anyway?" Funny how things work out.

Luckily for all concerned French is one of the easiest foreign languages to pick up since modern French and English share common roots. The English language we know today actually grew out of Old French following the Norman conquest of England at the famous Battle of Hastings in 1066. This makes it possible to get a basic understanding of French reasonably quickly.

Pronunciation
Perhaps the biggest difference between the two languages is pronunciation, a matter further complicated by the fact that some French words are spelt in exactly the same way as their English counterparts, yet pronounced very differently. To get started, let's look at how the vowels are pronounced:

a - like the first "a" in *marmalade*, or in cart, however less open;

e - like the second "a" in *marmalade*, or the "u" in cut;

i - like "ee" as in *bee*, however slightly shorter;

o - when in the middle of a word, like the "o" in *bottle*; and at the end, like "o" in *go*;

u - most commonly "u" as in *bush*, although it also has a sound that is hard to reproduce in English words, but has a sound similar to the German "ü";

French also contains accented vowels, which can look a little scary to English speakers who are used to plain old Roman characters without accents. In reality, these are simply a con, since most accents do not change the way the vowels are pronounced. The exceptions are:

é - Like the "ay" in *bay*.

è/ê - Both like é, but lean more towards the "e" in *tennis*.

In all other cases (à, ô, î, ù, etc), the vowels are pronounced in the same way as they are without the accent. So why have the accented characters in the first place? The main reason is because the French are extremely protective of their language and very reluctant to change it, particularly because many of the accented characters survive from Old French in which these unpronounced accents were used show the contraction of a sound. These contractions simply came about through evolution of the language; for example, the word hôpital (hospital) in Old French used to be hospital and the "ô" simply represents the contraction of the "os" sound. Likewise, hôtel (hotel) was formally hostel.

In addition to the plain and accented vowels the different pronunciations of a few vowel combinations are also useful to know.

ai - like the English combination "ay", as in *play*;

eau/au - like "oa" in *boat*;

er/et - pronounced like é;

eu/oeu - like "er" in flower, but not quite as long, unless followed by a "f" such as in oeuf (egg) or boeuf (beef), in which case it is more like the "urr" in purr.

in/ain - like "an" in *can*. Very important as when you ask for *vin* (wine) it is pronounced van.

ou - somewhere between the "u" in *bush* and the "oo" in *boot*;

oi - difficult to reproduce in English, but it is pronounced like "wha", for example the combination of the "w" in *wagon* and the "a" in *attack*.

on - a bit like the "ong" in *long*, however more nasally and without the "g" on the end;

ui - like two sounds "oo-ee". No similar sound in English;

Most consonants in French are pronounced roughly the same way as in English, however there are a few notable exceptions. Further, some are pronounced differently depending on their location within a word, and indeed which word follows in the sentence.

ç - pronounced like "ce" in *ice*.

ch - like "sh" in *English*;

d/n/p/r/s/t/x - are generally not pronounced when they are at the end of a word;

g - depends on the next character. a/u/o it is pronounced like "g" in *garden*. e/i like a French "j";

gn - pronounced "nya" like in *filet mignon*;

j - pronounced like the "s" in *leisure*;

h - in almost all cases "h" is silent in French when located at the beginning of a word. For example, *homme* (man) is pronounced "om".

ll - double "l" is almost always silent in French words. For example, the verb *travailler* (to work) is pronounced TRAV-AY-AY, ignoring the double "l";

r - a little softer than in English, closer to *air* than *arr* and with a slight roll;

s - when one "s" is in the middle of a word, it is pronounced like the "z" in *zoo*; when there are two "s" in a word, they are pronounced like the "s" in *snake*. Like English, French adds an "s" on the end of nouns to signify plural form, however this "s" is almost never pronounced.

y - a double French "i", for example, the French word *pays* (country) is pronounced PAY-AI.

Gender

Unlike words in English all French words have a gender; that is, they are either masculine or feminine. Definite articles are proceeded by le if masculine (pronounced LOO with a very short "oo") and la if feminine. Indefinite articles are un if masculine or une if feminine. Unfortunately, there are no hard and fast rules for determining the gender of a specific word; the only way is to learn them by heart. But don't worry too much if you mess up your genders as most French people will know what you mean.

Numbers
Your numbers are important, particularly for shopping and anything to do with money. It's all pretty straight forward until you reach seventy, which is literally "60 and 10" in French. Eighty is "4 times 20" and ninety is "4 times 20 plus 10" (no wonder there are no great French mathematicians!). Where the numbers stop below assume that they continue in the same format until the next number shown.

In the following sections words are shown with the following convention:

English Word - French Word - Pronunciation

1 - Un - UN
2 - Deux - DE
3 - Trois - TWAR
4 - Quatre - KAT-RE
5 - Cinq - SANK
6 - Six - SEESS
7 - Sept - SET
8 - Huit - HWEET
9 - Neuf - NURF
10 - Dix - DEESS
11 - Onze - ONZ
12 - Douze - DOOZ
13 - Treize - TRAYZ
14 - Quatorze - KATOEZ
15 - Quinze - CANS
16 - Seize - SAYS
17 - Dix-sept - DEESS-SET
18 - Dix-huit - DEESS-HWEET
19 - Dix-neuf - DEESS-NURF
20 - Vingt - VAN
21 - Vingt-et-un - VAN-TAY-UN
22 - Vingt-deux - VAN-DE
23 - Vingt-trois - VAN-TWAR

30 - Trente - TRONT
40 - Quarante - KARONT
50 - Cinquante - SANKONT
60 - Soixante - SWASONT

70 - Soixante-dix - SWASONT-DEESS
71 - Soixante-onze - SWASONT-ONZ
72 - Soixante-douze - SWASONT-DOOZ
73 - Soixante-treize - SWASONT-TRAYZ

80 - Quatre-vingt - KAT-RE-VAN
90 - Quatre-vingt-dix - KAT-RE-VAN-DEESS
91 - Quatre-vingt-onze - KAT-RE-VAN-ONZ

100 - Cent - SONT
1,000 - Mille - MEEL
1,000,000 - Un Million - UN MILLION

Days & Times

Monday - Lundi - LOONDEE
Tuesday - Mardi - MAR-DEE
Wednesday - Mercredi - MERK-RED-EE
Thursday - Jeudi - ZJHE-DEE
Friday - Vendredi - VOND-RA-DEE
Saturday - Samedi - SAHM-DEE
Sunday - Dimanche - DIM-MARSH

Today - aujourd'hui - OR-SURED-WEE
This Morning - ce matin - SEH-MAR-TAY
Tonight - ce soir - SEH-SWARR
Midday - midi - MEE-DEE
Midnight - minui - MIN-EW-EE

Yesterday - hier - YEHR
Tomorrow - demain - DER-MAY
Morning - matin - MAR-TAY
Afternoon - après-midi - APRAY-MID-DEE
Night - nuit - NEW-EE
Week - semaine - SAM-ENN
Month - mois - MWAR
Year - an - ON

Food & Eating

Breakfast - petit déjeuner - PET-EET DE-SURE-NAY

Lunch - déjeuner - DE-SURE-NAY
Dinner - dîner - DIN-AY

Meat & Poultry - Viandes et Volailles

Beef - bœuf - BERF
Lamb - agneau - AGNOH
Pork - porc - POR
Chicken - poulet - POOL-LAY
Rib Steak - entrecôte - ONT-RA-COT
Veal - veau - VOH

Seafood - Fruits de Mer

Fish - poisson - PWAR-SON
King prawns - gambas - GAMB-AS
Prawns - crevettes roses - CRAVETTE-ROS
Lobster - homard - OMARD
Tuna - thon - THON
Salmon - saumon - SOR-MON
Trout - truite - TROO-IT
Clams - palourdes - PAL-OORD
Squid - calamar - CALAMAR

Vegetables - Légumes

Asparagus - asperges - ASP-AIRG
Cabbage - chou - CHOO
Capsicum - poivron - PWAR-VRON
Cauliflower - chou-fleur - CHOO-FLER
Corn - maïs - MAYZ
Cucumber - concombre - CON-COM-BER
Garlic - ail - AY-LL
Gherkin - cornichon - CORN-EE-SHON
Leek - poireau - PWAR-OH
Lettuce - laitue - LAT-EW
Mushrooms - champignons - SHAMP-EEG-NYON
Onion - oignon - OARG-NYON
Peas - petits pois - PE-TEET PWAR
Potato - pomme de terre - POM DE TAIR
Pumpkin - citrouille - SIT-ROU-EE
Spinach - épinards - AY-PAN-YARD

Fruits & Nuts - Fruits et Noix

Almonds - amandes - AM-OND
Apple - pomme - POM

Cherries - cerises - SAIR-REES
Grapefruit - pamplemousse - POMP-EL-MOOSE
Grapes - raisins - RAY-SAN
Hazelnuts - noisettes - NWAR-SET
Oranges - oranges - OR-ONJE
Peach - pêche - PESH
Peanuts - cacahouètes - KAKA-HOUT-AYT
Pear - poire - PWAR
Plum - prune - PRUNE
Raspberries - framboises - FRAM-BWARS
Strawberries - fraise - FRAYS

Drinks - Boissons

Beer - bière - BEE-AIR
Orange Juice - jus d'orange - JOO-DOR-ONJE
Tomato Juice - jus d'tomate - JOO-D-TOMART
Red Wine - vin rouge - VAN ROOJE
White Wine - vin blanc - VAN BLONK
Water (Still) - eau naturelle - OH NAT-REL
Water (Sparkling) - eau minérale - OH MIN-ER-ARL

Useful Words & Phrases

Hello bonjour - BON-ZJURE
Good Evening - bonsoir - BON-SWAR
Goodbye - au revoir - OH-REV-WARR
Yes - oui - HWEE
No - non - NOHN
Right - a droite - A DWART
Left - a gauche - A GORSH
Straight Ahead - a doit - DWAR
Sorry - pardon - PAR-DOHN
Please - s'il vous plait - SIV-VOO-PLAY
Thank you - merci - MER-SEE

Thank you very much
merci beaucoup
(MER-SEE BOO-KOO)

Excuse Me
Excusez-moi
EX-KUSAY-MWARR

The Bill (check)
L'addition
LA-DISHOHN

I don't understand
Je ne comprends pas
(ZJUNE COMPRON PAR)

Where is...?
Où est...?
(OO-AY)

Go straight ahead
Continuez tout droit
(CONTIN-YOO-AY TOO DWAH)

Turn right
Tournez à droite
(TOOR-NAY A DWAHT)

Turn left
Tournez à gauche
(TOOR-NAY A GOHSH)

I would like...
Je voudrais...
(ZJE VOO-DRAY)

How much is it?
C'est combien?
(SAY COM-BEE-EN)

Can you take me to...?
Est-ce que vous pouvez me conduire
à ...?
(ESKA-VOO POO-VAY MER KOD-EER
A...)

Here is fine thank you.
Ici ça va, merci.
(EE-SEE SA VA MER-SEE)

Do you have any rooms available?
Est-ce que vous avez des chambres
libres?
(ESKA-VOOS AVAY DE SHARMBRA
LEEBR)

How much is it per night?
Quel est le prix par nuit?
(KEL-AY LA PREE PAR NOO-EE)

I would like a one-way ticket for...
Je voudrais un billet aller simple
pour...
(ZJE VOO-DRAY UN BEE-AY ALAY
SOMPLA POR...)

I would like a return ticket for...
Je vourdrai un billet aller retour
pour...
(ZJE VOO-DRAY UN BEE-AY ALAY RE-
TOUR POR...)

Could you let me know when we get
to...?
Est-ce que vous pouvez me dire
quand nous arriverons à...?
(ES-KE VOO POO-VAY MER DEER KA
NOOS ARREEVERON A...)

Is this...?
Est-ce que est...?
ESK-AY...?

appendix v
hotels and accommodation booking services

Finding somewhere to stay in Cannes during the festival will probably be your biggest challenge. This appendix contains an extensive list of hotels and accommodation booking services.

Remember to book your accommodation as far in advance as you possibly can to get the best deal, and don't be surprised when most of the hotels in Cannes itself tell you that they only take bookings for the entire festival period. Sadly, it's a seller's market.

Book Online
Cannes - A Festival Virgin's Guide has teamed up with Venere, one of the leading pan-European hotel and villa booking services. Visit the CFVG web site (www.cannesguide.com) to search hundreds of properties in and around Cannes. You can also make real-time online bookings.

And while you're at the site, don't forget to check out the Accommodation Exchange, a free message board where you can browse listings or post your own accommodation offered or wanted ad.

Hotels in Cannes (1-Star)

Albert, Hotel
68 Avenue de Grasse
Tel. 04 93 39 24 04
Fax. 04 93 38 83 75

Baume, Hotel La
65 Avenue du Maréchal Juin
Tel. 04 93 94 36 77
Fax. 04 93 43 56 73
www.hotel-labaume.com
info@hotel-labaume.com

Bourgonge, Hotel de
11 Rue du 24 Août
Tel. 04 93 38 36 73
Fax. 04 92 99 28 41
www.hotel-de-bourgogne.com
hoteldebourgogne@aol.com

Florella, Le
55 Blvd de la République
Tel. 04 93 38 48 11
Fax. 04 93 99 22 15
www.hotelflorella.com
reservations@hotelflorella.com

National, Hotel
8 Rue Maréchal Joffre
Tel. 04 93 39 91 92
Fax. 04 92 98 44 06
hotelnationalcannes@wanadoo.fr

Nord, Hotel Du
6 Rue Jean Jaurès
Tel. 04 93 38 48 79
Fax. 04 92 99 28 20

Hotels in Cannes (2-Stars)

Alize, Hotel
29 Rue Bivouac Napoleon
Tel. 04 93 39 62 17
Fax. 04 93 39 64 32
www.alizecannes.com
alizecannes@wanadoo.fr

Alnea, Hotel
20 Rue J. de Riouffe
Tel. 04 93 68 77 77
Fax. 04 93 68 77 78
www.hotel-alnea.com

Amiraute, Hotel
17 Rue Maréchal Foch
06400 Cannes
Tel. 04 93 39 10 53
Fax. 04 93 38 98 54

Appia, Hotel
6 Rue Marceau
Tel. 04 93 06 59 59
Fax. 04 93 39 43 38
www.appia-hotel.com
appia-hotel@wanadoo.fr

Ascott, Hotel
27 Rue des Serbes
Tel. 04 93 99 18 24
Fax. 04 93 99 12 26
hotelascott@wanadoo.fr

Atlantis, Hotel
4 Rue du 24 Août
Tel. 04 93 39 18 72
Fax. 04 93 68 37 65
hotel.atlantis@wanadoo.fr

Azurene Royal Hotel
28 Rue du Commandant André
06400 Cannes
Tel. 04 93 99 10 51
Fax. 04 92 98 05 37
info@azurene-royal-hotel.com
www.azurene-royal-hotel.com

Beverly Hotel
14 Rue Hoche
06400 Cannes
Tel. 04 93 39 10 66
Fax. 04 92 98 65 63
contact@hotel-beverly.com
www.hotel-beverly.com

Chalet de l'Isère, Le
42 Avenue de Grasse
Tel. 04 93 38 50 80
Fax. 04 93 68 73 22
perso.wanadoo.fr
chaletisere@voila.fr

Chantilly, Hotel Le
34 Boulevard Alexandre III
Tel. 04 93 43 05 95

Charmettes, Hotel Les
47 Avenue de Grasse
Tel. 04 93 39 17 13

Cheval Blanc, Hotel Le
3 Rue Guy de Maupassant
Tel. 04 93 39 88 60

Cigogne, Hotel La
14 Boulevard de Strasbourg
Tel. 04 97 06 91 80

Climat de France, Hotel
232 Avenue F. Tonner
Tel. 04 93 90 22 22

Corona, Hotel
55 Rue d'Antibes
Tel. 04 93 39 69 85
Fax. 04 93 99 09 69
cannescorona@aol.com

Cybelle Bec Fin, Hotel
14 Rue de 24 Aout
Tel. 04 93 38 31 33
Fax. 04 93 38 43 47

L'Esterel
15 rue du 24 Août
06400 Cannes
Tel. 04 93 38 82 82
Fax. 04 93 99 04 18
reservation@hotellesterel.com
www.hotellesterel.com

Etap Hotel Cannes Centre
48 Boulevard Carnot
06400 Cannes
Tel. 08 92 68 12 97
Fax. 04 93 38 20 20
h5493gm@accord.com
www.accord.com

Florian, Le
8 Rue du Commandant André
06400 Cannes
Tel. 04 93 39 24 82
Fax. 04 92 99 18 30
info@hotel-florian-cannes.com
www.hotel-florian-cannes.com

Ibis Cannes Centre
8 Rue Marceau
06400 Cannes
Tel. 04 92 98 96 96
Fax. 09 298 0568
www.accorhotels.com

Jumelles, Hotel Les
24 Avenue Francis Tonner
Tel. 04 93 47 07 84

Little Palace
18 Rue du 24 Août
06400 Cannes
Tel. 04 92 98 18 18
Fax. 04 93 68 65 73
little-palace@wanadoo.fr
www.cannes-hotel.com

Lutetia
6 Rue Michel Ange
06400 Cannes
Tel. 04 93 39 35 74
Fax. 04 93 39 94 41
lutetiahotel@free.fr

Madrilene, La
15 Boulevard Alexandre III
06400 Cannes
Tel. 04 97 06 37 37
Fax. 04 94 38 78
infos@hotel-lamadrilene.com
www.hotel-lamadrilene.com

PLM
3 Rue Hoche
06400 Cannes
Tel. 04 93 38 31 19
Fax. 04 93 99 77 15
hotel.plm@wanadoo.fr
www.hotel-plm.com

Select, Hotel
16 Rue Hélène Vagliano
06400 Cannes
Tel. 04 93 99 51 00
Fax. 04 92 98 03 12
hotel-select-06@wanadoo.fr
hotel-select-cannes.com

Hotels in Cannes (3-Stars)

Atlas, Hotel
5 Avenue Jean Jaurès
Tel. 04 93 39 01 17
Fax. 04 93 39 29 57
www.hotel-atlas-cannes.com
infos@hotel-atlas-cannes.com

Best Western Univers
2 Rue Maréchal Foch
Tel. 04 93 06 30 00
www.bestwestern.com

Canberra. Hotel
120 Rue d'Antibes
Tel. 04 97 06 95 00
Fax. 04 92 98 03 47
www.hotels-ocre-azur.com
hotelcanberra@hotels-ocre-azur.com

Cannes Gallia, Hotel
36 Boulevard Montfleury
Tel. 04 97 06 28 28
Fax. 04 97 06 28 29
www.cannes-gallia.com
info@cannes-gallia.com

Cannes Riviera Hotel
16 Boulevard d'Alsace
Tel. 04 97 06 20 40
www.hotel-cannes-riviera.federal-hotel.com

Cezanne
40 Boulevard d'Alsace
Tel. 04 93 38 50 70
Fax. 04 92 99 20 99
www.hotel-cezanne.com
contact@hotel-cezanne.com

Chanteclair, Hotel
12 Rue Forville
Tel. 04 93 39 68 88
Fax. 04 93 39 68 88

Citadines Cannes Carnot
10 avenue Font de Veyre
Tel. 04 93 90 52 52
Fax. 04 93 47 86 61

Comfort Hotel Atlas
5 Place de la Gare
Tel. 04 93 39 01 17
Fax. 04 93 39 29 57
www.hotel-atlas-cannes.com
infos@hotel-atlas-cannes.com

Embassy
6 Rue de Bône
Tel. 04 97 06 99 00
Fax. 04 97 99 07 98
embassy@wanadoo.fr

Festival, Hotel
3 Rue Molière
Tel. 04 97 06 64 40
Fax. 04 97 06 64 45
www.hotel-festival.com
infos@hotel-festival.com

Hotel de France
85 Rue d'Antibes
Tel. 04 93 06 54 54
Fax. 04 93 68 53 43
www.h-de-france.com
contact@h-de-france.com

Kyriad Centre
24 Boulevard de Lorraine
Tel. 04 92 59 44 44
Fax. 04 92 59 44 45
www.hoteliereduphare.fr
kyriadcannescentre@wanadoo.fr

Ligure
5 Rue Jean Jaurès
Tel. 04 93 39 03 11
Fax. 04 93 39 19 48
www.hotel-ligure.com
hotelligure@wanadoo.fr

Mondial
77 Rue d'Antibes
Tel. 04 93 68 70 00
Fax. 04 93 99 39 11
www.hotellemondial.com
reservation@hotellemondial.com

Orangers, Hotel des
1 Rue des Orangers
Tel. 04 93 39 99 92
Fax. 04 93 68 37 55
www.charmhotel.com
infos@charmhotel.com

Paris, Hotel de
34 Boulevard d'Alsace
Tel. 04 93 38 30 89
Fax. 04 93 39 04 61
reservation@hotel-de-paris.com
www.hotel-de-paris.com

Provence, Hotel de
9 Rue Molière
Tel. 04 93 38 44 35
Fax. 04 93 39 63 14
contact@hotel-de-provence.com
www.hotel-de-provence.com

Regina, Hotel
31 Rue Pasteur
Tel. 04 93 94 05 43
Fax. 04 93 43 20 54
reception@hotel-regina-cannes.com
www.hotel-regina-cannes.com

Renoir, Hotel
7 Rue Edith Cavell
Tel. 04 92 99 62 62
Fax. 04 92 99 62 82
contact@hotel-renoir-cannes.com
www.leshotelsdeprovence.com

Ruc Hotel
13-15 Boulevard de Strasbourg
Tel. 04 92 98 33 60
Fax. 04 93 39 54 18
ruc.hotel@wanadoo.fr
www.ruc-hotel.com

Splendid, Hotel
4 Rue Félix Faure
Tel. 04 97 06 22 22
Fax. 04 93 99 55 02
accueil@splendid-hotel-cannes.fr
www.splendid-hotel-cannes.fr

Suite Hotel Cannes Carnot
46 Boulevard Carnot
Tel. 04 97 06 77 77
Fax. 04 97 06 77 78
h3460@accord.com

Vendome (Villa Claudia)
37 Boulevard d'Alsace
Tel. 04 93 38 34 33
Fax. 04 97 06 66 80
hotel.vendome@wanadoo.fr

Villa Tosca, Hotel La
11 Rue Hoche
06400 Cannes
Tel. 04 93 38 34 40
Fax. 04 93 38 73 34
contact@villa-tosca.com
www.villa-tosca.com

Hotels in Cannes (4-Stars)

314 Hotel
5 Rue François Einesy
Tel. 04 92 99 72 00

All Suites Residence
12 Rue Latour Maubourg
Tel. 04 93 94 90 00
Fax. 04 89 88 40 25
www.theresidence-cannes.com
info@theresidence-cannes.com

Amarante Hotel
78 Boulevard Carnot
Tel. 04 93 39 22 23
Fax. 04 93 39 40 22
www.jjwhotels.com
amarante-cannes@jjwhotels.com

Beau Sejour
5 Rue des Fauvettes
Tel. 04 93 39 63 00
Fax. 04 92 98 64 66
www.cannes-beausejour.com

Belle Plage, Hotel
2 Rue Brougham
Tel. 04 93 06 25 50
Fax. 04 93 99 61 06
www.cannes-hotel-belle-plage.com
belleplage@wanadoo.fr

California's Hotel
8 Traverse Alexandre III
Tel. 04 93 94 12 21
Fax. 04 93 43 55 17
www.hotel-californias.com
nadia@californias-hotel.com

Cannes Palace Hotel
14 Avenue de Madrid
Tel. 04 93 43 44 45
Fax. 04 93 43 41 30
contact@cannes-palace.com
www.cannes-palace.com

Cavendish, Le
11 Boulevard Carnot
Tel. 04 97 06 26 00
Fax. 04 97 00 26 01
www.cavendish-cannes.com

Cristal Hotel Best Western
13-15 Rond-point Duboys d'Angers
Tel. 04 92 59 29 29
Fax. 04 93 38 64 66
www.bestwestern.com

Croisette Beach Hotel
13 Rue du Canada
Tel. 04 92 18 88 00
Fax. 04 93 68 35 38
croisettebea@aws.fr

Eden, Hotel
133 Rue d'Antibes
Tel. 04 93 68 78 00
Fax. 04 93 68 78 01
www.eden-hotel-cannes.com
reception@eden-hotel-cannes.com

Excellior, Residence
93 Boulevard Carnot
Tel. 04 93 39 76 65
Fax. 04 89 88 40 25

Grand Hotel, Le
45 Boulevard de la Croisette
Tel. 04 93 38 15 45
Fax. 04 93 68 97 45
www.grand-hotel-cannes.com
info@grand-hotel-cannes.com

Novotel Montfleury
25 Avenue Beauséjour
Tel. 04 93 68 86 86
Fax. 04 93 68 87 87
www.novotel.com
h0806@accor-hotels.com

Riviera Eden Palace
5-9 Boulevard de Lorraine
06400 Cannes
Tel. 04 92 59 16 12
Fax. 04 92 59 16 13
www.eden-palace.com
reception@eden-palace.com

Sofitel le Mediterranee
Tel. 04 92 99 73 00
Fax. 04 92 99 73 29
www.sofitel.com
h0591@accor-hotels.com

Sun Riviera Hotel
138 Rue d'Antibes
Tel. 04 93 06 77 77
Fax. 04 93 38 31 10
www.sun-riviera.com
info@sun-riviera.com

Victoria, Hotel
Rond-Point Duboys d'Angers
Tel. 04 92 59 40 00
Fax. 04 93 38 03 91
www.hotel-victoria-cannes.com
contact@hotel-victoria-cannes.com

Hotels in Cannes (5-Stars)

Carlton Intercontinental
58 Boulevard de la Croisette
Tel. 04 93 06 40 06
Fax. 04 93 06 40 25
www.ichotelsgroup.com
carlton@ichotelsgroup.com

Gray d'Albion, Hotel
38 Rue des Serbes
Tel. 04 92 99 79 79
Fax. 04 93 99 26 10
www.lucienbarriere.com
graydalbion@lucienbarriere.com

Noga Hilton – Palace Croisette
50 Boulevard de la Croisette
Tel. 04 92 99 70 00
Fax. 04 92 99 70 11
www.hiltoncannes.com

Majestic Barriere
10 Boulevard de la Croisette
Tel. 04 92 98 77 00
Fax. 04 93 38 97 90
www.lucienbarriere.com
majestic@lucienbarriere.com

Hotels in Cannes la Bocca

Amangani Resort Hotel
61/65 Avenue du Dr Picaud
06150 Cannes La Bocca
Tel. 04 93 47 63 00

Bagatelle Pension
4 Chemin des Arums
06150 Cannes La Bocca
Tel. 04 93 48 32 30

Brasserie du Marché, La
10 avenue Monseigneur Jeancard
06150 Cannes La Bocca
Tel. 04 93 48 13 00

Cannes Beach Residence
11 Rue Pierre Sémard
06150 Cannes La Bocca
Tel. 04 92 19 30 00

Cannes Verrerie
6 Rue de la Verrerie
06150 Cannes La Bocca
Tel. 04 93 90 72 00

Chateau de la Tour
10 Avenue Font de Veyre
06150 Cannes La Bocca
Tel. 04 93 90 52 52

Du Midi
88 Avenue Michel Jourdan
06150 Cannes La Bocca
Tel. 04 93 47 14 67
Ibis Cannes la Bocca
23 Avenue Francis Tonner
06150 Cannes La Bocca
Tel. 04 93 47 18 46

Jumelles, Les
124 avenue Francis Tonner
06150 Cannes La Bocca
Tel. 04 93 47 07 84

Kyriad
204-212 Avenue Francis Tonner
06150 Cannes La Bocca
Tel. 04 93 48 21 00

Neptune, Hotel
06150 Cannes La Bocca
92 Avenue Francis Tonner
Tel. 04 93 47 04 47

Paris Provence
68 avenue Francis Tonner
06150 Cannes La Bocca
Tel. 04 93 47 10 48

Villa Francia
33 Avenue Wester-Wemyss
06150 Cannes La Bocca
Tel. 04 92 98 20 00

Hotels in Le Cannet

Sunset
Avenue du Campon
Tel. 04 93 45 35 35

Ibis
87 Boulevard Carnot
Tel. 04 93 45 79 76

Virginia
41 Boulevard Carnot
Tel. 04 93 45 43 87

De la Grande Bretagne Hotel
Boulevard Carnot
Tel. 04 93 45 66 00

Hotels in Vallauris

Palm Hôtel
17 Avenue la Palmeraie
Tel. 04 93 63 72 24

Siou Aou Miou
Quai St Sébastien
Tel. 04 93 64 39 89
Val d'Auréa
11 Boulevard Maurice Rouvier
Tel. 04 93 64 64 29

California
222 Avenue de la Liberté
Tel. 04 93 64 39 89

Chez Claude
162 Avenue de la Liberté
Tel. 04 93 63 71 30

Etap Hôtel
Rte de St Bernard - Font de la Cine
Tel. 04 93 65 48 08

Formule 1
3030 Route de St Bernard
Tel. 04 93 65 20 20

Hôtel du Stade
48 Avenue Georges Clémenceau
Tel. 04 93 64 91 27

Hotels in Golfe Juan

Auberge du Relais Impérial
21 Rue Louis Chabrier - Golfe Juan
Tel. 04 93 63 70 36

Hôtel de Crijansy
85 Avenue J.Adam - Golfe Juan
Tel. 04 93 63 84 44

Lauvert RN7
Impasse Beau Soleil - Golfe Juan
Tel. 04 93 63 46 06

Hotels in Antibes - Juan les Pins

Aigue Marine
1 Avenue du Pylone
Tel. 04 93 33 48 76

Auberge Provencale
61 Place Nationale
Tel. 04 93 34 13 24

Les Capucines
Boulevard President Wilson
Tel. 04 31 61 18 04
Hotel de la Gare
6 Rue du Printemps
Tel. 04 93 61 29 96

La Jabotte
13 Avenue Max Maurey
Tel. 04 93 61 45 89

Hotel Du Lys
81 Boulevard Poincaré
Tel. 04 93 61 53 77

Nouvel Hotel
1 Avenue du 24 Août
Tel. 04 93 34 44 07

La Parquerette
Route de la Badine
Tel. 04 93 61 59 60

Parisiana
16 Avenue de l'Esterel
Tel. 04 93 61 27 03

La Petite Reserve
20 Boulevard James Wyllie
Tel. 04 93 61 55 86

Les Tamaris
37 Rue Bricka
Tel. 04 93 61 20 03

Trianon
14 Avenue de l'Esterel
Tel. 04 93 61 18 11

Villa Christie
Rue de l'Oratoire
Tel. 04 93 61 01 98

Alexandra
Rue Pauline
Tel. 04 97 21 76 51
Hotel du Cap – Eden-Roc
Boulevard Kennedy
Cap d'Antibes
Tel. 04 93 61 39 01
Fax. 04 93 67 13 83
www.edenroc-hotel.fr

appendix vi
your packing list

Travel always brings with it that nagging feeling of "I think I've forgotten something" so we've prepared this helpful checklist of essential items for your festival odyssey. While you might be wearing the same pair of underwear for two weeks, at least you'll have all of the necessary kit to see you successfully through Cannes.

Mobile Phone (aka cell phone)
You'll need to be contactable at all times while in Cannes and having your own mobile phone is the only way to be sure of this. Don't rely on hotel messaging services or third-parties. Bring your own or rent one locally, which may be cheaper.

Hangover Kit
One night you'll be partying hard into the wee hours, the next morning you'll need to be bright eyed and bushy-tailed for your pitch meeting. Whatever works for you, bring plenty of it.

Formal Gear
If you want to get into the evening screenings and many of the parties, you'll need to remember to bring your Sunday best. It might be a hassle if you're staying in a tent, but it's better than hanging around outside while everyone else has fun. And for the blokes... don't forget your bow-tie; lest you find yourself being forced to buy one at an extortionate price while you stand in line outside the Palais.

Beachwear
You're going to need a break at some stage so you may as well enjoy the beach when you get the chance. Locals tend to be a bit less inhibited by the clothing thing, but perhaps you would prefer to be a little more modest and go out in your favourite beach kit.

Umbrella
One day you will be soaking up the sun in beautiful 25°C (77°F) heat, the next you will be dodging a deluge which has decided to come right when you need to skip down the Croisette to an important meeting. Save yourself a soaking and bring a brollie.

Shoes
A successful trip to Cannes requires two pairs of shoes. The first should be the most comfortable pair you own (to provide some consolation to your feet for the amount of running around you'll be doing). The second pair should be your knock 'em dead shoes to match your Sunday best; although ladies, it's advisable to keep your glam shoes as sensible as possible since it's conceivable that some fancy footwork may be required to pull off entry to a party.

Credit Cards
An essential tool for any traveller. Credit cards allow you to manage your spending more effectively and in some cases, put off the payment pain until later. They also bring the added bonus of more favourable exchange rates on your purchases, since the currency conversion is done by your card issuer at home rather than locally. Savvy travellers

always bring at least two credit cards just in case one doesn't work for some reason or happens to meet an untimely end.

Business Cards
You never know who'll you'll meet or when so you should carry business cards with you at all times. At minimum they should contain your vital statistics: name, telephone number, and email address. Don't get bogged down with fancy job titles – they mean nothing to the film industry. At best, no one cares, and at worst, people will just think you're a loser.

Sun Protection
Even though May in Cannes is technically still spring the sun can be quite strong, particularly if your skin has yet to come out of hibernation after the northern hemisphere winter. If you're going to be spending a reasonable amount of time outside (e.g. running around between meetings or hanging in one of the pavilions) you'll need to apply sunscreen to prevent your skin turning pink. A good pair of sunnies is also a must as the morning glare off the water can feel like it's melting your retinas.

For those coming to Cannes with a film in tow, you'll also need to be packing the following materials:

Press Kit
A good press kit is essential for those who are looking to drum up interest in a film from either a distributor or the media. If you're working with a sales agent and/or publicist, they will have already made you go through this process, however if you're trying

it on your own you'll have to create one yourself.   A decent press kit includes a short synopsis of your film (one paragraph); a long synopsis of your film (3-4 paragraphs), bios of principle cast and crew, 1-2 pages of production notes describing how your film was made, and set of good stills (ideally in both digital and hard copy formats).

One Copy of Your Script
People won't read scripts in Cannes so sacrificing a forest will only have one effect: making the printers and the excess baggage people rich. However, if you're trying to drum up interest in your project bring one printed copy of your script just in case.

A Disk
Containing electronic versions of all your support materials and script. You may need to print more while you are in Cannes, so it's always best to come armed with all the information you need.

Realistic Expectations
Perhaps the most important thing to bring with you.

about the author

Benjamin Craig started his media career at the tender age of just 18 months when he was cast as the new child of the main family in "Certain Women", a popular 1970s Australian Broadcasting Corporation (ABC) soap opera. After leaving the show aged three, Craig spent the remainder of his childhood growing up in Perth, Western Australia.

Always more comfortable behind the camera than in front of it, Craig spent much of his teens working backstage in theatre before starting a media production degree at Curtin University of Technology in 1990. Graduating in 1994 with a Bachelor of Arts (English), Craig divided his time between developing short film projects and working in the fledgling new media industry before moving to Europe in 1996.

In addition to his work in theatre, film, television, and new media, Craig is an accomplished freelance writer. He is the author of the leading film festival travel series, A Festival Virgin's Guide, with titles on the Cannes and Sundance film festivals. He has also freelanced for a variety of magazines including Vogue, GQ, and Condé Nast Traveller, and is the editor of one of the web's oldest filmmaking resources, filmmaking.net.

Benjamin Craig is currently chief executive of cross-media production company Cinemagine Media Limited and resides in London.

map of cannes (centre-ville)

This is a basic map of the central area of Cannes. Free city maps are available from the tourist offices in town. Get yours as soon as you arrive.

City Places

1. Gare du Cannes (train station)
2. Tourist Office
3. Gare Routière (bus station)
4. Gare Maritime (ferry port)
5. Forville Market
6. Hotel Majestic Barrière
7. Hotel Grey d'Albion
8. Grand Hotel
9. Noga Hilton Hotel
10. Carlton Intercontinental Hotel
11. Hotel Martinez
12. La Poste (post office)
13. Cannes English Bookshop
14. Hôtel de Ville (town hall)
15. Monoprix (supermarket)
16. Musée de la Castre (old fort)
17. Petit Majestic (bar)
18. Petit Carlton (bar)

Festival Places & Cinemas

19. Palais des Festivals
20. Espace Riviera
21. Village International
22. Théâtre Palais Croisette (cinema)
23. Espace Miramar (cinema)
24. Les Arcades (cinema)
25. Olympia (cinema)
26. Star (cinema)
27. Cinéma de la Plage (beach cinema)
28. Village International Pantiero

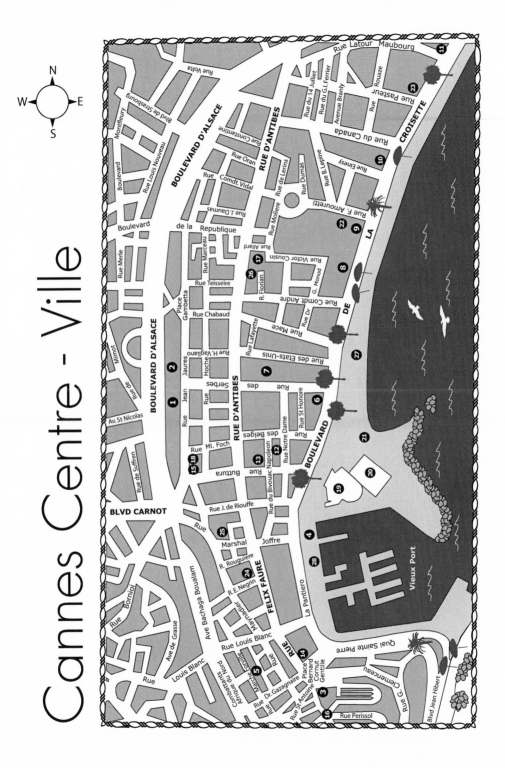

Cannes Centre - Ville